S. Sidwell

E gate

Crockich

Bedford haute

S. Steue

S. Mary

bal

S. Peroks

Bishops pallace

Frents

South gate

the Maut line

Lork Beam

Radfort place

Holloway

S. Leonard

Albalores

S. Mary Stepps

West gate

Water gate

Crane Sellar

The Kay

S. Leonard weare

New haven

CIVITAS EXONIÆ
(vulgo Excester) VRBS
PRIMARIA IN CO:
MITATV DEVONIÆ.

Flyers hayes

S. Thomas

EXETER IN 1618.

from Braun & Hoghenbergh's 'Civitates Orbis Terrarum.'

The Story of
Exeter

Lionel Aggett's *The Medieval Exe Bridge, Exeter.*

The Story of
Exeter

Hazel Harvey

 Phillimore

2011
Published by
PHILLIMORE & CO. LTD
Andover, Hampshire, England
www.phillimore.co.uk

© Hazel Harvey, 2011

ISBN 978-1-86077-678-6

Printed and bound in Malta

Manufacturing managed by
Jellyfish Solutions Ltd

Contents

List of Illustrations

Frontispiece: Lionel Aggett's The Medieval Exe Bridge, Exeter.

Acknowledgements

The following organisations kindly supplied illustrations and/or permission to use them:

Lionel Aggett (Lark Studio), frontispiece; Bodleian Library, Oxford, 44; Devon and Cornwall Constabulary, 157; Devon and Exeter Institution, 26-8, 30, 38, 39, 41, 45, 47, 62, 68, 75, 76, 89, 96, 103, 138; Exeter Cathedral Library, 14, 25, 99-101; Exeter Civic Society, 12; *Express and Echo*, 125, 132, 135, 142, 147; Isca Collection, 149; National Railway Museum, York, 123-4; Ny Carlsberg Glyptotek, Copenhagen, 1; Railway Studies Collection, Newton Abbot Library, 95; Royal Albert Memorial Museum, 15, 34, 69; The Royal Society, 97; University of Essex, 171; Victoria and Albert Museum, 43; Walter Scott (Bradford) Ltd, 144; Westcountry Studies Library, 31, 82, 90-1, 108, 127 and endpaper maps.

Illustrations have also been taken from Dr Thomas Shapter, *The History of the Cholera in Exeter in 1832* (1849), 51, 53, 58, 77-81. Angela Pedder of the Royal Devon and Exeter Hospital kindly allowed use of exerpts from my *A Better Provision* (50 Years of the NHS), and Jenny Lloyd from *People Talking*, recorded for the Fountain Community. The author is indebted to the late P.V. Pitman for allowing reproduction of her drawings (86-8, 120) and for lending postcards; the late John Andrews for lending postcards; Gillian Baker, 35; Francis Harvey, 161; Monica Hoare for lending postcards published by her grandfather's firm, Worth and Co.; Deryck Laming, 10, 23, 52, 54-5, 59, 63, 65, 83-5, 152-3, 162; Mrs G. Price, 141; the Sclater family, 115-16; Gilbert Venn, 107, 139, 150, 194; Nigel Watts, 151, 164; Bob and Betty Youngson, 140. Other photographs are by the author.

The author also wishes to record her appreciation of the generous help given by the *Express and Echo*'s nostalgia specialist, Geoff Worrall; and the friendly cooperation of John Allan, Merriol Almond, Jane Baker, Roger Brien, Katharine Chant, Roy and Monty Chrisholm, the late Aileen Fox, Ian Maxted, Richard Parker, Rosemary Petheram, the lat Michael G. Smith, Liz and Bob Snowden, Sheila Stirling, Martin Stoolman, Robert Sweetland, Peter W. Thomas, Lorna Till, Christine Trigger, Ray Vail, Peter Weddell, Brian and Angela Wilkinson, Peter Wiseman and the late Michael Woollacott.

Britons and Romans

I Here the mature Vespasian is portrayed, after he had become emperor in A.D. 69. At the time of the Roman Conquest of Britain he had been recently promoted to command of a legion. His previous responsibility had been to keep the streets of Rome free of litter and filth.

Exeter lies where the invading Romans built a fortress in about A.D. 50, on a steep-sided spur overlooking the river-crossing, where a natural shelf served as a quay. In A.D. 43 the emperor Claudius had sent forces to subdue the south of Britain. His general Vespasian and the Second Augustan Legion had worked their way east to west, capturing a total of 19 strongholds before they arrived here. Medieval chronicles report a seven-day siege at 'the camp on the hill by the great wood' before the local British king and the Roman commander came to terms.

The inhabitants of the western peninsula were called Dumnonii. They lived in small farming settlements among the wooded hills, raising cattle, sheep, goats and grain. Their major defensive forts were several miles north and east of the future site of Exeter, but they had a camp a mile north of the river-crossing and a small trading-post near the river-bank. The prehistoric ridgeway, the Icknield Way, which ran across the whole breadth of Britain, came along the spine that is now occupied by Sidwell Street and High Street, to terminate on the cliff-top above the river. The great glowing globe of the sun setting in the west – greatest of all traffic lights – still fills the High Street on winter afternoons.

Strabo the geographer, writing about half a century earlier, recorded that the British exported gold, silver, iron, grain, hides, slaves and hunting dogs; it rained a lot and on fine days it was foggy; the British were long-limbed, towering over the tallest Romans; they kept their cattle in clearings in the woods. 'The forests are their cities', he wrote. The name Dumnonii may come from the Celtic word for 'deep' or 'mysterious', and may denote worshippers of the Mysterious God or dwellers in the deep valleys, or (like the names of many tribes) it may simply mean 'us here', 'the people', as opposed to 'them'. 'They' at this point were the Roman invaders, who seem to have met with little resistance after the initial siege. The Dumnonii were proud and fierce, with their own kings, but they were not tightly organised. They did not issue their own coinage, although neighbouring tribes did.

2 The bend where upper Paul Street meets Gandy Street preserves the line of the path where the guard patrolled just inside the fortress ramparts. The fortress boundary has also been excavated in Friernhay Street and elsewhere, and subsidence cracks in the museum and in St Stephen's church reveal that they stand on the fortress ditch.

3 Dr John Salvatore demonstrates being trapped in a 'Punic profile' ditch.

4 A fragment from the mosaic floor of the bathhouse, showing hooves, perhaps from a depiction of the insignia of the Second Augustan Legion, Pegasus. The cubes for the pattern in red, white and grey-blue were cut from old tiles, East Devon limestone and local siderite.

Vespasian's camp-prefect, Publius Anicius Maximus, supervised the construction of a temporary fortlet above the quay. He or his successor, Poenius Postumus, oversaw the building of a full-scale military fortress, enclosing 38 acres, on the top of the spur. A road ran from this fortress due south parallel to the river, as far as the port of Topsham. Ancillary Roman forts have been found adjacent to this road, one in Topsham, one each side of Holloway Street and most recently (2010) on the site of the vacated St Loyes College in Countess Wear, cleared for the development of a retirement village. This latest discovery may have been used for storage or workshops or tented accommodation; it does not reveal traces of barrack blocks or metal working, but pottery shards date it to the time of the legionary occupation of the city-centre fortress. It was defended by deep ditches and ramparts. The outer ditch had a classic military Roman V-shaped profile, while the inner ditch has a 'Punic' profile – vertical on the outer side and sloping on the other, making it virtually impossible to scramble out of once one has leapt in to attack.

The Roman military presence lasted for 20 to 30 years, with all the shouting and clatter of barracks, workshops, hospital, kitchens and stabling for the horses and mules. There was a hill-top signal station to the north (near the British camp) where beacons could be seen from as far as Dorchester. Its ditch is still visible from the air, outlined by the trees round the practice yard of the present riding-school.

Pennsylvania Road lies on the route that Roman messengers took from the legionary fortress guarding the river-crossing to the signal-station and look-out 600ft above sea-level. In the 19th century a Roman signet-ring of iron was found under the road, and also the upper third of an amphora.

No clear evidence of military occupation was found in excavation in 1956-7, but the soldiers would have been living in tents inside the ditches and ramparts. It was possibly used again in the late 3rd to 4th centuries by a civic militia watching the estuary, as is suggested by the discovery of a coin of Carausius.

The fortress held tightly packed barrack blocks and possibly a hospital on the later site of the deanery. A bath house was erected in about A.D. 60. It was one of the first stone buildings put up in Britain, and was the finest bath house north of the Alps at that time. It consisted of the usual three rooms: hot, tepid and cold (caldarium, tepidarium and frigidarium). The entire suite of rooms was roofed with a series of concrete vaults. At each end of the baths there were apses holding round stone basins.

Rosemary Sutcliff's *Eagle of the Ninth* opens in the fortress at Isca in AD 128. Marcus is a young Roman who has been posted here as a centurion. The local British are rampaging on horseback on the river banks. They attack the fort and Marcus receives a serious wound to his thigh. His stoicism during painful treatment draws on the author's experience in hospital.

Another inspiration for Exeter children is *A Beacon for the Romans* by David Rees. A boy and a girl move to the higher slopes of St Thomas and discover Roman remains in the garden which bring Isca alive for them. David Rees also wrote *The Ferryman*, set in the time of Exeter's cholera epidemic, and he won a Carnegie medal for his book *The Exeter Blitz*.

Derek Gore's *Isca* is set in the last days of the Roman town and draws a vivid picture of the chaos and dilapidation as it collapses into disrepair.

5 (Left) Excavations in 1972 on the site of St Mary Major revealed the legionary bath-house from *c*.A.D. 55, with underfloor heating, cut through 50 years later by the walls of the administrative *basilica* of the Romano-British town. The substantial remains were recorded and grassed over. The Royal Albert Museum has a comprehensive display of the finds.

6 (Above right) Squared blocks of purple volcanic stone quarried from Rougemont can be seen in several stretches of the surviving walls (here in Northernhay Gardens.) The stone has a characteristic honeycomb surface.

7 (Below right) An earth bank still standing inside the city walls at 14 Cathedral Close.

The floor of the hot room stood on stacked tiles where hot air circulated from outside furnaces. The walls were finished with Purbeck marble, and fragments of mosaic have been recovered from the floor: the earliest fragments of mosaic known in Britain. The amount of water needed for these baths may have been as much as 70,000 gallons a day. This was piped in from the Sidwell Street ridge, along the hillside just behind the present church, and was then fed along pipes around the knoll of Rougemont to enter the fortress through the wall by the present Habitat shop.

During Boudicca's rebellion in A.D. 60-1 Poenius Postumus failed to respond to a call for reinforcements, and then killed himself for shame because he had denied his legion this chance of gaining glory. In *c*.A.D. 75-8 the legion dismantled the fortress palisades and carried them to Wales. The military bath-house was demolished, and in its place there rose grand stone civic buildings for the regional civitas capital, Isca Dumnoniorum. A combined forum and basilica complex accommodated municipal offices and shops, with public baths nearby in the form of an open-air pool surrounded by colonnades.

Isca was the Celtic name for a river rich in salmon. The fortress had been completely Roman, neat and tidy and under military discipline, with officers from Italy and soldiers from various parts of the empire housed in close-packed

rectangular barrack blocks. The British who settled outside its walls had built wattle and daub workshops and huts in which food remains and broken pottery lay messily mingled with industrial waste from working bronze and enamel, and leather scraps and lumps of iron slag. In contrast, the town that succeeded the fortress must be described as Romano-British, since it assimilated enterprising individuals enticed in from life in the countryside, who set up stalls and workshops along the streets; some of them eventually participated in local government as council members, magistrates and tax-gatherers, settling disputes, collecting market-tolls and making sure that the streets were clean.

Until *c.*160 the town of Isca had no outer defences. Cemeteries lay beside the main exit roads (two on the sites of the future churches of St Sidwell and St David, and one outside the south gate). Vineyards and orchards covered the sunny slopes. The defences of the military fortress had been levelled, and the ditch had been forgotten when a grand town-house was built on the future site of St Catherine's almshouses. Part of the mosaic floor of its corridor was found in modern times: it had folded at right angles into the fortress ditch. Traces of another town-house found near Carfax in 1994, in the middle of the High Street, show that the Roman street grid did not coincide with the modern one.

Some time after A.D. 160 an earth rampart was thrown up to enclose 93 acres, including the red volcanic knob at the north-east corner. (The earth bank survives behind the wall in Rougemont Gardens, in the garden of the Bishop's Palace, and in the grounds of 14 Cathedral Close). After *c.*A.D. 200 the rampart was reinforced with massive stone walls, over 15ft high and 9ft thick. Timber gatehouses were replaced by stone ones, which have also long since gone, although the outlines of the Roman south gate have recently been marked out in brickwork in the pavement of South Street. The walls themselves, generally embedded in the work of later generations, can still be seen in an almost complete circuit. They run along the crest of the low cliff above the river, make a right-angled turn to run east above the deep valley of the northern brook, and circle the volcanic knob to reach Eastgate. On the south-eastern side the terrain is less precipitous, sloping more gently to the southern brook. Roman masonry is visible in many stretches, mainly in the lower courses. Herringbone work is exposed just to the left of the archway that leads from Rougemont Gardens to Northernhay. The massive thickness of the core can be seen near Maddocks Row in Paul Street car-park, and characteristic squared blocks in Northernhay Gardens, in Post Office Street, Quay Lane and many other places.

The line of the Roman walls still defines Exeter's centre, forming an irregular rhomboid, or, as John Hooker put it in the 16th century, 'It is not altogether fowre square but declinethe somewhat towards a rowndeness'. In the 18 centuries since the wall was built the city has engulfed neighbouring villages, and even two towns (St Thomas and Topsham), but the original site of Roman Isca provides the civic focus, containing castle, cathedral, guildhall, civic centre, law courts, main shopping areas, libraries, museums and historic churches.

To judge by the number of coins found, the Romano-British town flourished as a centre of trade. From A.D. 212 no distinction was drawn between Roman and British – all free men were full citizens of the empire. The town's population grew from about 1,000 to twice or three times as many by the late 4th century. There were plentiful supplies of grain, vegetables, dairy foods and fish. Venison was enjoyed more widely

8 This pipe-clay figurine of Venus, or possibly of a Celtic fertility goddess, was found in a late 2nd-century context in the Trichay Street area (but almost immediately stolen). Many similar figures were made in France in the preceding century and were widely distributed.

9 This miniature portrait head, found in the Goldsmith Street area in a 4th-century context, was probably made in the 1st century A.D. from white Mediterranean marble. It is as small as a pear but precisely carved to show a bald dome, lined forehead and deep-set eyes. It may have been set up as a memorial bust in a private home.

10 St Pancras Church, nestling in the Guildhall Shopping Centre.

than it would be in the Middle Ages, and large amounts of beef, pork, duck and oysters too. Native hazelnuts and introduced walnuts, plums, apples, grapes, mulberries and cherries were all available.

There were Roman-Britons in Exeter for about 350 years. They may have dug the first leats that drained and divided Exe Island, Shilhay and Bonhay, and they may have set mill-wheels in the leats. They probably either bridged or paved the ford across the main stream. Whether they crossed by bridge, ferry or ford, the starting-point was Shilhay. Many Roman coins have been found there, showing either that travellers threw a coin into the water for luck or that many accidentally dropped their payment. (The modern equivalent is the scattering of coins near bus-stops, a welcome subsidy for cyclists.)

The western bank was low-lying and marshy. Alphington Road runs on a causeway for part of its length and the section of Cowick Street from the railway-bridge to Old Vicarage Road may owe its straightness to origin as a Roman causeway. The straight section ends precisely at the point reached by the floods in, for example, 1800 and 1810.

There is evidence that Christianity has been practised in Exeter for over 1,600 years. The religion had gained tolerance under the Emperor Constantine in A.D. 313. A chi-rho sign scratched on a sherd from a 4th-century black-burnished cooking pot has been found in South Street. The little church of St Pancras has been rebuilt several

11 The Heavitree yew. The present tree by the tower of the parish church has been estimated to be a 450-year old shoot which sprouted from a much older tree, which was probably cut down when the tower was first rebuilt in 1541.

times, but its dedication is to a 4th-century Roman martyr, and its alignment seems to predate the medieval street-grid.

In about A.D. 380 the forum was remodelled, but by then the town was beginning to decline. Fewer coins came in to be mislaid or deliberately buried. When the Roman administration withdrew from Britain in A.D. 410, Isca's buildings began to fall into disrepair. Rubbish pits were dug in the centre of town; paved streets disappeared under briars and brambles; furze and fern reclaimed the slopes. Some British families continued to occupy the north-west corner inside the walls, where the ground drops steeply on two sides. They had lived in this area before the Romans arrived and they stayed on after the Romans left. This quarter continued to be called Britayne for centuries afterwards.

It was the British Dumnonians who maintained Christian practice in Exeter between the decline of the Roman town and the arrival of the Saxons. A few 5th- to 7th-century graves have been found in the area of the demolished forum, alongside a building that may have been used as a church. Of the many medieval city churches those dedicated to Celtic missionary saints (Kerrian, Petrock, Pol de Leon) stood near the British quarter, but the British had never been true city-dwellers. Isca came and went, a 'mere parcel' cut out of the royal estates.

The kings of Dumnonia probably continued to hold their assemblies at the traditional landmark tree at Wonford, a mile east of Exeter, where the main road across the south of England crosses the ancient ridgeway coming down from Stoke Woods, along Polsloe Road to the river. Wonford was later the name of the huge estate that encircled Exeter, reaching west nearly as far as Okehampton. When the Normans took over from the Saxon kings Wonford was already a royal estate, and it is known that the Saxons held court here.

The name Heavitree comes from the Anglo-Saxon heafodtreow, or 'head tree', head as in headquarters or capital or summit meeting-place. Today there are several yew trees in Heavitree churchyard, but one of particular significance stands by the west door of the church. A great authority on the history of ancient yew trees, Allen Meredith, visited this tree in 1991. Its trunk is hollow, and was given a constricting 'corset' of old stones and rubble by the Victorians who rebuilt the church tower. He examined the tree very carefully, looking at the branches, bark, fallen berries, trunk size and general proportions, and came to the conclusion that what we see today is a side-shoot about 450 to 500 years old from a much older tree. This main tree was cut down: you can see the tops of the old roots over a wide area round the surviving trunk. Yew tree roots go down, not sideways, so these show where the main large trunk was; when it was cut down this section sprouted again. Meredith dated the tree without knowing anything of the history of the church, and the church tower had in fact been completely rebuilt in 1541. You cannot get much nearer than that: 1541 to 1991 is 450 years; and 19th-century etchings show a stump by the church door.

Meredith said that the main trunk could well have been there in Saxon times. Yew trees were often used as landmark trees and as meeting places for hundred courts, because they were evergreen and stood out even in the winter months; while their wood is hard and they cannot easily be cut down. They are also very long-living: Saxons planted them in their burial grounds, and so did Celts: Meredith has found yew trees in churchyards that are 3,000 or 4,000 years old, much older than Christianity itself, and he thinks that the yew tree at Heavitree could well be older than the church building. St Augustine saw a yew tree in the churchyard at Canterbury when he arrived in A.D. 597. He did not destroy it: he blessed it and poured holy water on it.

The Romans left imposing reminders of their centuries here: squared masonry, mosaic floors, coins, pottery, sculpture, the city walls and the remains of the bath-house. Because of this, and because we know about them from their literature and inscriptions, their history has overshadowed that of the British population, whose 'greener' life-style left few tangible traces. The Dumnonii have not provided any of the illustrations for this chapter, but it should be remembered that the British were here long before the Romans, they played a full part in the Romano-British town, and they were still here for centuries afterwards, even after the Saxon settlers arrived.

2
Saxons and Danes

From the middle of the 6th century the West Saxons were trying to expand into Dumnonian territory. Many British emigrated to Brittany during this period, possibly after poor harvests or illness, or because they had been driven from their farms and many of their men had been killed. The chronicles record battles but do not give details of Saxon settlement. For centuries the British occupied the high ground, for safety, and also because the lighter upland soil was easier to till. The ploughs of the Saxon incomers could cope with the heavy red-brick clay of the east Devon valleys. The landscape pattern still visible today – Saxon villages in the valleys surrounded by large fields, alongside older British farmsteads on the slopes – reveals the state of play when the fighting stopped.

Exeter stands at the border between the two types of soil and the two ways of life. At this time the town was home to only a few British families. Sometimes more gathered there to hold the walls against the Saxons: in A.D. 568 against Cealwin, King of Wessex, and in A.D. 632 against Penda, King of Mercia. In A.D. 658 the British lost: Cenwealh of Wessex beat them at Pinhoe and then took Exeter. Three years later he beat them again, near Crediton. It may have been Cenwealh, baptised in A.D. 644, in possession of the Devon royal estates since A.D. 658, who with the fervour of the newly converted built the first church at Wonford next to the head tree. In A.D. 670 he founded an abbey at *Exanceastre*, possibly requisitioning the small British church in the central burial yard.

Some 10 years later the small Saxon boy called Winfrith who was to become famous as Boniface, apostle to the Germans, came from Crediton to receive his early education under Abbot Wolfhard here. The long life of Boniface is fully documented: his further education, his journeys to Rome, the chain of monasteries that he founded in the German forests, his personal correspondence, and his martyrdom at a great age at the hands of the Frisians. (His cousin Walpurgis, who also took Germany as her mission field, is said to have come from Devon too.)

The solidity of the record of the life of Boniface makes his alleged contemporary, Sidwell, seem a creature of fairy-tales: a devout Saxon maiden who was beheaded by her father's farm-workers in the fields outside Eastgate, 'since when God has performed miracles there at her shrine'. In A.D. 930 King Athelstan confirmed ownership of her remains to the minster, and in 1072 Leofric included them in his list of cathedral relics.

12   The figure of St Sidwell on the store next to the church is by Frederick Irving, 1969.

Along the flank of the Sidwell Street ridge are numerous springs of pure water. These have been of overwhelming importance in the history of the area. The geological explanation is that they bubble up through the red sandstone where it adjoins the Culm clay. The Celtic explanation was that all wells and springs are sacred entrances to the Other World. In rituals and legends wells were particularly associated with severed heads. The Romans came with their own cult of water-deities; their name for a pure source was *aqua virgo*. By the time written records begin we find that two of the local springs have been named after decapitated Christian virgin martyrs. A nearby well is named after St Anne or Agnes, another maiden who was stabbed in the neck, in Rome in A.D. 306. The policy of the Christian church from the 7th century was to incorporate holy places into the cult of appropriate saints. We shall see that obstinate resistance to religious innovation remained a peculiar characteristic of the local population down to the 19th century – and the impossibility of eradicating nature-worship is shown by the fact that we still have wishing wells. When Princess Margaret came to Crediton to commemorate Boniface – the 8th-century missionary to the Germans who felled their sacred oak – she did it by planting an oak tree.

The parish boundaries of St David's, St Leonard's and St Sidwell's are not recorded before 1222, but they may nevertheless represent the extent of the land belonging to the Roman city. The valleys were wooded, *sylvestris*, but on the more level ground outside the east gate the Romans had their grain fields, land sown with crops, *sativus*. The earliest documents referring to St Sidwell give her Latin name, *Sancta Sativola*: it is an adjective, not a true name, and could be a descriptive title taken from the sacred burial area among the cultivated fields. We know that there were already Christians in Exeter in Roman times, because of the chi-rho sign on a 4th-century pot found in South Street; and 5th-century Christian burials were found on the St Mary Major site. *Saedefulla* could be an Anglo-Saxon translation of *Sativola*, made when the first English came to Exeter in the middle of the 7th century, *saede* meaning 'land sown with crops'. By the time the English form of her name appears in surviving records, early in the 11th century, it was understood to be the adjective *sidefulla* or *sedefulla*, the normal Old English for 'modest ' or 'chaste', applied to any virtuous maiden. (The seventh bishop of Crediton, 973-7, was given a similar name, Sidemannus.)

In Middle English (1100 onward) the Devon dialect developed *sedefulla* to *sidevel* and forgot the Old English meaning; but the saint's connection with the holy well was still lively enough for the second part to be taken to mean 'well'. The first part was close enough to 'scythe' for the 14th-century east window in the cathedral to depict St Sidwell with scythe and well, a rebus on her name that was also appropriate to the legend that Bishop Grandisson spun in 1335 to supply an improving story for reading out annually on her feast-day. Introducing a wicked stepmother, a lunchtime errand and a miraculous spring of water, Grandisson's version embroiders the bald statement in the earliest record ('this innocent virgin was slain by her father's hay-makers, and afterwards Almighty God displayed many miracles at her tomb'). It supplies a motive for the murder (her stepmother coveted her inheritance), reasons to revere the saint (she was Christian, obedient and courageous) and details of the miracles (water sprang from the place of martyrdom, light shone from the corpse and many pilgrims have been healed at her tomb). We may never know the true story, and we do not even know the girl's real name. She may have been a late Roman martyr, a British princess or an English contemporary of Boniface. She may even have been an early Sydenham, a name that recurs frequently among local landowners.

By the middle of the 10th century Sancta Sidefulla without Exanceastre was listed in the tourist literature of the time, a pilgrims' guide to the resting-places of the saints. Among the open fields cultivated by the Saxons a stone-built church probably stood on the hillock above the Longbrook valley, which is also the site of today's church.

West of present-day Pennsylvania Road was the Hoperneland. Hoopern meant 'house for making barrel-hoops'. St Sidwell's Fee, containing well-watered pastureland and withybeds, stretched over the triangular flank of the hillside between modern Pennsylvania Road and Rosebarn Lane. The latter was called 'the highway leading towards Stocdoune' in 1312, and later Mary-bone-lane, Mary Bow Lane or Mary Port Lane. From the earliest written records its junction with the present Pennsylvania Road has been called Marypole Head; the older forms are Marpoole, Marypoole, Marepoll and Marpool, the first element probably going back not to the Blessed Virgin but to the Old English for boundary, now familiar to us as 'march' as in the Welsh marches. The name would then refer to a boundary pool, unless it marks the limit of Poll's land, now Polsloe.

The Venerable Bede described the forests of the south-west in the 8th century as full of deer, boar and man-eating wolves. The Saxon kings often visited Exanceastre to enjoy hunting in the steep wooded valleys north of the town. For example, Edward the Confessor was invited to hunt when he came to preside at the installation of the first bishop in 1050.

The hedge along Belvidere Road is one of the oldest in Exeter. It has been estimated to be about 900 years old. Duryard makes up a large part of the parish of St David's. It stretches from the edge of the city as far as Cowley Bridge and Wreford's Lane. The Manor of Duryard was given to the city in 950 by King Athelstan. The name Duryard is often taken to mean 'deer park' – and deer still occasionally leap into the gardens of houses in Hillcrest Avenue and Argyle Road. However, if Duryard was a deer park it would have needed a surrounding high bank or fence, to stop the deer leaping out – and there is no trace of this. But there was also an Anglo-Saxon word door-yard, meaning land owned outside one's gate. Domesday Book mentions that Exeter owned 960 acres outside the city's gates – so was Duryard the city's door-yard? It is interesting to note that some old English words and pronunciations have survived in America when they have died out in England. For example, T.S. Eliot wrote of 'the April dooryard' in 'The Dry Salvages' in 1942. In the 19th century Walt Whitman wrote 'When lilies last in the dooryard bloom'd'.

King Ine of Wessex asserted dominance over King Geraint of Dumnonia soon after A.D. 700, and the bishop of Sherborne negotiated with Geraint about standardising the timing of Easter celebrations. In A.D. 712 King Ine introduced Peter's Pence. Every householder with goods worth 20d. had to pay 1d. to the pope every Lammas Day. But each Saxon king had to make a fresh agreement with the British. A century later they held out against King Egbert from 800 to 816 before agreeing to the usual arrangement: that they could continue to live under their own laws if they paid an annual tribute.

In the early 9th century Vikings began to raid the south coast. In A.D. 851 the men of *Defenascire* drove them off. In A.D. 876 the 'Danish pagans' came riding overland from Dorset, pursued by King Alfred and his men. The Danes reached Exeter, and overwintered inside the walls. The following year Alfred drove them out, and took steps to keep them out of the country. He ordered longships to be built: the shipwrights of the Exe thus helped inaugurate England's royal navy. Alfred also established a stronghold or burgh in each of four royal possessions in Devonshire – Exeter, Totnes, Lydford and Barnstaple – where the burgesses paid dues direct to the crown. Exeter's Roman walls were repaired. Parts of the modern street plan may date from this time: Fore Street may preserve the width and straightness of Alfred's new main street; Gandy Street, St Martin's Lane and Catherine Street are surviving examples of the narrower side-streets that formed a regular grid. The blocks were divided into rectangular burgage plots of equal size, each with a frontage onto the street. Alfred established a mint for silver pennies in each burh, and made an impromptu gift of the church at Exeter, with its possessions 'in Saxon and Cornish areas', to his friend and biographer Asser, a bishop from Wales. The western diocese was still based in Sherborne, but when Asser died in A.D. 909 a bishop's seat was established in Crediton.

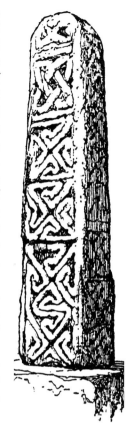

Alfred's daughter was given in marriage to an ealdorman of Mercia. Ties with Mercia may explain the dedication to the Mercian martyr St Osyth of a cross outside Westgate.

In A.D. 893 the Danes could not penetrate the new defences and besieged Exeter instead, until they heard that Alfred was coming to disperse them, and they fled.

Alfred's son, Edward the Elder, chose Exeter to hold his conference of earls and priests (Witanagemot) in A.D. 918. The king spoke about keeping the peace of the realm, and the meeting enacted a body of laws relating to the protection of property, the impartial administration of justice and the punishment of transgressors.

Alfred's grandson, Athelstan, held royal councils in Exeter in A.D. 928 and 935. Until then the British were still occupying their quarter, under their own laws, which ranked equally with English law. Athelstan tidied up the town by expelling 'that filthy race' to beyond the Tamar (including their king, Howell); he repaired the walls and added defensive towers. Present-day Athelstan Road runs along part of his eastern defensive dyke.

Athelstan divided the city into four hundreds or wards, north, south, east and west, with an alderman over each. He also refounded the minster as a house of Benedictine monks dedicated to the Blessed Virgin Mary. A manuscript written in Anglo-Saxon lists the large number of relics that King Athelstan sent well-funded emissaries to collect for him to donate to the minster of St Mary and St Peter. While visiting Exeter he had realised that 'with perishable treasures he could gain imperishable ones'. The 'honest men' whom he sent overseas to purchase the relics found pieces of the greatest significance, including fragments of the cross, of the Lord's tomb, of his garment, of the manger, water from Jordan, a piece of the spear which pierced his side, part of the table from the last supper and of the burning bush, bits of Mary's robe, head-dress and hair, of the body and clothes of John the Baptist, of the beard, hair, neckbone and robe of St Peter, a piece of the head of St Stephen, the first martyr, some of his blood and the stone that killed him, a relic of St Jerome who translated the Bible into Latin, St Augustine the sagacious bishop, St Nicholas, St Petroc, the stone that St Silvin carried three times to Rome, a finger-bone of Mary Magdalene, four of St Agatha's teeth, a relic of St Sidwell and many other apostles, martyrs, confessors and virgins, 146 in all, all identified by labels.

13 Toisa's Cross is a late-Saxon granite praying-cross the height of a man, tapering slightly, and carved on all four sides with interlaced patterns. T Oisa is thought to be a local pronunciation of St Osyth. This may be the cross described as broken in 1316, when it stood outside Westgate near the river crossing.

It was believed that a monastery without a library was like a castle without an armoury. Books were important for education and for use in services. Before the advent of printing, books were laboriously copied out by hand by monks using quills and parchment and ink made from oak galls. This made books extremely expensive. Not many copies were made of each text, unless they were very important or useful. If they were destroyed that work was lost.

The minster's scriptorium produced fine manuscripts, and it is now thought that 'the large English book with everything cast as verse' known as The Exeter Book was written there, in its beautiful square minuscules. This is one of only four surviving collections of Old English poetry, which do not completely overlap in their contents. The Exeter Book contains many works, including the Crist and Juliana of Cynewulf, many elegiac poems and two important works of the heroic age, Widsith and Deor. One melancholy elegy, 'The Ruin', seems to describe the remains of the Roman baths from half a millennium before, with their crumbling walls – lichen-grey and stained with red, broken arches and streams of heated water: 'Bright were the buildings, many the bath-chambers, high were the gables, great the sound of merriment …'

The book preserved dozens of jokey Anglo-Saxon riddles about such things as a cuckoo, a ship and a weathercock (although the answers were not supplied so these are guesses). They are meant to catch you out. The swelling that a young women hides under a cloth does not show that she is with child: she is putting bread dough to rise. The hairy round object with a stalk sticking up that makes a girl cry is not what you might think: it is probably an onion. In the following centuries, when the monks could no longer understand Anglo-Saxon, the book seems to have been used as a sturdy cutting-board. It was slashed by knives and splashed by glue pots. Gleaming gold fragments between the pages suggest that gold leaf was stored there when the scriptorium was producing illuminated manuscripts, in the 14th century.

In A.D. 968 King Edgar the Peaceful sent a group of monks from Glastonbury, led by Abbot Sidemann, to reform the minster. Henceforth the scribes were to copy only theological texts. Sidemann was tutor to Edgar's son Edward, so the martyr king might have been a schoolboy here. Perhaps they let him read the riddles. Edgar also reformed the mint in A.D. 973. From that time all coins had the king's head on one side, and the mint and moneyer's name on the other.

Of Edgar's peaceful reign a Saxon poet sang: 'There was no fleet so proud, no host so strong as to seek food in England while this king wielded the sceptre. He reared up God's honour, he loved God's law. He preserved the people's peace. God was his helper and kings and earls bowed to him, and obeyed his will, and without battle he ruled all as he pleased.'

Edgar had a very tall and very strong friend, Ordgar Earl of Devon, founder of Tavistock Abbey and father of Edgar's third wife. One day he and Edgar visited Exeter, found the Eastgate shut and the gatekeeper nowhere to be seen. Ordgar was so angry at the want of respect that he dismounted from his horse, pulled off the bars of the gate, taking part of the wall with it, set his teeth, placed his foot against the gates and burst them open.

Edgar often came hunting in Devon. He tried to settle the problem of wolves in the woods by accepting 300 wolves' heads instead of cattle for the annual tribute; while Edward's half-brother Aethelred tried to settle the Danish problem. Raids had intensified in the 980s, and payments of danegeld were siphoning off hundreds of the

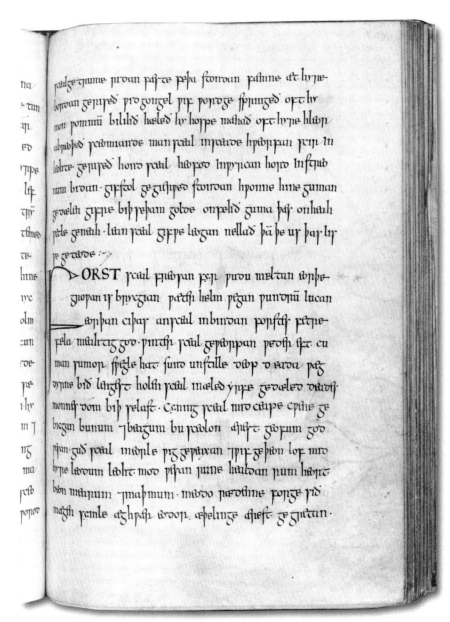

14 Incantations and etiquette meet in the Anglo-Saxon maxins written on vellum in square miniascules on this page of the 10th-century Exeter Book.

FROST shall freeze, fire burn wood, earth grow … and mighty God shall break frost's fetters.

At the foot of the page:

In handing around the mead-cup she must quickly reach the frist drink to her lord.

new pennies. Aethelred asked the Norman ports not to harbour the raiders, and took Emma of Normandy as his wife. After devastating raids in 1001 he ordered all the Danes in England to be slaughtered on St Brice's Day, 13 November 1002. King Swein's sister was amongst them; and in 1003 Swein came rowing up the Exe to take revenge on the favourite town of the Saxon kings: Emma held Exeter as a dowry, the 'morning-gift' made after the wedding-night. (This began the tradition of making each royal bride the lady paramount of Exeter.) Emma had installed a Norman bailiff, Hugh, to collect her revenues. He opened the gate to Swein and his men, enabling them to destroy the town and burn down the abbey and its library. Swein levelled the city to the ground from east to west and put all the citizens to the sword. The traitor Hugh was dragged off in chains by the enemy, and the king paid a huge sum, £36,000, for a truce.

When Swein's younger son, Cnut, became King of England in 1016 he ended 200 years of wars which had killed 300,000 men in 54 land battles and 38 fights at sea. He called himself King of England and Denmark and the Norwegians and part of the Swedes. He was a Christian, went on pilgrimage to Rome and negotiated free passage for English merchants and pilgrims. Cnut married the widowed Emma, rebuilt Exeter's walls, houses and churches, and made the town once more prosperous and secure. The Exeter mint was the fifth or sixth largest in England. In 1019 he gave a charter to the new Abbot of Exeter that all present and future brethren in the monastery should have all previous rights and privileges. The royal signature was attested by the Archbishops of Canterbury and York, five bishops, five dukes, five abbots and five officers.

In the early 11th century royal protection was given to four national highways, of which one was the Icknield Way leading to Exeter. The Lammas Fair was already being held each year on Exe Island at the beginning of August.

Most of the city's buildings were timber and cob, with thatched roofs. The churches were stone-built, but little of the original fabric can be seen today. The tower of St Olave's, now enclosed by the later aisle, may have been part of the 11th-century church founded soon after the saint died in 1030, and some of the original volcanic blocks of stone from Northernhay can be seen re-used in its outer walls. St George's stood on the west side of South Street until 1843, when it was cut away for road-widening. After the Second World War a remaining Saxon arch was moved across the road, where it stands in the ruined hall of the vicars choral. St Martin's proclaims a consecration date of 1065, but this may be the date of a re-consecration of the foundation. There is Saxon work in the crypt of St Stephen's. Saxon work is characterised as 'long and short work', where individual stones are laid at the corners alternately horizontally and vertically.

In 1042 the throne was restored to Saxon kings. Edward, son of Ethelred, who became known as the saintly Edward the Confessor, repaired St Peter's Monastery and moved the bishop's seat there from Crediton. Bishop Leofric had obtained permission directly from the pope to move from the small town to the walled city. His personal friend King Edward said: 'I, Kynge Edward, taking Leofricus by his right hande, and Editha, my Queen, by his lefte, do enstalle hym the fyrste and most famous Byshoppe of Excester, with a great abundance of blessynges to all such as shall furder and encrease the same, but with a fearful and execrable curse to all such as shall diminish, or take away anything from it.' This scene was enacted in the newly elevated small abbey church to which Boniface had come, west of the later magnificent Norman cathedral.

In the 1970s the cathedral planned an underground car park in front of the west front. Demolition of St Mary Major seemed to clear the way, but archaeologists found not only the extensive remains of the Roman legionary bath-house but also different generations of St Mary Major: beneath the Victorian church there was the 15th-century church and beneath that the original apsed abbey church, which became Leofric's cathedral. The site is marked by an iron cross in the grass of the western close.

Edward dispatched the monks to the new abbey he was building at Westminster. Exeter Cathedral was therefore never a monastic foundation and would not be affected by the Dissolution of the Monasteries. It is still organised according to the charter of 1050, and is thus the oldest surviving institution in the land, centuries older than the United Kingdom itself.

15 This silver penny of 'long cross' type was issued by the moneyer Wulfsige of Exeter in the reign of Aethelred the Unready between A.D. 997 and 1003.

The bishop's charter was witnessed by several members of a powerful local family. Godwin had married a kinswoman of Cnut called Gytha, and had been made Earl of Wessex by Cnut. One of their sons, Harold, was to succeed Edward in January 1065-6. They had also forced Edward to contract a nominal marriage with their daughter Edith in 1045. All these individuals, and Harold's brother Tostig, were among the witnesses named in 1050.

The area vacated by the British in A.D. 928 had become known as 'the earl's burh': Godwin had a mansion there, and Gytha may have lived there in her widowhood (1053-66). Her daughter the queen was dismissed by King Edward, but continued to hold the royal estate of Wonford.

Saxons had displaced the British, but they themselves were soon to yield to the Normans.

The smells, street stalls, pub brawls and brothels of 12th-century Exeter are brought to life in Bernard Knight's series of medieval murder mysteries about a fictional Exeter-based coroner, one of the first to hold such a position and second only to the county sheriff. 'Crowner John's' office is in the gateway of Rougemont Castle; his house is in Martin's Lane.

Bernard Knight became a Home Office pathologist in 1965 and was appointed Professor of Forensic Pathology at the University of Wales College of Medicine in 1980. He is also a barrister. Professor Knight discovered that the position of coroner was established in England in the 1190s, primarily to raise fines to help pay the ransom of Richard Coeur de Lion. He would have preferred to set his stories in his native Wales, but coroners were not appointed there until later.

The first coroner in Exeter whose name is known held the office in about 1211. Bernard Knight felt free to choose a name for his main character, and so 'Crowner John' was born.

The author of this series makes every effort to make his narratives as historically accurate as possible. He spends long hours in the Westcountry Studies Library and the cathedral archives. He reckons he knows every medieval cobbled street in Exeter, the little churches, the cathedral yard, humpy with many burials, the noisy traders in the High Street, the rowdy alehouses and stinking workshops. For the names of his characters, Bernard Knight rings the changes on names that are documented as having existed in Exeter in the 1190s.

Another gripping story set in a thinly disguised 12th-century Exeter is Ken Follett's *The Pillars of the Earth*, about the building of the Gothic cathedral. Follett also wrote *World Without End*, set two centuries later, clearly based on Exeter. As the wool trade develops, extra profit is made from using scarlet dye, and the bridge over the river collapses dramatically.

3

Castles and Cathedrals

16 King William, a mosaic portrait by Elaine M. Goodwin in the multi-storey car-park on the site of the Norman siege of Eastgate.

Exeter was a centre of Saxon opposition to the Norman Conquest. King Harold's sister, Queen Edith, still held the royal estate of Wonford. Their widowed mother Gytha took refuge in the town-house of the Earls of Wessex. Harold's sons were gathering support in Devon and Cornwall. William led 500 horsemen westwards in late autumn 1068 to demand allegiance from Exeter. A delegation met him 4 miles outside the city: they agreed to a compromise, and gave hostages. The two parties then progressed to the gates, only to find that the citizens refused to open up until they were assured that the city's

17 An inside view of the gatehouse, showing the adjacent modern gateway dating from the 1770s, when the castle was rebuilt and the approach was realigned.

18   The gatehouse of Rougemont Castle, built for William in 1068, is the oldest Norman military arch surviving in Britain. Long-and-short stonework and triangular window heads probably indicate that Saxon masons were employed. The entrance was fitted with a drawbridge over a ditch.

tribute would remain unchanged at £18 (£12 to the queen, £6 to the bailiff), payable only when London, York and Winchester were taxed. William, furious, had a hostage blinded in front of them but the citizens remained adamant. The Normans laid siege to the city, mined under the east gate and camped outside, growing impatient as the weather became wintry. After 18 days part of the wall collapsed and the citizens agreed on a conditional surrender. William swore on the cathedral's holy relics that he would leave Exeter's tax status unchanged, and Gytha was allowed to depart. The king would not be defied again: he decided to plant a castle inside the walls, towering over the rest of the town on the red hill called *rougemont* in Norman-French. William created his friend Baldwin Sheriff of Devon, with responsibility for building and manning the castle (and one at Okehampton). To make way for Rougemont Castle and its sprawling earthworks 48 houses (a 10th of the housing stock) were demolished. The massive ditch

19 The 11th-century undercroft of St Nicholas Priory.

20 The surviving western range of St Nicholas Priory contains the guest-hall, kitchen, chambers and main entrance. An alley now divides it from the surviving north side of the cloisters where the monks ate.

is still a feature of Rougemont Gardens, and the steep slope above Gandy Street by the arts centre is a remnant of the outer earth bank.

William confiscated the earl's estate in the north-west quarter (including Gytha's church of St Olaf) and gave it to the Benedictine monks of the St Martin's Abbey, which he had founded in Battle. They set up a priory, dedicating its church in 1087 to the 4th-century bishop Nicholas.

When Muslims overran Nicholas's shrine in Turkey, Italian merchants stole his remains and took them to Bari in Apulia, in the Norman kingdom of Sicily. St Nicholas

was not only the patron saint of sailors, children and merchants but also pawnbrokers: his emblem of three golden balls figures on the present gate to the cloister. This also relates to the story that Nicholas secretly threw three bags of gold into a poor man's house, as dowries for his three daughters to save them from prostitution. To this day Santa Claus brings his gifts secretly down the chimney.

The priory is said to be the oldest standing building in Devon and contains examples of architecture from every century from the 11th onwards. There are Norman vaulted cellars in the western range, used for storage of the priory's food and drink. A huge church stood on the south side of the cloister, and by 1102 its bell was eliciting complaints from the cathedral clergy. A chapter house stood on the east side. The church and the chapter house were demolished during the Dissolution of the Monasteries. The refectory, still standing, completed the enclosure of the cloister. In the early 16th century the refectory and the guest hall in the western range were given fine arch-braced roofs. A round-roofed fountain house stood in a corner of the cloister near the refectory.

The monks followed the Benedictine order, taking vows of poverty, obedience and chastity. Their days were divided into periods of worship, teaching, study and gardening in the priory's field and 2½ acre orchard. Their duties included hospitality to visitors and charity to the poor. The monks slept communally in a dormitory and ate together in the refectory.

Under King Henry I guilds or fraternities were established 'for the better government of trades and mysteries'. This weakened the feudal system and the power of the barons, and raised the opulence of cities. Countrymen flocked into the towns. If they were unclaimed by their liege lord during a year and a day they were no longer vassals and could join a guild.

Meanwhile a new cathedral was rising in shiny milky-white stone, in contrast to the more than 30 little churches and chapels built of local red Heavitree stone, served by

21   The Norman font of St Mary Steps.

22   The church of St Mary Arches was enlarged in the 15th century but still has its Norman pillars.

23 Matthew Miller Clock
on St Mary Steps Church.

a streetful of priests in Preston Street. Bishop Osbern had not felt the need to extend or replace the Saxon minster cathedral. After his time the bishop's seat was vacant for four years. Then the king appointed William de Warelwast, a nephew of the Conqueror, in 1107. Tithes from the recently discovered rich veins of tin near Tavistock helped finance a grand Romanesque church, which would accommodate the growing number of clergy celebrating mass at many altars. In the still largely deserted city there was plenty of space within the walls for the new cathedral to be sited further away from South Street and High Street.

Today we still see the massive twin towers that were retained in the succeeding Gothic cathedral. We also know that the Romanesque cathedral was of similar length and width to its successor, because masonry in the aisle walls was kept up to window sill level. The pillars were thicker and stronger than the Gothic ones, and the round-headed windows let in less light. There were polygonal chapels radiating out from an ambulatory apse.

By 1133 the canons were able to process from the old church and begin to use at least the new eastern choir end, while building continued in the nave under the next five bishops. The west front was completed under Bishop Henry Marshal by 1204. The remains of Leofric and Osbern were reinterred in the new choir.

Exeter children are lucky to have a real Norman castle, Rougemont, where they can play attackers and defenders on the steep slopes of the former moat. Exeter's other Norman castle, by Howell Road, is harder to appreciate. It was a siege work, thrown up in 1136 to threaten Rougemont across the Longbrook valley. But the walls of the prison block the view across to Rougemont, and the slopes of the new reservoir tower over the little earthwork. It has an interesting history.

King Henry I died in 1135. For the next 19 years his daughter Matilda and his nephew Stephen fought for the throne. Henry had named Matilda as his heir but Stephen managed to get himself crowned first. Exeter's citizens were loyal to King Stephen, but the Earl Baldwin of the time held the castle for his own cousin, Matilda. He put his wife and children into Rougemont Castle for safety, protected by a garrison of 'valiant youths in shining armour'. Stephen's men built the little castle above Howell Road and besieged Rougemont for three months. They built siege towers, dug tunnels under the walls, and slung stones and burning torches over the walls. Baldwin's troops sallied out through secret passages to fight with swords, or sent down showers of arrows from inside the castle walls. Baldwin's men held firm when the castle wells ran dry – they used wine for drinking, cooking and putting out incendiaries – but then the wine ran out, and they surrendered.

For a century or so the earthwork was referred to as the New Castle, but by about 1700 the campaign was forgotten and people thought it dated from the Danish sieges of Exeter. In 1833 the water company built a reservoir where the fire station is now. They converted this to filter beds in the 1850s and built a larger reservoir on top of the castle mount, slicing off the top of the earth ramparts and dumping the spoil in the ditch. In 1905 houses were built alongside in Danes Road. In the 1990s South West Water decided to rebuild the reservoir and make it 'half the size for a more compact supply'. Members of the Archaeological Field Unit were delighted to find that the Norman siege castle was still there. It had been covered up rather than destroyed 140 years before. South West Water built their new reservoir further back from the road and gave the little Norman castle to the city as a public open space. There is an interpretation board

with an excellent drawing by Piran Bishop that shows how it looked during the siege of 1136. Even after all the publicity the houses built next to the site were marketed as a chance to live 'on the site of a Viking castle'.

Across the river the manors of Cowick and Exwick were not part of the city, but shared its fortunes. It was this river that originally hollowed out the valley floor that St Thomas stands on, and caused Exeter to grow at this particular junction of cliff and crossing. Until the Middle Ages sea-tides came to the quay, and when they ebbed one could wade across or urge a horse through the shallow water. Ships could unload, and travellers could pass to west and east. The river runs along one side of its flood-plain, leaving a wide flat valley to the west. Flat ground is in short supply in Exeter. Over the centuries every activity, industry or sport that needs elbow-room has found it west of the river: space to dye cloth and hang it to dry, space for iron-foundries, plant-nurseries, wrestling, the Easter Fair, factories, the gasworks, the cattle-market, a railway and houses for the railwaymen, an industrial estate, Park and Ride, and even supermarkets and sports centres.

According to Domesday, before the Conquest the manor of Coic was held by a Saxon called Ailmar, with land that eight ploughs could till. There were eight villeins (smallholders), three bordars (who held a smaller portion of land), two serfs, one rouncey (small horse), three beasts (oxen for the ploughs), 40 sheep (no cows mentioned), one mill, 3 acres of woodland and 3 acres of meadow. Essoic (Exwick) was held by Eureuuacus (Earwaker), and likewise had eight ploughs; there were nine villeins, five serfs, 40 sheep, a mill, 3 acres of meadow, 50 acres of pasture and 3 acres of coppice.

25 Exeter Domesday is the draft of the return for the south-west countries. This page lists the lands of St Peter's church in Exeter in Devonshire, i.e. of the cathedral, held by Bishop Osbern (1073-1103), who was one of the Domesday commissioners. His income from this large diocese made him the sixth wealthiest bishop in England.

Between Buddle Lane and the river lay Haia (Hayes), held by Edric, next to Sotrebroc (Southbrook), held by Aluiet.

At the Battle of Hastings one of William's generals was his nephew-by-marriage, Baldwin of Brionne. Baldwin was made Sheriff of Devon and entrusted with the construction and care of castles at Rougemont and Okehampton; he was also made lord of 159 manors in Devon, including Cowick and Exwick. Baldwin's home in Normandy was near the famous Benedictine abbey of Bec (their London property is still called Tooting Bec). It was a prior of Bec, Lanfranc, who became the first Norman archbishop of Canterbury; Anselm made the same career-move in 1093. Baldwin's father had helped to found Bec, and when Baldwin's son inherited the family lands and obligations on both sides of the Channel he made a gift to the French abbey of two of his English estates, Cowick and Exwick. This must have been between 1090 (when Baldwin died) and 1107 (when his son died).

We know the names of some Cowick people in 1090-1100, because the Exeter Book and Leofric's Missal carry records of serfs being sold or freed at the hundred court there. Regenere bought Alfrith from Regenolde, the monk of Cowick. Edith, daughter of Leofric Locc (Lock), bought the freedom of herself and her children. Godwin Blaca (Black) bought himself, his wife and offspring from William Hosethe. The witnesses representing Cowick included Edmaer the priest, Alfric Hals and Agilword Pudding. There is even mention of a Sewin Pinca, surely an early Cowick Pince.

Bec set up a small daughter-priory in Cowick. 'Priory Ruins' are marked in Flowerpot field in some maps, but it is more likely that the little community took over Cowick Barton farmhouse, and the Saxon burial ground next to it, gradually adding cells, cloisters and church. William Warelwast (Bishop of Exeter 1107-36, himself a Norman, indeed another nephew of the Conqueror) helped Cowick's building-fund by promising 60 days off purgatory for visiting the relics there. The cathedral's collection of relics included a piece of St Andrew's staff. Did Warelwast lend this to the new priory, thereby giving it a dedication? Visitors to St Andrew's will have had a good view across to the bishop's rival enterprise, the construction of the Norman cathedral.

The priory church was functioning by 1150. The monks also built guest rooms for travellers and pilgrims, a bakehouse to provide bread for the poor, a great grange to store the produce of the two manors and a great porch. One monk called Walter (possibly a prior of that name in the 1180s) had a vision of the terrors of purgatory, put on a hair-shirt and was revered after his death as St Walter, attracting crowds of pilgrims on his name-day even 300 years later. Many little Exonians were named after him.

There was another small monastic building not far away, at Marsh Barton: St Mary of the Marsh, built by Plympton Priory for monks visiting Exeter. It had its own water-mill.

There were chapels at each end of Exe Bridge, still only a narrow footbridge made of 'clappers of tymbre'. (Bulky traffic or impoverished travellers used the ford alongside.) The chapel at the city end was dedicated to St Edmund, as Saxon chapels on bridges often were, since the king once escaped from the Danes by hiding under a bridge. The chapel at the western end was dedicated to Thomas Becket. He was murdered and canonised in the 1170s, so the chapel may have dated from then, or an existing chapel might have been renamed to annoy Bishop Bartholomew, an enemy of Becket. If so, this was not the only time that space was found just across the river for something forbidden within the city walls.

The mills at Exwick and Cowick had been grinding grain since Saxon times. In 1189 the priory bought 2 acres of river-meadow from Duryard to build a new weir for Exwick leat. The Cowick mill drew its water off the end of the bridge-weir. Merchants and tradesmen built dwellings, workshops and warehouses on Exe Island and along the approach-roads to the bridge. There were soon enough residents in Cowick to call it a township. Tanners, brewers, metalworkers, clothmakers and dyers plied their smelly trades. The leats around Exe Island alone were driving at least nine mills. The weavers began to produce more cloth than could be cleansed and felted by trampling on it in cold water, and carried it to be pounded mechanically in tucking or fulling mills.

A manor-house stood on each estate. One at Barley is mentioned in 1189. Randolf de Haga (1125) may have occupied the house on Hayes that preceded one fortified in the Civil War. The neighbouring estate, Southbrook, was beginning to be called Floyerhayes. Today's place name Flowerpot is probably a corruption of Floyer. Floyer Hayes is documented as the name of the land near the riverside as early as the 1170s. The Floyers have an unusually long record of their family tree, going back to before 1066, when a local Floyer was a witness to the freeing of a serf. By the time of Domesday Book the family already had a mansion and 30 acres of land near the Exe. One John Floyer was a churchwarden in 1412 when the parish church of St Thomas was relocated from the flooded river-bank to its present site on Cowick Street. In 1567 William Floyer transferred a piece of his land to the city for the excavation of the canal. The 1587 Hogenberg map of Exeter has a little drawing of the Floyers Hayes mansion, standing among trees on the Alphington Road, and 200 years later Tozer's 'Plan of the City and Suburbs of Exeter' also draws in, and names, Floyers Hayes on Alphington Road, just before the turnpike gate. However, by this time it was the Georgian mansion of 1770, which had replaced the earlier house.

The grand mansion on Haven Banks survived until 1979. All that now remains is the high garden wall decorated with granite balls. Gone are the balustraded roof, the vast reception rooms and the grand sweeping staircase. The service rooms on the right had flagstone floors, and there was a huge scullery with a grate furnished with cooking-spits. There was a pump in the yard.

One reason for recording the family history so carefully was that the Floyers had married into the family of the founders of Wadham College, Oxford, and were entitled to a free place if they could prove their descent. Another perk was the collection of tolls for Exe Bridge, as the agent of their liege lord, the Earl of Devon; in return they had to be ready to supply one soldier in time of war. There was also a more picturesque duty. A silver bowl was carefully passed down from father to son, and whenever the Earl of Devon set foot on Exe Island the Floyer of the time had to stop whatever he might be doing and step forward 'decently apparelled with a fair sweet towel on his shoulder, a flagon of wine in one hand, and a silver bowl in the other, and offer to serve his lordship with drink'.

For many generations the lord enjoying this roadside service-station was a Courtenay. The Courtenays came to England with Eleanor of Aquitaine. They married into the Redvers family and into other branches of the Brionne family, gaining within 200 years control of the greater part of Devon, including most of the Exe valley. Exeter's own jurisdiction did not extend an inch outside the city walls, while the Courtenays controlled the river-banks, including the area between Bartholomew Street and the river, and even the river itself. Indeed our own Earl wrote in 1966: 'I think I am the only non-royalty who owns part of the river-bed.'

In 1180 Robert de Courtenay was the lord of Exe Island. He granted to Nicholas Gervase 'all his water which Thomas the Fuller holds outside the West Gate between the corn-mills and Crickenpette'. Gervase was a prominent citizen who owned mills and warehouses near the bridge. He saw many travellers drown on the ford, and the wooden bridge swaying in the winter floods. He determined to rebuild the bridge in stone, and dispatched his son (Walter!) to collect donations from near and far. It took many decades at the turn of the 13th century to complete the work. The bridge had to be about 700ft long, crossing not only the stream but also the salt-marshes. Half still stands, enjoying a peaceful retirement in the drained marshes between Frog Street and Edmund Street.

Drawings of this bridge done in the 1660s and 1760s show the central pier with a door at water-level, leading to a 'Pixy House'. This has been explained as yet another chapel, housing a sacred pyx; or a pixhay, a fairy house, a public urinal; or was it something piscatorial, a place to spear salmon as they leapt upstream? Three 17th-century travellers mentioned the fishing. Risdon wrote in 1605: 'The River Ex [is] well stored with salmon; which are reputed the best in this land, for at most times you shall find some come new from the sea with lice on their backs, and then they are best. ' A lieutenant from Norwich in 1635 saw 'a faire stone Bridge of 20 arches, under which the dainty Salmon Trouts come trolling'. Celia Fiennes in 1695 recorded that 'they catch the salmon as they leap, with spears'.

Back to when the bridge was young: in the 1240s a devout woman settled on it as a hermit, blocking the traffic for more than five years while the city tried to formulate a bye-law against squatting. The obstruction must have inconvenienced many, including the Cowick monks (who at this time were all Frenchmen, sent over from Bec; they wore white undyed wool, not monastic black.)

Soon after 1250 the bridge chapels were upgraded to parish churches. Bishop (Walter!) Bronescombe installed John as rector of St Edmund's in 1259, and Henry as vicar of St Thomas in 1261. Cowick Priory provided stipend and manse for Henry, and the little flood-damaged chapel was rebuilt in stone. (An archway from this building is preserved in the north porch of the present parish church.) As the river-bank could not be used for a graveyard, the parishioners continued to bury their dead next to the priory. A small cemetery chapel, St Michael's, was built there in the 1270s.

A grander project dominated the view of the city. Bishop Bronescombe was rebuilding the entire nave of the cathedral, for which an immense amount of stone was needed. One of the quarries listed in the fabric rolls for 1324/5 is Barley. An inventory of the priory's possessions from the same year enables us to picture cartloads of stone trundling down Dunsford Road past fields of barley and of rye, oats, wheat, beans and peas. The priory's livestock that year amounted to 4 horses, 11 oxen, 116 sheep, 41 pigs and 3 peafowl (still no cows; cheese was made from ewes' milk). The monks had 24 free tenants and 10 unfree.

The monks' Courtenay overlords had inherited the obligations of their original patron. When Sir Hugh died near Colyton in 1291 he was brought to the priory for burial. A stone coffin and a lead chalice were found on the site in 1887; the coffin may well have been Sir Hugh's. It is on display at present in St Nicholas's crypt. In 1328 Sir Hugh's widow died in London and was brought to Cowick to lie next to him. Their son, another Hugh, and his wife, who died shortly before him in 1340, were also interred at Cowick. This Hugh had revived the title of earl in 1335, and the present numbering of the Earls of Devon starts with him. He it was who in 1311 blocked the gap in Countess Isabella's weirs, preventing ships and salt water from reaching Exeter quay. His elaborate funeral took up a long weekend. On the Friday virtually all of Devon's nobility, gentry and top clergy escorted the coffin from Tiverton to Exeter, where it lay in the cathedral for solemn vespers and a mass. The procession re-assembled on the Monday and walked to Cowick, where Bishop Grandisson presided over the interment in the choir. A tile-floor patterned with the Courtenay arms may date from then. Hugh's successor died in 1375 and was buried in the cathedral, but he had remembered Cowick in his will: 'Jeo devise a la meson de Couwyk cent soulds.' In 1376 William Courtenay, Bishop of London, ordained 99 clerics at Cowick, including yet another Hugh Courtenay.

Before 1160 Exeter had a leper hospital for not more than 13 sufferers at a hygienic distance from the south gate, on the further bank of the southern brook. Dedicated to St Mary Magdalene, its name lives on in the street that led there.

In 1154 William of Malmesbury wrote of Exeter: 'By reason of its stateliness, the wealth of its citizens, and the great resort of strangers, it so abounds with all sorts of merchandise that nothing is wanting that can be reckoned useful.'

In 1189 Richard Lionheart granted a charter to the city releasing the merchants from certain taxes. From 1191 the city paid the royal dowry to the Lionheart's queen, Berengaria, Lady Paramount of Exeter. It also paid a large sum towards Richard's ransom when he was captured on his way back from the Holy Land. He had been attended on the outward journey by Joseph, 'the swan of Isca'.

In about 1200 Exeter was famous as the birthplace of the poet Joseph, who wrote Latin hexameters that were regarded as the equal of those written in classical times. He was called 'the miracle of his age in classical composition'. Surnames had not yet become fully established, so people were called after their trade or referred to as the son of so-and-so. Anyone who made a reputation far from home might be called after the place he came from. This happened in Joseph's case. He was called Joseph of Exeter, or in Latin Iscanus.

Joseph was born in about 1160 to a humble family but he probably benefited from being the nephew of Baldwin of Exeter, who was already a well-known writer and later became Bishop of Worcester and then, in 1185, Archbishop of Canterbury. Baldwin probably made sure that young Joseph had a good start at the school run by the cathedral, and later Joseph studied in Reims in France. King Richard the Lionheart set out for the Third Crusade from Dartmouth in 1190. He was accompanied by his archbishop, and Baldwin was accompanied, very reluctantly, by his nephew Joseph.

Baldwin died during 1190 and Joseph was released from the obligation to follow the crusaders any further. Instead he went to Belgium and became a schoolmaster. He composed a major Latin epic called *De Bello Antiocheno* relating the king's exploits in the Holy Land, but the manuscript has been lost. Leland saw it in the 16th century and recorded that it included a description of Exeter. Joseph also wrote a Latin epic about the Trojan war, *De Bello Troiano*. Several copies of this have survived, including one made at Battle Abbey, the mother house of Exeter's St Nicholas's Priory. The Plantagenets were keen on the story of Troy, since they claimed to be descended from the Trojans. They believed the legend that the great-grandson of Aeneas, Brutus, had landed at Totnes at the spot marked by the Brutus Stone, and gave his name to Britain.

As an aside, it is interesting to note that a history of cricket says that bat and ball games have been played for centuries, but that the first mention of a game where the batsman defends stumps is in writings by Joseph of Exeter dating from 1183.

In 1200 King John granted Exeter the power to elect a chief magistrate or 'mayor' and two bailiffs or stewards. Previously the Earl of Devon had nominated provosts. Exeter was therefore the earliest town to have a mayor, after London and Winchester.

26 An impression of the silver Common Seal of the City of Exeter which uses the image of the new Norman cathedral and probably dates from about 1200. It is the earliest civic seal in England (although the cathedral chapter were using one with a similar, but simpler design half a century before).

In 1217 the nine-year-old Henry III came to the throne, and asked Robert Courtenay, whose family now held Rougemont, to vacate one chamber and the great hall for the use of the dowager queen. Two years later he had to repeat the request. In 1228, fully grown, Henry gave the revenues from Exeter to his brother Richard, Earl of Cornwall, later Holy Roman Emperor. From that date the castle was traditionally assigned to the Earls of Cornwall. Earl Richard was a friend and patron of the Franciscans at Oxford. Soon after the death of St Francis in 1226 a little group of eight came to Exeter, perhaps encouraged by Richard. They settled behind St Nicholas's Priory, living in poverty and caring for the poor and sick. They were known as grey friars from the colour of their cloaks. The street that led to their first house is still called Friernhay.

On the opposite side of town, in the south-east quarter, Bishop Brewer established a priory for the followers of Francis's friend Dominic, known as black friars. In September 1232 the king gave them permission to quarry stone for a church from the side of Rougemont, from a spot where it would not undermine the castle.

William Brewer, bishop from 1224 to 1244, was away from 1227 to 1235 leading crusaders to the Holy Land, and then escorting the king's sister Isabella to Germany to marry Emperor Frederick II. Before he set out he appointed Serlo to the new office of dean. When Brewer came home he may have brought drawings of exotic Asian beasts and news of the latest European literature – which would explain the choice of decorations for the cathedral misericords, the oldest set surviving in England. The carvings include mermaids, grotesques, an elephant, foliage and parrots. There are knights in 13th-century surcoats, chain-mail and flat-top helmets acting out scenes from Arthurian romances, including Lohengrin in a boat pulled by a swan (his brother had been turned into a swan to guide him over the sea). The Alexander Romance supplied the figure who is trying to fly by sitting in a basket pulled by two hungry griffins tempted by meat-tipped spears. The images are pagan, not Christian, of good and wicked tree-spirits, soul-birds not angels, brave knights not saints. Each image was carved from a single block of oak wood. A misericord (meaning 'pity') is a ledge beneath the seat that offered relief to the bottoms of clergy during long services when they had to stand.

By this time Exeter had a water supply running through underground tunnels, possibly drawing from the same springs as the Romans had done. Frontinus, author of a handbook on hydraulic engineering and aqueducts, was governor of Britain in A.D. 74-7, and it was he who ordered the Second Augustan legion to move from Exeter to Caerleon. A generation later the Roman town was bringing water from outside Eastgate, round the north side of Rougemont, to cross the town-ditch near present-day Maddocks Row in a wooden aqueduct datable to A.D. 101. During the following centuries an Iscan engineer may have devised a shorter route, maintaining the necessary downhill gradient by tunnelling a short distance under the hump by the east gate. When the new cathedral was begun in the 12th century it was sited to the east of the Saxon church. This work blocked the spring used by the bishop's household, and once again water had to be brought in from the eastern ridge. The first written references to the underground passages constructed for this purpose date from 1226. The supply was divided between the cathedral staff, the monks of St Nicholas and the townsfolk. At first the water ran along the floor of the tunnels, then in 1347 lead piping was laid and the passages were made large enough for maintenance men to walk along. In 1420 the City Chamber (as the governing body was called until 1835) built its own separate system. Today the complex network of burrows provides a fascinating tourist attraction under the east gate.

From 1228 to 1230 it seemed to rain non-stop. In 1234 plague swept through England, brought probably by returning crusaders, and more than two-thirds of Exeter's population died.

27   The many daily masses sung in the chapels of the new cathedral required a back-up team of vicars choral. In 1387 a college was built for them behind the deanery, in Kalenderhay. It had a strong gatehouse, a row of little houses left and right (one for each member) and a common kitchen and dining-hall at the far end.

In 1270 Bishop Bronescombe began to rebuild the eastern end of the cathedral to accommodate liturgical changes. Once the modernisation was started it seemed to acquire its own momentum: it was continued by succeeding bishops until only the two towers remained from the Norman building. The nave was extended in one unbroken avenue of slender, soaring, branching pillars, clasped by jewel-like bosses where they met far overhead. The vaulting shafts spring from clustered pillars set diamond-wise, known as the Exeter pillar.

In 1276 the Lammas Fair was moved from Exe Island to Southernhay (then called Crulditch). Many foreign merchants thronged to this event. Part of the city walls stood between noisy Crulditch and the cathedral, preserving the peaceful seclusion of the

28 The hall of the Vicars Choral had no doorway onto South Street while it served their college.

bishop's grounds. The other sides of the cathedral yard were surrounded only by a low wall – and criminals sometimes jumped into the consecrated ground to avoid arrest. In November 1283 there was a serious incident. Walter de Lechlade, the cathedral precentor, was attacked and killed as he walked the short distance from a night-time service to his lodgings in the chantry. Various cathedral officials and the mayor himself were implicated, and the dispute dragged on. Two years later King Edward I and Queen Eleanor came to spend Christmas with the bishop in order to settle the matter. The king gave permission for the cathedral yard to be enclosed by a high wall, and for all access gates to be locked at night.

It is thought that before the 1280s the main street curved north, round the sprawling burial-ground, then south of St Petrock's and down Smythen Street and Stepcote Hill to the west gate and Exebridge. The new cathedral defences ran through the sites of today's Royal Clarence Hotel, old Tinley's and St Petrock's, displacing the High Street to its present line and moving the Carfax to its present position at the junction with Fore Street, North Street and South Street. The town conduit was also resited.

In 1287 the Franciscans were allowed to move from the increasingly unhygienic site behind St Nicholas's Priory to the airy height above the quay, still called Friar's Walk. They dedicated their church there to St John the Baptist.

Exeter has many claims to fame: the first mention of an English theatre, the first pound-lock canal in England, the first shilling-in-the-slot gas-meter. Trainee town-planners are taught that the first planning appeal was Exeter's complaint to the crown in 1461 that the Countess of Devon had 'made a great nuisance by erecting a weare … salmon fishing is now destroyed on this side. Boats and vessels laden with wine and merchandise cannot come up.' In the 1290s Countess Isabella, who owned land on both sides of the estuary, had built weirs for her mills, leaving only a small gap in midstream. Her successor completed the blockage. For centuries Exeter's loss was Topsham's gain: ships had to unload at Topsham quay and pay dues there. But the Courtenays continually fell into royal disfavour; the city made haste each time to petition the sovereign to restore access to Exeter quay – but to no avail for 250 years.

29   In 1285-6 the cathedral yard was walled off from the town, after the murder of the precentor one dark night. Access was thereafter through gates at St Martin's, St Petrock's, St George's, the Deanery, the Palace and (here) Broadgate, also called St Michael's.

In 1307 Edward II appointed his childhood friend the frivolous Piers Gaveston as Earl of Cornwall and Lord of Exeter. Edward III raised the earldom to a duchy (also the first in England), granted it to the Black Prince and enhanced Exeter's value by adding to it the manor of Bradninch. Exeter's castle began to be regarded as the manor-house of Bradninch, giving its surroundings the title 'Precinct of Bradninch'.

St Katherine's Priory, known as Polsloe Priory, was a Benedictine sister-house to St Nicholas's Priory, founded before 1160 and rebuilt in about 1300. The priory consisted

30 St Katherine's Priory at Polsloe was the only house for Benedictine nuns in the diocese. It was founded before 1160 and rebuilt in about 1300. In January 1320 the bishop had to remind the sisters to speak more softly, to use Latin, to come to services and meals promptly, and not to have so many visitors through this gate.

of a square of cloisters enclosed by buildings: the church formed the north side, standing higher than the rest, and the Mincing stream ran past the eastern range. What we see today is the western range, which contained the guest-house, the prioress's chamber and possibly the priest's room. It is of plum-coloured Heavitree stone, rebuilt in about 1300 but re-using the original 12th-century back wall and possibly some of the timbering. The entrance doorway with its old oak door has a two-centred arch with an original oak beam above. The first floor would originally have been reached by outside stairs. The sloping line of the roof can be seen on the middle buttress. A remarkable oak screen survives at the southern end of the guest hall It is possibly unique in this country, with three (originally four) two-centred arches without capitals. The prioress's room at the northern end is screened off by a wall made of oak posts, laths and cob. The fireplace is 13th-century, and there are two stone corbels – one a man's head, one a women's, in head-dresses of about 1300; these originally supported ceiling beams. In the corner is the medieval garderobe, or toilet, set in a turret. The gate dividing the nuns from the outside world, the 'foreyne porte', can still be seen in the neglected cob-wall round the grounds.

The priory's deer-park, which stretched as far as Mount Pleasant, gave way in 1899 to the Exeter Brick and Tile Company founded by A. and H. Bradbeer. These brothers later bought the priory, thinking it a decayed farmhouse, but when it was recognised for what it was they presented it to the city in 1934. The 17th-century linenfold panelling was removed to the Guildhall muniments room. The priory was used as a council store until it was carefully restored, and in June 1982 it became a local community centre.

In about 1300 Wonford manor became the property of the Montacute family. In 1345 William de Montacute married the sister of Bishop Grandisson. She it was whose fallen garter was picked up by Edward III, who alledgedly said, 'Honi soit qui mal y pense', and made it the motto of the Order of the Garter, founded in 1348. French was still the language of the royal court.

In 1348 and 1352 Bishop Grandisson instructed his archdeacon to ban a 'sect of malign men' who were mocking the leather-dressers in the theatre at Exeter. Apparently the leather-dressers had been overcharging, but it was thought that public satire might provoke a riot.

In the years of the Black Death (1349-51) Exeter was one of the worst-hit areas, losing half of its population, and then a quarter of the survivors when the plague returned after 13 years. Building of the cathedral was interrupted, and the unglazed windows were stopped up with wattle and daub to keep it weatherproof. Clergy visiting the sick and burying the dead succumbed one after the other. Bishop Grandisson was given papal permission to ordain 100 replacements, but he was unable to find enough candidates. Nevertheless religious and commercial life continued. In 1353 Exeter was recognised as one of the main markets for wool, leather skins and lead. Also in 1353 the minstrels' gallery in the cathedral, decorated with angel musicians, was finished in time for the Palm Sunday procession. By 1369 the cathedral was declared complete. Bishop Grandisson had written to his friend Pope John XXII that it was marvellous in beauty, and would surpass every Gothic church in England or France. The west front was finally exposed to view, with ranks of angels, saints and prophets carved in stone and painted in red and green, yellow and white. The cathedral had a simple timepiece as early as 1284. The Fabric Accounts of 1327 and 1376 refer to it as the *horologium qui vocatur clokke*. Here an English word bobs up, an assurance that Anglo-Saxon was still the language of the street whatever was being spoken in the castle and the Bishop's Palace.

People often ask why Mint Lane is the name of the alley broken through between the main wing of St Nicholas's Priory and its refectory along the line of the western side of its cloister garden. It was not the site of the Saxon or the Norman mints.

In Saxon times the silver penny was the basic unit of money. A hundred thousand English pennies have been found in Scandinavia, Viking booty. All mints were controlled by the king. Silver pennies were first minted in Exeter during the reign of Alfred the Great (871–99). After King Edgar's reform in 973 all coins had the king's portrait on the obverse. The peak of production was reached during the reigns of Æthelred II and Cnut (1016–35) when the Exeter mint was the fifth or sixth largest in Britain. From 1042 to 1060 coins of Edward the Confessor were struck in Exeter. The Norman kings left the system unchanged. William I and William Rufus both issued Exeter pennies. It is not known where the mints were housed during these centuries.

In St Nicholas's Priory's Norman undercroft there are two round holes in the window-sill, which may have held crucibles for Exeter's Civil War mint, striking emergency payment for the Royalist soldiers. The stone ceiling and massive walls made it a secure place to deal with precious metals. Gold and silver plate was collected, melted down and stamped into coinage.

There was also a mint set up in 1696 for a short period, said to have been in a house in the neighbourhood of Mint Lane, possibly in Mary Arches Street.

4

Carpenters and Kings

In 1403 Henry IV greeted his second bride, Joan of Navarre, at Falmouth, and brought her to Exeter for two nights on the way to their wedding at Winchester. As they approached Exeter from the west they would have seen the white cathedral towering over the low, tightly packed houses on the city's slopes. A few thatched houses stood beside the approach roads, but at this time (and for the next 400 years) market gardens and orchards encircled the city. There were still wooded hills all around but also many fields of pasture, grazed by the vast numbers of sheep kept for their wool. There were also large green areas within the walls: the enclosed castle grounds, the cathedral yard, the Dominicans' domain and the land of St Nicholas's Priory. The townsfolk were crammed into the remaining space, merchants living above their shops along the main streets, artisans in cottages, mainly in the west quarter where the land falls away to the river.

The 15th century saw a building boom. Red sandstone quarried at Heavitree was near at hand and easily worked. Many cartloads rumbled in as the city's churches were enlarged or completely rebuilt, almshouses were founded, splendid halls were raised by corporate bodies and merchants' premises were upgraded.

At the top of Sidwell Street there is an important road fork. To the left was the main route to Tiverton and North Devon, from ancient times until the New North Road replaced it in 1834, whereupon it became the Old Tiverton Road and was disturnpiked; to the right the way to Pinhoe and beyond, which in 1775 became the coaching road to Bristol and Bath. At the fork stood a hermitage annexed to a small chapel. Was the saintly hermit a man or woman? Were travellers given a blessing and directions for their journey, a last chance to confess and to fill their water-flasks? Bishop Grandisson introduced the cult of the Virgin's mother in about 1350. The chapel is known to have been rebuilt in 1418, and for the next 500 years its name was often used as a landmark when describing plots of land – 'near St Anne's hospital' or 'by St Agnes' Chapel'. Which was the original dedication, Agnes or Anne? What is the connection with St Anne's

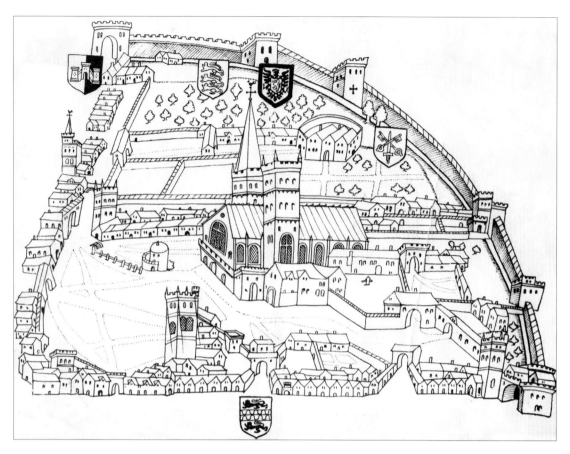

Well, which lay 150yds to the north? The peasant in the Wenceslas carol lived 'By St Agnes' fountain'. But St Anne's name was given to the holy well at Great Malvern, and the most famous English shrine of St Anne is at Buxton, a spa that was known to the Romans: they called it *Aquae Arnemetiae*. Before the Romans reached Exeter or Buxton there may have been temples of Arnemetia, Celtic goddess of the waters.

After the Dissolution the property was purchased by Oliver and George Mainwaring and endowed by their family in 1561, 1570 and 1617 as almshouses for eight poor men and women, each having two small rooms and 'a garden plat'. Burials in St Sidwell's register include in 1597 'John Crosse, an Almesman of St Ann Chappell' and in 1616 'Charitie Courtise in St Anne Chapple'. The fabric was damaged in 1646 when it served as a fort against the Parliamentary forces advancing down the roads to both sides of it. When St Sidwell's decided to build a second church in the parish in the 1830s there were plans to demolish St Anne's and to erect a chapel of Grecian design with patio and pediment, but this was not permitted, and St James's was built 50yds to the north instead.

St Anne's Chapel is small, about 15ft by 15ft, has a perpendicular east (or rather north-east) window with three lights, a ceiled wagon-roof, and a piscina with a canopied niche on either side. Extensive restoration work was done in 1907-10 by the Dean and Chapter; they removed a house that was partly within the chapel, demolished the chaplain's house, and rebuilt two of the almshouses in red brick and 'half-timbering'. They also gave new oak fittings to the chapel, and it was re-dedicated on St Anne's Day

31 This drawing, based on a map in Hooker's *History of Exeter* (1587), shows the city walls from Eastgate to Southgate, the gates to the cathedral close, and the large area between the cathedral and Eastgate occupied by the Dominicans.

32 These may be the two houses 'north of St Martin's Church' which a mason contracted to build in 1404 for £6 6s. 8d. He did a good job: they still enhance the corner of the cathedral yard.

(26 July) 1910. St Anne's Day was then said 'to have been observed here from time immemorial'. The porch was rebuilt in 1927 and provided with a clock – now gone.

More recently the chapel was used for weekday services by St James's Church, but it is now on loan to the local Orthodox community. The almshouses have passed from the Dean and Chapter to the Feoffees of St Petrock's and Heavitree. The rear two 'cottages' preserve the 16th-century fabric of Heavitree stone.

Bowhill is an important 15th-century manor house, so important that the Historic Building and Monument Commission was rumoured to be spending another 500 years

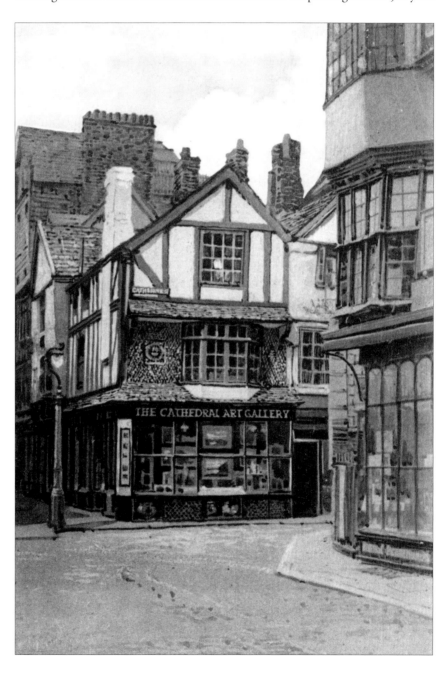

restoring it. Its glory is the wagon-roof of the great hall in the east wing, but the south range along the road, and part of the kitchen wing to the west, also survive from the original quadrangle. The walls are roughly built of red Heavitree stone and volcanic trap. The house, named Bogehull ('curved hill') after the estate, was started in 1422 and probably just finished when its private chapel was licensed in 1429 for Richard Holland, who was MP for Devon in 1430. His son and grandson also served as MPs for Exeter. The fine roofs of the great hall and of the solar in the south wing are thought to be late 15th-century, perhaps from 1488 when the Holland heiress in the next generation married a Carew. The hall has four large square-headed windows with external decorations of carved human heads, and internal signs that shutters were used. There was a screen in the south range, which has lost its panelling but retains the original moulded doorways with pointed arches. The large kitchen fireplace also survives, with a joggled segmental stone arch. (How many fitted kitchens from the 1980s will last five centuries?)

The Carews held the manor for many generations, although John the regicide forfeited the honour and his life in 1661. In 1662 Charles II restored the manor to Thomas. He had no sons, and the property passed to the Sawle family by marriage. In 1792 the surrounding land was sold. In 1799 the house itself was sold to be used for the new St Thomas Hospital for Lunatics, accommodating 15 patients. This institution soon erected its own buildings lower down the hillside.

At one time Bowhill was the residence of the grandparents of General Gordon of Khartoum. On 18 January 1884 he was in the porch of the parish church, about to visit their memorial, when he was summoned to London and thence to his martyrdom in the Muslim uprising. For the past century or so Bowhill has been an ordinary farmhouse, the great chamber partitioned, the great hall given an extra floor to store many tons

33 Bowhill stands above the flood plain on the western slopes facing the city. It was built in the 15th century for the Holland family, who supplied Exeter's member of parliament for three generations. In 1488 the Holland heiress married a Carew; it was possibly then that the fine arch-braced roof was added to the great hall in this southern range.

34 This is a plate from an early 'hornbook' mislaid in about 1500, and untypically made of copper alloy. Saracen dress was fashionable in the later 15th century. Children learnt their letters from the alphabet in upper and lower case at the top, then 'a' stands beside the archer.

of apples, and the chapel used as a barn. The Sclater family ran the extensive Bowhill nurseries and orchards for several generations.

Within living memory the hillside from here to Crossmead was covered with orchards and nurseries. Some of the road names acknowledge this: Greenway, Parkway, Orchard Gardens, Orchard Hill.

In 1435 William Wynard endowed a hospice on Magdalen Road for 12 infirm paupers and a priest. Wynard owned the White Hart Inn in South Street, sagging a little now but still a credit to its builders.

Henry VI and Queen Margaret toured their troubled realm in 1452. They were met at Clyst Honiton on 16 July by the nobles and gentlemen of Devon, then by the Exeter civic party, numbering 300, all in mulberry-red gowns and black velvet capes, with the shoulders embroidered with the city's arms: a castle triple-towered. The clergy and friars awaited the king at Livery Dole, then joined the procession as it continued to the south gate, where the high cross was 'gorgeously apparelled'. Old Bishop Lacy, who had been at Agincourt, waited at the Broadgate, where the king dismounted. The Carfax conduit ran with wine (achieved by inserting a hogshead of claret behind the spout). The king's son was not yet even conceived, so the king himself was both sovereign and seigneur of Exeter. (Ten years earlier he had appointed an Exeter man as clerk of works for his new foundation of Eton College. This may explain why Eton Chapel had a wall-painting of Exeter's St Sidwell.)

In 1457 the east gate suddenly collapsed one midday, with no loss of life; but it had to be rebuilt in those uncertain times. In 1466 the city's muddy streets and alleys were paved with stone after a gap of 1,000 years. A remarkable series of elaborate timbered hall-roofs survive from this century: the arch-braced roofs of Bowhill are two of them. The law library at 8 Cathedral Close has a roof with hammer beams ending in horizontal angel figures, comparable in beauty and quality to the roof of Westminster Hall made in 1399. Bishop Lacy began building a chapter house before the middle of the century, and Bishop Bothe had it raised higher under an ornate beamed ceiling in 1470.

Exeter had long prided itself on its loyalty to the crown, but during the Wars of the Roses it was no simple matter for the mayor to welcome the right party. The rival factions of York and Lancaster were fighting bloody battles, and the main figures suddenly changed sides, or were murdered, or slain in the fighting. In 1453 King Henry became mentally ill and the Duke of York seized control. In 1459 the Earl of Warwick fled to Exeter with York's son (the future King Edward IV). Warwick's brothers were in positions of power here: one was Marquis of Montacute, and the other was the new young bishop, George Neville. However, the townsfolk were loyal to the crowned king, Henry, and Warwick found it advisable to lie low at Nutwell, on the estuary, and then set sail from Lympstone to France. In 1461 he returned with Edward to proclaim him king, Prince of Wales, Duke of Cornwall and Lord of Exeter. The Guildhall accounts for 1468-70 survive only in part, but it is thought that the elaborate timbered roof was built at this time. At first glance the carved supporters seem to be the bear and ragged staff of Warwick's insignia, but a closer look reveals a monkey and staff, a dog and staff, and so on. Could it be deliberate mockery of the turncoat Warwick? By 1469 Warwick had switched allegiance to Henry's queen and young prince, another Edward, and had married one of his daughters to the Duke of Clarence, the disloyal brother of King Edward. In the spring of 1470 Henry's party was on the run. The Duchess of Clarence took refuge in the bishops's palace, and a thousand of his followers found lodgings with the canons. Bishop Bothe fled. King Edward's local adherents, led by Sir William Courtenay, began a siege of the city on 16 March, breaking down the bridges and cutting off much-needed supplies of food. No markets could be held for 12 days: there was a real danger of famine. The supporters of the white rose and of the red rose each asked the mayor to hand over the keys of the city, but he refused. He said he would yield them only to the king, since the city yielded revenue only to the king; but 'certain canons of the cathedral' mediated between the parties and the siege was raised. Three weeks later, on 3 April, Warwick and the Duke of Clarence fled south (chased by King Edward and 10,000 men), and joined the party in the palace while they hastily arranged evacuation by ship from Dartmouth. The king arrived on the 14th, 'but the birds had flown'. The mayor handed him the keys and a purse containing 100 gold nobles, and the king rested with his men for three days, including Palm Sunday, when he joined in the procession; then they all set out for London. By September Warwick had married his other daughter to the young prince, Edward. He came back to Devon, raised 60,000 men and reinstated Henry as king in October. Edward IV fled to Holland, but in spring 1471 he came back, Clarence returned to his side, and on 13 April they slew Warwick at the battle of Barnet. On the same day Henry's queen, Margaret, and Prince Edward landed at Weymouth, came to lodge with the Black Friars at Exeter and raised another army. They were defeated on 4 May at Tewkesbury. Prince Edward was killed. On 21 May King Henry was murdered in the Tower of London. Edward IV was king again.

While the dynasties clashed, and sudden tides of armed men swept through Exeter, the city's merchants minded their own business. Several trades guilds gained charters of incorporation at the end of this century and the beginning of the next. The wealthy Guild of Weavers, Tuckers and Shearmen, who controlled the main local industry, the flourishing woollen trade, built themselves a grand stone meeting-place in 1471. The hall, which has a fine wagon roof, can still be visited in Fore Street. The barbers and cappers each had a guild, as did the butchers and brewers, bakers and cordwainers, glovers and skinners, smiths and cutlers. A trade supplied a living and often a surname too, as the skills and 'tools of the trade' were handed down in the family.

35   The Bishop's Palace from the garden.

In 1471 the causeway leading to Cowley Bridge, a muddy way alongside the river, was paved single-handed by a priest doing seven years' penance for debauching, impregnating and murdering a young woman in Duryard Wood.

From September 1479 to the end of November 1480 'incredible numbers' of people were swept away by pestilence in London and in Exeter.

When King Edward died in 1483, Richard of York allegedly had the young heirs killed in the Tower of London, had himself crowned in York and came to Devon to

36 The town hall was simply called *Gihalde*, meaning simply Guild, from the 12th century until the 15th, since when it has been called Guildhall. It was always been used as a court room; there are prison cells at the rear.

37 Bishop Peter Courtenay is thought to have had this dial fitted to the cathedral clock in 1484. It shows the earth in the centre, the moon revolving around it (and turning to show its phases) and a fleur-de-lys sun circling the earth every 24 hours while also pointing to the day of the lunar month.

38 Wynard's Hospital was built in 1435. In the Civil War it was used as a fortification and damaged. It was restored in 1863 but this did not spoil the serenity of its red stone walls, cobbled courtyard and cool chapel.

stamp out local hostility. The king was challenged, as Shakespeare says in *Richard III*, by 'Sir Edward Courtenay, and the haughty prelate, / Bishop of Exeter, his elder brother, / With many more confederates in arms'. Richard was greeted by the mayor at the east gate and given a purse of 200 gold nobles. He lodged in the palace; Bishop Courtenay had fled, and he and his brothers were declared outlaws. At the trial of conspirators in Torrington two gentlemen were found guilty of high treason. One was the king's own brother-in-law, Sir Thomas Leger. They were brought to the Carfax in Exeter to be beheaded by the sword.

In 1485 Richard was killed at the Battle of Bosworth, and Henry Earl of Richmond was crowned as Henry VII. Shakespeare used an anecdote about Exeter in *Richard III*. The king had once been told that he would die soon after he saw Richmond. When the mayor was showing him round Exeter in 1483 he mentioned that the castle was called Rougemont. The king heard it as Richmond, 'whereat he fell into a great dump'.

Under Henry VII the Courtenays were back in favour, and Bishop Peter Courtenay could return to his palace. In an unusual gesture the Earl of Devon, Sir Edward Courtenay, was made freeman of the city. His son Sir William had married a daughter of Edward IV, Katherine Plantagenet.

In 1496 some pleasant jobs were available: 'Aletasters were apoynted for serching that holsome Drynke shold be made.'

In 1497 the city suffered two assaults. Firstly 16,000 Cornishmen marching to protest against a 'subsidie' demanded by the crown were denied entry. When the mayor found no support forthcoming from the lords of the shire, he grudgingly allowed the angry captains to pass through, but their men had to go grumbling round the outside of the walls and rejoin them at Eastgate. An explosive situation was defused. Soon afterwards a smaller band collected at Bodmin when Perkin Warbeck arrived there in pursuit of his claim to be the younger of the 'princes in the tower'. He reached Exeter on 17 September with an army of 4-5,000 and found the gates shut against them, but this time the Courtenays were inside, lodging with the Black Friars, ready to help defend the city – having been reprimanded for not turning up the last time. Warbeck's

men tried to burn down the north gate but found their losses were too great there, where the defenders were safely inside and on higher ground. They moved to the flatter approaches of the east gate and managed to break it open, then started fighting their way toward the castle. The Courtenays, father and son, came rushing out with their men, there was furious fighting on the High Street and Warbeck's band withdrew, to make for Taunton. Meeting the king, Warbeck surrendered to him, and was brought back through the east gate as a prisoner on 7 October.

The king lodged at the treasurer's house, which abutted the north tower of the cathedral. (The marks of its gable can still be seen.) Warbeck was sent to the Tower of London; the other leaders were condemned to be hanged and quartered on Southernhay Green. The rest were brought before the king's window with nooses around their necks: the window had been enlarged for the occasion, and several trees had been felled to clear the view. The men begged for pardon, swore to be loyal in future, and were released.

That year there had also been trouble over deciding on a mayor. The king laid down election rules, imposed his own choice of mayor for that year, 'and to encourage the mayor and citizens to continue dutiful and obedient subjects as tofore, he took his sword which he then wore about his middle, and gave it to the mayor together with a hatt of mayntenunce', to be borne before him and his successors, 'as it is used in the Citie of London'. The city's right to bear a sword has been proudly exercised ever since, a symbol of loyalty to the crown and a reminder of times when men lived and died by the sword.

5

Reformation and Resistance

An incident in 1501 presaged the turbulent times still to come. The bishop had negotiated a marriage between the king's eldest son, Prince of Wales, Lord of Exeter, and the 15-year-old Spanish Infanta. Escorting her on a long and stormy journey to what would be two marriages, a short one ending in widowhood, then a long one ending in divorce, he lodged the royal party at the deanery. 'The weather was very foul and windy … the weathercock upon the Church of St Mary the More … did so whistle that the princess could not sleep'. A workman braved the wind and dark to climb the steeple and take down the squeaking weathercock on St Mary Major, which was disturbing young Catherine of Aragon.

In 1511 Sir William Courtenay died of pleurisy, and his young widow, the Countess Katharine (who was proud of being daughter, sister and aunt of kings), retired to Devon to live off her estates, including Columbjohn near Exeter. Her household accounts for 1523-4 reveal some local supplies (cream, apples for pies, eels) but also many luxuries imported via Topsham and Exeter – including sour and sweet oranges, licorice, caraways, rices, figs, ginger, cloves, sugar loaf, cherries; velvet, satin, linen and furs. She was obviously fond of marmalade: Hull of Exeter had sent her a box of it the previous year (and the recipe?). This predates the earliest use of the word marmalade cited in the *Oxford English Dictionary*: a letter mentioning a box of it sent to Henry VIII in 1524 by (presumably the same) Hull of Exeter.

The religious upheavals of the Reformation rocked the West Country. A Master of Arts from Cambridge, Thomas Benet, came to Exeter in 1525 and ran a small school in Smythen Street. In 1531 he began pinning placards to the cathedral door proclaiming such Lutheran sentiments as 'We ought to worship God only and no saints'. Benet was not discovered until he laughed during a cathedral service, when the 'heretic' was publicly cursed by bell, book and candle and condemned to be burnt. The mayor refused the use of Southernhay, Benet refused to retract his beliefs, and

39   As part of the dissolution of the monasteries the 13 nuns in St Katherine's Priory were pensioned off in 1538. The surviving western range, containing guest-rooms, prioress's chamber and priest's accommodation, became a manor-house, then a farmhouse, more recently a council store, and now a community hall, with a unique 14th-century oaken screen and corbel heads.

40   Similarly, the surviving western range of St Nicholas' Priory contains the guest-hall, kitchen, chambers and main entrance. An alley now divides it from the surviving north side of the cloisters, where the monks ate and slept.

died at the stake at Livery Dole on 15 January 1532. By this time Henry VIII was already in the process of breaking with Rome. He soon sent Bishop Hugh Latimer on a tour to preach the Reformation, and he reached Exeter in June 1534. First he spoke to a crowd in the churchyard of the Greyfriars outside Southgate. They were undeterred when it began to rain. As he continued to preach very earnestly his nose began to bleed, which the friars took as a sign of God's displeasure, but their own warden, John Cardemaker, was won over (to the extent that, like Latimer himself, he would be burnt in 1555, after Queen Mary had restored the supremacy of Rome). Latimer also preached in St Mary Major, although the clergy complained that it would interfere with the celebration of their feast day. Such a great crowd gathered in and around the church that its windows were broken to allow those outside to hear. One Thomas Carew Esquire heckled loudly, and called Latimer to come down from the pulpit or he would pull him by the ears.

In 1535 the king sent commissioners to dissolve the smaller monasteries. In Exeter they began by viewing St Nicholas's Priory, then retired for dinner after ordering a workman to pull down the rood loft. But the priory's tenants rushed to defend it: they depended on a distribution every Friday of a 2d. loaf, a pottle of ale, a piece of fish and a penny in money. A number of women came running with shovels and pikes and sticks, broke open the church door and chased the workman up the tower. He jumped out of a window, breaking a rib. Somebody fetched Alderman Blackaller to pacify the women, but Elizabeth Glandfield 'gave him a blow and sent him packing'. The women barricaded themselves in the church until the mayor came and arrested them, and allowed the commissioners to continue their work. By 1539 the priory's church and cloister had been demolished. Some of the stone was bought for the mayor's new project, a hall for a weekly yarn market to rival the one in Crediton. Other loads of the stone were used to repair Exebridge, where a central arch had collapsed one night, together with the dwelling house on it. Henry Courtenay, Marquis of Exeter, had been required to send 200 well-armed men to confront northern rebels in the Pilgrimage of Grace, and one of his men was John Cove, whose house it was on the bridge. Jenkins reports: 'On the night of his return home from Doncaster part of his house near the river, swelled by excessive rains, fell down and the servants who slept in the upper part were drowned, but he and his wife were carried away, bed and all, by the current, when desiring his wife not to stir he, by exerting his arms and legs, kept on the western bank out of the stream's current and providentially got upon a hillock where the water was shallow and thence he and his wife recovered the shore in safety.'

The surviving wings of the priory, the west wing and the refectory were purchased and converted into mansions for well-to-do citizens. New wooden windows were inserted, elaborate plaster ceilings installed and painted decoration added. The owner of the site from 1562 was Robert Malet, but he leased it to two generations of the Hurst family. Later poorer tenants were housed in smaller apartments, eventually described as 'a mere rookery of tenements'. In 1913 the city council acquired the west wing for a museum and stripped the building back to reveal its medieval character. Recently, painted panelling has been reinstalled, and a visit to the priory is presented as occurring when William Hurst and family lived there. The refectory wing was rescued in the 1990s by Exeter Historic Buildings Trust, and converted into a house and an apartment.

In 1537 Henry VIII granted Exeter a charter making it an independent county separate from Devonshire; it could elect its own sheriff. An Act of 1550 clarified the boundaries. The extramural parishes of St David's and St Sidwell's were included, but the castle and its precincts were not. On 6 August 1564 the city's arms were confirmed as the 'castle triple-towered' with the addition of supporters in the form of two winged horses (although the College of Arms cannot have known that Pegasus was the insignia of the Second Augustan legion, or that this legion founded Exeter). The citizens were proud to use the description 'city and county of the city of Exeter' until they lost the privilege in the 1972 reorganisation of local government.

A Dominican, the Bishop of Dover, was appointed to dissolve the Exeter friaries. The Greyfriars' site, with 300 elms, was subsequently leased to a member of the family of marmalade importers, John Hull, who lived at neighbouring Larkbeare. The Dominican house, with church, belfry and churchyard, was included in a large grant from the king to Lord John Russell, who was overseeing the reformation in the West. Russell used it as a residence and called it Bedford House.

Cowick Barton public house is the mansion built for Russell in about 1540 after he dissolved St Andrew's Priory, doubtless re-using the stones. It has mullioned windows and a Tudor-arched entrance to the projecting three-storey porch in the centre. Short wings at each end are probably later additions. Lord Russell had a town house in the city, so Cowick was probably built for his bailiff. It remained

41   The hall of the Vicars Choral was fitted with linenfold oak panelling in the 16th century. A visitor in 1635 found there 'a Cup of good Ale, wch I liberally tasted off, with their honest Organist, and some of the merry Vicars …'

in the Bedford family for 100 years, passing to the Pate family in 1641. An ornate overmantle dated 1657 commemorated some now-forgotten event. A more intriguing plaster relief forms the overmantel in the function room in the east wing. On the left a nun or the Blessed Virgin is caring for several children, and on the right is a maiden with long hair, she and the Virgin standing on the head of a fat doll-like friar. Three children in medieval costume are being led by an angel and dragged back by a little devil. There is a cryptic Bible reference, 'Phil. III, 14', which is interpreted as a coded instruction to activate a secret panel to a priest-hole: 'I press towards the mark.' Under the carpet there is a trap door leading to the cellars and passages. Robert Pate and his son each left annuities for a schoolmistress to teach four poor children. Perhaps this was a schoolroom.

The Pate family passed the property down to a Mr James White by 1830, and it remained for five generations with Whites, or White Abbots. John White Abbot (1763-1851) was a surgeon and a fine watercolourist who painted Devon views, some held in Exeter Museum. He will have appreciated the rural surroundings of the Barton. The Rev. John Swete described them in September 1789: 'On the northern side of this House is a grove of uncommonly large Elms. Through a break amid the successive ranges of Elms, Exeter is beheld, with its turreted Cathedral, rising with lordly grandeur over the subjacent city.'

When drains were dug in 1887, 13th- century remains of the priory were found east of the house. White Abbott's grandson and namesake carefully restored the house in 1895.

The 'Agricultural Property' of Cowick Barton was sold by auction in 1920. It comprised 75 acres divided by Cowick Lane, and Barton House with its extensive range of farm outbuildings, some of which still stand to one side of the car park: 'Five-stall Stable and Loose Box, Four-stall Cow House and Root House, 12-stall Cow House, Hay House, Piggery and Slaughter House, barns, Bullock House with loft over, and Double Cow Shed for Ten. Brick Cart Shed with corrugated-iron roof. Granary on stone piers, wood with slate roofing.'

The Courtenays suffered a great fall from grace. Henry Courtenay had been a favourite of the king, even named as heir to the throne before Henry VIII had any children of his own. But in 1538 he was accused of treason, and was executed the following January. His possessions reverted to the crown. This time the city's long-standing complaint was heeded: an Act of Parliament of 1539 authorised the clearing of obstructions from the river. However, the Courtenay weirs proved too solid to uproot; they would have to be bypassed with a canal, and work began in 1545. Silver plate was collected from the city's parish churches towards the great expense. Francis Drake suggested enlarging the mill-leat at Countess Wear, which ran a straight course along the eastern bank. Little progress was made until the engineer John Trew was engaged in 1563. His workmen found themselves cutting through solid rock, so Trew proposed routing 'the new haven' through the softer ground west of the stream. Work began again in 1564. By 1566 ships were able to pass to Exeter quay through seven sluices, six of them paired, making this the first pound-lock canal in England. A new stone quay was constructed below the city walls, furnished with a crane.

William Floyre of Floyrehays transferred to the city in 1567, in language that conveys the great muddy mess made by the workmen, 'All that ground, soil & terrytory as well now digged trenched & caste up for a new water course … digged, banked, moyned,

W.H.Worthington, sculp!

EDWARD COURTENAY, EARL OF DEVONSHIRE,

From the Enamel painting by H. Bone Esq.r R.A after the
Original of Sir. A. More in the collection of His Grace
The Duke of Bedford. at Woburn?

42 Sir Edward Courtenay (1526-56). After his father's execution he spent 14 years of his boyhood in the Tower of London, where he is said to have carved the words *Ubi lapsus? quid feci?* The death of Edward VI saved this Courtenay from the block. Queen Mary created him Earl of Devon.

trenched wrought, levyed & cast up or measured out, for & towards the better brynging, carrying, & recarrying of Botes & vessels with Wares & mechandices or other things from the High sea … to a place beneathe Bole Poole called Old Exe'.

In 1542 plague swept through the parish, killing 106 in a population of 500 to 700.

Meanwhile the religious turmoil continued. The vicar of St. Thomas's during these changes was Robert Welshe, appointed by Tavistock in 1537 and retained by Russell in 1539. When Henry VIII frowned on dedications to Becket, Welshe shortened the church's name to plain St Thomas's, which could mean the martyr or the apostle. Edward VI, coming to the throne in 1547, ordered all images of saints to be removed from the churches. The Latin mass-book was to be replaced by the Book of Common Prayer, an innovation particularly resented by the Cornish because it imposed the English language on them. Whitsunday 1549 was the deadline for the change from Latin masses and Roman vestments to services according to the new prayer book. Cornishmen, passionate to retain the old rites, set out to march to London to protest. They were joined by crowds of Devon churchgoers who also loved their familiar form of Latin service. The demonstrators reached Exeter on 2 July 1549 in a solemn procession headed by priests and a banner portraying the five wounds of Christ. The rebels had formulated their demands: 'We will not receive the new Service because it is but like a Christmas game. We will have every priest in his mass pray specially by name for the souls in Purgatory as our forefathers did …' Other demands were that there should be a limitation on the number of servants kept by gentry, and that holders of monastic lands should give back half to establish two abbeys in each county, Devon and Cornwall. They burned copies of the new prayer book in their camps. The rebels hoped to find support and supplies in Exeter, but the gates were shut against them. Robert Welshe tried to control them during the subsequent siege. His contemporary, John Hooker, portrays him as a straightforward, sportsmanlike, unfoppish man: he was 'of no great stature, but well sett and mightelie compacte he was a verie good wrasteler, shott well, bothe in the longe bowe as also in the crosse bowe, he handeled his handgonne and pece verie well he was … suche a one as wolde not geve his hed for the pollinge nor his bearde for the washeinge …'

There were violent incidents during the five-week siege, and bloody clashes in the surrounding countryside. One of Lord Russell's messengers was captured, tried by the mob and hanged from an elm tree on Exe Island. One hot-head even proposed burning down the city by firing red-hot shot onto the houses in North Street. The vicar of St Thomas, Robert Welshe, persuaded him that this would benefit nobody. Welshe was a Cornishman himself and sympathised with the rebels, but he tried to moderate their violence. They had captured St Sidwell's Church, as it lay outside the walls, and they held prisoners in its tower, including Sir Walter Raleigh senior, who had told off an old woman for carrying a rosary. Inside the town the citizens were reduced to eating horse-meat and then the redundant horse-fodder. They were relieved after five weeks by Lord John Russell. He sent most of the surviving rebels home to Cornwall, but made an example of the ringleaders, and Robert Welshe was condemned as a traitor. Treason is a political crime, but his execution was played out as a gruesome spectacle that made it only too clear that the quarrel was about religious practices. Welshe was hauled to the top of his own church tower, in his 'Romish vestments', and the Old Religion was hanged there with him in the shape of 'a holye water bucket, a sprinkle, a sacringe bell, a payre of beddes and such other lyke popyshe trashe …' His corpse

43 (Far left) Nicholas Hilliard (1547-1619) was born in Exeter, son of a goldsmith, and appointed limner and goldsmith to Queen Elizabeth I at the age of 24. He became the first great painter of miniature portraits, and made this self-portrait in 1577.

was tarred and left dangling on the tower-roof until Mary came to the throne – four years later. The city was rewarded for standing firm against the rebels; it was granted the manor of Exe Island, which still included land on both sides of the river.

Russell's chaplain during this campaign was Miles Coverdale, who had made the English translation of the whole Bible, which Henry VIII had ordered in 1538 to be set up and used in every church. In 1551 Coverdale became Bishop of Exeter. He was preaching in the cathedral in July 1553 when the news came that Mary was queen. He stopped preaching and fled, later leaving the country for the duration of Mary's reign. Other leading Protestants in Exeter also found it prudent to go into voluntary exile – but less courageous people bowed to the prevailing wind. William Horne, parson of the mayor's parish church, St Petrock's, stated publicly during the reign of Edward VI that he would rather be torn with wild horses then say mass again. Seeing him saying mass as soon as Mary became queen, the mayor reminded him of what he had said. Horne replied in front of the congregation, 'There is no remedy, man.' Now Protestants suffered again.

It is believed that Benet's death in the flames at Livery Dole was witnessed by an illiterate child called Agnes Prest. Years later she settled near Launceston with a husband, who welcomed the return of Catholicism under Queen Mary. He ordered Agnes to attend mass and confession, but she refused and fled to Exeter, returning because she missed her children. In Launceston she was accused of heresy against the sacrament of the altar and for speaking against idols. Bishop Turberville told her she should be burned to death, but she replied that calling a piece of bread God and then worshipping it was absurd and blasphemous. She was visited in prison by Walter Raleigh's mother. On 15 August 1557 Agnes was led outside the city walls to Southernhay and burnt at the stake. She and Thomas Benet are commemorated by a tall obelisk in Denmark Road: the Protestant Alliance meets every October here, equidistant from the two martyrdom sites. They lay wreaths and remember the Protestant martyrs. Harry Hems created the memorial, and carved scenes and inscriptions on it. The inscription on the southern elevation reads:

IN GRATEFUL REMEMBRANCE OF THOMAS BENET, M.A. WHO, SUFFERED AT LIVERY DOLE, A.D. 1531. FOR DENYING THE SUPREMACY OF THE POPE, AND OF AGNES PREST, WHO SUFFERED ON SOUTHERNHAY, A.D. 1557, FOR REFUSING TO ACCEPT THE DOCTRINE OF TRANSUBSTANTIATION. 'FAITHFUL UNTO DEATH '. TO THE GLORY OF GOD & IN HONOUR OF HIS

44 (Above left) Thomas Bodley (1545-1613), the distinguished diplomat, was born in Exeter, son of a leading citizen, a printer and a Protestant, who took his family (and the young Nicholas Hilliard) to Geneva during Mary's reign. Hilliard painted this miniature of his fellow Exonian and friend in 1598, the year in which Bodley refounded the library of Oxford University. (Poole Portrait 73).

45 (Right) The Guildhall – the oldest municipal building in the country still in use – is documented from 1160, but the solid oak door and distinctive portico were not added until 1593-4. The pillars are of Dartmoor granite. Until the early 19th century drunkards were punished by an hour in the stocks. This drawing is from a vignette in Roque's map of 1744.

FAITHFUL WITNESSES WHO, NEAR THIS SPOT, YIELDED THEIR BODIES
TO BE BURNED FOR LOVE TO CHRIST AND IN VINDICATION OF THE
PRINCIPLES OF THE PROTESTANT REFORMATION, THIS MONUMENT WAS
ERECTED BY PUBLIC SUBSCRIPTION, A.D. 1909.

THEY BEING DEAD YET SPEAK.

Exeter was to have a Catholic martyr in 1599 when James Dowdall denied the queen's
spiritual supremacy. He was hanged, drawn and quartered at the castle.

Protestant Elizabeth succeeded Catholic Mary in 1558 and once again there came
the command that the (recently replaced) images of saints should be destroyed. By
September her emissaries were lodged in the deanery supervising the stripping of
the cathedral of its statues and ornaments, and their destruction on a bonfire in the

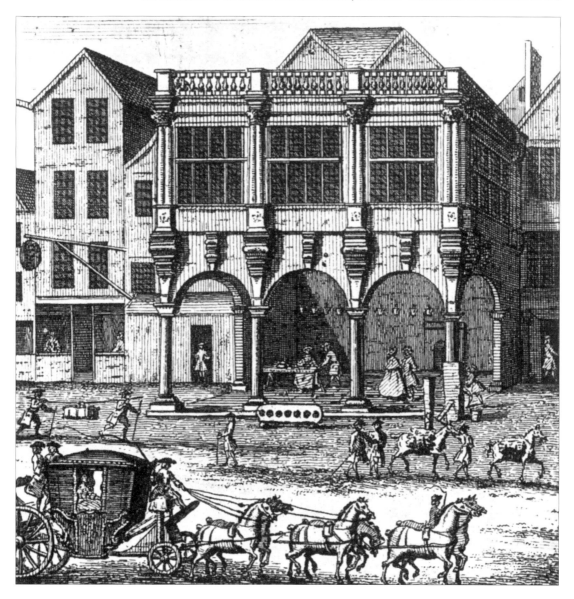

46 Three centuries after the Elizabethan sea captains met here in the first-floor room, Mol's Coffee House had become Worth's Art Gallery. A plain pointed roof-line was replaced in the 1980s with the ornate gable seen here.

churchyard. The new individual responsibility for one's soul did not make everyone virtuous immediately, but it led to one odd incident. John Hooker records that the cathedral exchequer was robbed in 1566, 'but the thieves had such good conscience that when they had carried home the money and found it to be more that they needed, they carried back the overplus'.

During Elizabeth's reign various civic improvements were undertaken. In 1568 the City Chamber chose three sites for 'common jakes'. One was at the Snayle Tower, in the steep north-western angle of the walls. In 1575 the mayor, Thomas Prestwood junior, had boundary stones set up at the limits of the city-shire, at Marypole Head, Scarlet's Cross (now Stoke Hill roundabout), at the top of Blackboy Road and so on. (Two hundred years later these would be the sites of the tollgates for the turnpike roads.) Prestwood was a wealthy merchant who had a pair of four-storeyed houses built in the High Street (now nos 225-6), with ornate façades. Another tall timber-framed house is a landmark at the corner of the cathedral close. In the 1590s it was owned by an Italian, Thomas Mol, and the premises were used as a coffee-house from about 1700. The first-floor casement has been compared to the poop of an Elizabethan galleon: the panelled room that it lights is believed to have been the meeting-place of the great Devon 'sea-dogs' Drake, Raleigh, Gilbert, Hawkins and their like. In Exeter they could hear the latest news from Europe brought by returning merchant-ships, or news from London brought by waggoners or the riders for the Royal Post. Exeter has been called 'hell for horses', the way being uphill in nearly every direction coming or going. To remedy this a little, the deep valley in Magdalen Road was filled and paved in 1599, and the dip in Holloway Street in 1605.

Many of these glimpses into the life of the city come from John Hooker (1523-1601), appointed Exeter's first chamberlain in 1555. He loved Exeter and had trees planted in every available space in the city. He also sorted out the accumulated archives, compiled a history of Exeter up to 1583, and in 1584 put into print the duties of the various officers. For instance, the porters 'must, every night, shut and make fast the City's Gates, Ten of the Clock at Night in the Summer, and at Nine of the Clock in Winter: and must open the said Gates at Four of the Clock in the Morning in the Summer, and at Five of the Clock in the Winter. Also, if any Post happens to come … Also, if any Hue-and-Cry shall happen to be … Also, if any Tumults, Uproars, Escapes of Prisoners, Firing of Houses … forthwith close and make fast the Gates.' The piped water-supply was to be kept clean and orderly by the scavengers, who also had to see 'that no private Person do incroach the Common Commodity of the Waters therein for Brewing, Washing, or any such like use, other than for Dressing of their Meats, and such like'. In other words, the trickle of spring water from the conduit spouts was only for drinking and cooking; river-water was to be used for washing and cleaning.

Hooker's nephew Richard, 'Judicious Hooker', was born in Heavitree in about 1553 and died in 1600. His statue has sat on the cathedral green since 1907. While a clerk at Corpus Christi he walked to and from Oxford each term for three years, until his patron, the Bishop of Salisbury, lent him a horse. He was ordained in 1581, and wrote a famous defence of the Church of England as established under Elizabeth I, *Of the lawes of ecclesiasticall politie*, promoting charity and tolerance towards Catholics and Calvinists. Although its purpose was to supply a philosophical and logical basis for the Anglican Church, it is also regarded as a landmark in English literature because of 'the stateliness and grace of its language'. It has been said to have 'more philosophical value than theological, and more literary value than either'.

One Sunday in 1581 a crowd was watching bear-baiting near Paris Street when the wooden stand collapsed. Seven were killed and many injured. On 7 August 1582 there was a happier entertainment. After the wedding in St Stephen's Church of the Earl of Bath and the daughter of the Earl of Bedford, Elizabeth, who had been born

47 Several other important buildings also had elaborately carved doors. This is 10 Cathedral Close. The centre part would admit a person; the whole door would open for horses entering the yard.

in Bedford House, the citizens presented them with a silver-gilt jug and basin, and laid on a grand cavalcade or 'triumph' in Southernhay.

Exeter paid towards the cost of supplying three ships when the Spanish Armada threatened the realm in 1588. Queen Elizabeth wrote to thank the 'ever-faithful' city. Exeter adopted the phrase as its motto: *Semper fidelis*.

6

Serges and Sieges

By the early 17th century Exeter's woollen trade was steadily increasing in volume and value. Dyeing yellow, blue, green and black began to be practised on an industrial scale; red dye was expensive and used more sparingly. Exeter specialised in light-weight serges, exporting them not just across the Channel and the North Sea but also to the lands of the eastern Mediterranean. The ships came home (if they escaped the dreaded Algerian pirates) laden with spices and wines, bringing large profits to the city's merchant venturers.

A school for their sons was started in 1633. This had roots going back 400 years, and branched out to create four of Exeter's main educational establishments. The Long

48 St John's Hospital School before the 1859 rebuilding. The frontage onto the High Street was lost when the former priory church building was demolished to make way for a new post office building in 1880. One of the Blue Boy statues was placed in Princesshay in 1957 to mark the position of the entrance to the main school buildings.

59

brothers had endowed a hospital just inside the east gate in *c.*1238, assigning to it family property bordering the nearby brook (therefore already known as the Longbrook). The hospital was a religious foundation, dedicated to St John the Baptist, housing five priests, six singing boys and twelve poor people. It was shut when the priories were dissolved, but the solid stone buildings and large church were subsequently used for dwelling-houses, a fleece market, a gunpowder store, a boys' workhouse and a grammar school. The church nave was divided into two floors; Latin and Greek were taught upstairs, and the Free English School occupied the ground floor. The latter supplied the pupils with uniform gowns and caps, leading to their nickname of Blue Boys. The buildings were modernised in 1859; in 1877 the name of the school was changed to St John's Hospital School, and the school survived until 1931. Hele's (now part of St Peter's) and Exeter School moved to new premises in 1840 and 1880 respectively, and both claim descent from the grammar school. A Blue Maids' School was opened in Mary Arches Street in 1656, the forerunner of the Maynard.

In Exwick Cleave, Cleve, Cliffe or Great Cleave is an old estate sited below a strong spring of water. John de Nethereclyve is recorded in 1339. It passed down in the family of Joel de Buckington and came to John Holland. In the early 1600s it was occupied by Thomas Malet, then Zenobia Mallet, then owned by Benjamin Oliver, followed by Robert Gubbs. The estate was purchased by a Thomas Northmore in the reign of Charles II; his heir and namesake, who extended the house, and died in 1713, was MP for Okehampton. Some of the interior dates from Gubbs's time. Northmore's house was L-shaped, the long main wing being two rooms deep and two storeys high, each with seven windows looking across a flat meadow towards Duryard. Some of the plaster ceilings date from the late 17th century. The façade was altered in the late 18th century, adding a central Tuscan porch below a Venetian window, and a stucco finish.

For nearly 100 years Cleave was the residence of one branch of the Snow family. Their ancestors were mayors, MPs and bankers in Exeter; now there were Snows at Franklyn, at Cleave, in the Quarries, at Weircliff and at Whitestone House. At Christmas the Snow charity provided every Exwick child with a bright new sixpence and an orange.

At the beginning of the last century some of the employees of the Cleave estate lived in thatched cottages each side of the drive – two on the left, five on the right. The infants' Sunday School treat was held in the big house, and they were collected in a

49   The Blue Boy statue in the new Princesshay still marks the site of St John's Hospital School.

50   Matthew Locke, the most important English composer between the Elizabethans and Purcell, or, as Roger North put it, 'since Jenkins fell off', received his musical training in the cathedral choir and carved his name in the stonework of the organ loft in 1638. He later became composer to Charles II and organist to his queen.

horse-drawn mill-wagon. From 1950 Cleve House was owned by the Guide Dogs for the Blind Association, and used as one of seven regional training centres. Additional bedrooms and kennels were built at the side and behind the main house. On 5 May 1988 Princess Alexandra re-opened the centre after major renovations and extensions. It has now been converted for residential use.

A lieutenant from Norwich came sightseeing in 1634. He reported that the cathedral had 'a stately rich high Seat for the Bishop' and also 'a delicate, rich and lofty Organ which had more additions than any other, as fayre Pipes of an extraordinary length, and of the bignesse of a man's Thigh, which with their Vialls, and other sweet Instruments, the tunable Voyces, and the rare Organist (John Lugge), together, makes a melodious and heavenly Harmony ...' At this time the choirmaster was Edward Gibbons (elder brother of Orlando) and Matthew Locke was a chorister. Locke's later career at court may have sprung from meeting the future King Charles II in 1644, when the prince lodged at the deanery from 28 July until September, or perhaps their paths crossed later, when they both took refuge in the Netherlands.

By 1637 the cathedral yard had become the last resting-place of so many Exonians in the space of 1,000 years that the rising ground level threatened to darken the cathedral windows; it was decided to close the yard to burials for 16 years. It was levelled and railed in, using 100 oaks from the city's stock in Duryard. A new cemetery was consecrated on 24 August 1637, St Bartholomew's Day, which gave the name Bartholomew to the street alongside it, previously known as Britayne. A plaque on the wall of the cemetery read:

FIDELIS IN ETERNVM

REPOSITORIVM DEI FIDELIVM DORMITORIVM

This platte of grovnde was given by ye Cyttie of Exon fytted and encompassed by the concurrent charge of both the Chvrche and Cyttie with the carefull overseeynge of ROGER MALLACK, MARCHANTE then MAIOR and was solemlie consecrated by the REVERENDE JOSEPH HALLE then LORD BISHOP of EXON vpon Sainte BARTHOLOMEWS DAYE Avgvste XXIIII; 1637 PRETIOSA IN CONSPECTV DEI MORS SANCTORVM

This is now one of the loveliest green spaces in the city centre. It is shaded by mature trees, and the view to the north is through treetops across the Longbrook valley to the soaring spire of St Michael's Church. The land falls away sharply. This is the edge of the hilltop defended by the Romans –and probably by the Britons before them. One only has to look over the railings and down into the valley to see how difficult it would be to attack from below.

In about 1640 Barley and Franklyn (and many other estates in Cowick) changed hands. The Russells were liquidising all their assets to pour into their great Fen-draining project in East Anglia. The Goulds became major landowners. William Gould had bought Cowick from the Russells and Hayes from the Peters; he died in 1635, leaving money for a school in St Thomas. William's brother, Henry Gould, owned Floyerhayes and bought Lew Trenchard from General Monk's father. A Gould heiress married a James Buller in 1739. This is how the lordship of the riverside manors passed from Baldwin to Courtenay to Russell to Gould to Buller.

During the Civil War Exeter was constantly under siege or attack from one party or the other. At the outset a majority in the City Chamber supported Parliament. Exeter

became the Puritans' headquarters. It withstood assaults by Cornish Royalist armies in November and December 1642, and in the following spring the Earl of Bedford had the walls strengthened to carry cannon and to withstand artillery. Provisions were stockpiled; the areas outside the city gates were cleared of trees and houses; defensive ditches were dug. The Royalists captured key positions outside the walls and besieged the city from 19 June 1643 until 7 September.

The Royalists had garrisons at Columb John and Poltimore House. Some of them seized St Anne's Chapel and almshouses at the fork of Old Tiverton Road and the Bath Road – a key position, which was a source of great annoyance to the Parliamentarian garrison in the city. The Royalists had fortified the most substantial buildings in Cowick Street, the church, the gaol and the West Indies Inn, and Hayes manor-house. On 31 July more than 1,100 Roundheads sallied out over the bridge with muskets and cannon. They took more than 80 Royalist prisoners and drove the others back to the higher ground. Excavations on Flowerpot in 1986 found little musket-balls and a 1lb cannon-ball against the yard walls, and signs that the house had burnt down.

The rest of Devon was falling to Prince Maurice, the king's nephew. The Duke of Bedford changed sides and the Exeter garrison surrendered, marching out of the gates on 7 September. Sir John Berkeley took over as governor, and set up a mint to pay the troops. He restored Royalists to the principal offices in the city. Exeter became a

51   Bartholomew Yard by moonlight, looking northward over the city walls. This peaceful scene records the midnight burial of the last cholera victim in August 1832, after which the cemetery was closed.

52   The Tudor House probably took its name from the local Tedder family. Prettily shaped slates originally covered the entire façade. Inside, a one-piece newel post rises through all four floors, and a musket-ball embedded in a beam of an upstairs room shows that the house stood through the sieges of the Civil War.

Royalist headquarters for two and a half years under Royalist military government. In 1644-5 wounded Royalists were nursed in 'Cowack House'.

In May 1644 Queen Henrietta fled to Exeter from Oxford for safety, arriving on 1 May. She was delivered of her ninth and last child in Bedford House on 16 June. Little Henrietta was christened in the cathedral. The register records that 'Henrietta daughter of our Sovereign Lord King Charles and our gracious Queen Mary was baptized the 21st July 1644.' The queen fled to France before the christening: only two weeks after the birth her doctor walked alongside the litter in which she was carried to Falmouth. He then had to hurry back to Exeter to care for the baby princess, who was suffering convulsive fits. Her father, busy fighting, saw the baby briefly on 26 July. The City Chamber gave the king £500. He could see that the city was prospering, and mentioned that his army could do with new shoes. Exeter gave him another £200 to buy 3,000 pairs. In September he was given a further £500.

In January 1646 General Fairfax encircled Exeter – pressing close to the St Thomas stronghold. On 30 January the church had been burnt down, probably deliberately to prevent his making use of it. In early February he occupied Barley House. He went to fight in North Devon and Cornwall, but on 31 March he came back over Redhill and through Exwick and Cowley. That night the city surrendered, but no treaty was signed until the Royalists had ceded 'Hunkses Fort' in St Thomas (probably the fortified prison).

The city had held out against Parliament for two and a half years, but agreed terms with Fairfax in April 1647. The Treaty of Exeter, which marked the end of the Civil War, was negotiated at Poltimore, in the Bampfyldes' Tudor mansion 3 miles outside Exeter. Six representatives of each side, Fairfax's Council of War and Exeter's City Chamber, argued from 3 April until Wednesday 8 April. Their aim was a bloodless surrender and this was achieved; but the occupying Royalists would not be satisfied until they had been assured of a list of safeguards. The city's castle and fortifications and all its supplies and weapons were to be ceded to the Parliamentarians, and in return all officers, soldiers and civilians who wished to leave the city could do so, if they paid a fine because they had supported the Royalists. The little princess was to be allowed to leave with her household and possessions. (In 1661 she would be married to the younger brother of Louis XIV, and by 1670 she was dead, possibly poisoned for acting as go-between for the French court and her fond eldest brother, Charles II.) The cathedral, churches and clergy were not to be harmed, but this last undertaking proved worthless. The unruly Puritans ran into the cathedral to convert it into an ammunition store. They smashed the window glass, destroyed the books and struck the heads off the statues. They tore down the cathedral organ pipes and 'went up and down the streets, Piping with them, and meeting some of the Choristers … scoffingly told them "Boyes we have spoyled your trade, you must go and sing hot Pudding Pies".' They also broke down the gates to the close and turned elderly canons out of their houses, which were used for hospitals or slaughterhouses or set on fire. The Bishop's Palace became the stable for their oxen and sheep. The figures on the west front had their features destroyed. The Parliamentarians had a legal basis for these actions. A few years before Exeter surrendered, Parliament had passed ordinances for the speedy demolition of all organs, images and all manner of superstitious monuments in cathedrals, parish churches and chapels throughout England and Wales.

From 1657 to 1662 the cathedral was divided into East Peter's and West Peter's by a brick wall, for the separate worship of the Congregationalist Independents and the Presbyterians. The lady chapel was converted into a library.

Only four of the city's 19 parish churches were to be retained for worship: St Mary Arches, St Edmund's, St Petrock's and St Mary Major. The others were to be sold. In many cases the parishioners bought them back. Allhallows on the Walls was an exception: it had taken a battering during the war and was left to deteriorate.

53 John Gendall's view of St Thomas from Exebridge shows the Seven Stars on the right. This inn had provided an upstairs room for George Fox to hold a Quaker meeting in 1657, and in 1728 John Gay's company performed *The Beggar's Opera* there.

St Stephen's Church tower had been partly burnt down. This church 'with the cellar beneath' was sold for £250 in 1658 and used for stables, and when Charles II came to the throne the congregation raised the money to buy it back. It had an extraordinarily long history and is mentioned in Domesday. A drawing from 1826 shows Saxon or early Norman pillars with carved capitals in the crypt.

St Thomas's Church was so badly damaged that it had to be completely demolished. The vicarage and church houses were 'also pulled down in the Warr time'. A public

appeal was launched in 1654, and the church was rebuilt in 1656-7. The new tower was taller. Its dedication was explicitly to Thomas the apostle. Cromwell ruled. St Thomas had a Presbyterian minister until 1662, when John Reynolds (grandfather of the artist Joshua) was installed as an Anglican vicar. Houses were built in Cowick Street to replace those destroyed in the Civil War, and were themselves destroyed in 1959 and 1962 during road-widening.

Quakers had begun to hold private meetings in Exeter. They were arrested and imprisoned if discovered, having their property seized. When George Fox came to Exeter in 1657 he took care to lodge outside the city, and Friends from Plymouth, Land's End and elsewhere joined him 'at the sign of the Seven Stars, an inn at the bridge foot', and they had a 'blessed heavenly meeting'. Fox continues: 'Next morning Major Blackmore sent soldiers to apprehend me; but I was gone before they came. As I was riding up the street, I saw the officers going down. The soldiers examined some Friends after I was gone, "what they did there"; but when they told them that they were in their inn, and had business in the city, they went away without meddling any further with them.'

At this time, manna from heaven, an incredible number of larks were found on the south side of the city, fat and plentiful, and were sold for 2d. a dozen.

Roads had potholes and worse. One January the rector of St Mary Clyst was returning home on horseback from Exeter with his wife perched behind him. As they were going down Paris Street they all fell into a well, nearly 40ft deep but not properly covered over. They were pulled out unhurt with ropes, but the horse was bruised and died.

Royalists plotting to restore the monarchy used to meet at an inn just beyond the city's boundary-stone on the Bath Road. The swarthy complexion of Charles, the next king, had caused his mother to call him 'My black boy', and the inn-sign was a coded reference to this. Citizens rejoiced when his accession was proclaimed on 11 May 1660, and a hogshead of good claret was fixed in each of the three public conduits. The siege trenches and dilapidations of the war were made good. Trinity Green was consecrated as an additional burial ground in 1664; the rest of Southernhay was levelled, and planted with 200 young elms. Another 200 were planted on Northernhay, to restore its charms as England's earliest pleasure-garden: it dated back to 1612. In 1672 the king gave the city a portrait of his Exeter-born sister, now dead.

The king was restored and the bishop was reinstated. Dr John Gauden was met by a grand cavalcade of coaches and some hundreds of horses carrying the principal gentlemen of the county of Devon. He was received at the Eastgate by the mayor, Chamber and incorporated trades, and some thousands of citizens who conducted him to the cathedral 'with great testimonies of joy and respect'. The musical waits were to be restored, and John Loosemore installed a new organ.

Over the centuries, whenever infection struck, the victims were nursed and sometimes buried outside the city. In 1665 the Corporation prepared for the Great Plague. They acquired a house and barn at the top of what is now Devonshire Place, facing Withybed Lane, which was thereafter often called Pester Lane or Pesterhouse Lane. On 14 November 1665 a 'public colleccon' was made to provide '8 bedsteads, 8 bolsters, flock, 2 prs of middling Blanckquilts, 3 prs ordinary.' However, Exeter was spared that outbreak of the plague: the pesthouse was not needed and was rented out under the name of Marlpool Cottage, until destroyed by bombing in 1942.

Jenkins reports that in June 1669 a huge sturgeon was caught in the Exe 'opposite the red rock or Good-Man's-Well on this side of Topsham, 'nine and a half feet long and six feet in girth'. By then monarchy had been restored, so it probably had to be delivered to the king.

The canal was extended to Topsham in 1676 and made deep enough for barges up to 16 tons. Ships off-loaded into seven lighters owned by the city. The Elizabethan quay was extended to make a waterfront twice as long, 483ft instead of 230ft. A handsome custom house was built in 1680, with cellars for storage and accommodation upstairs for excise officers, who were responsible for collecting dues on goods landed anywhere between the rivers Axe and Teign, not just the cargoes being unloaded below their windows. They had to chase local smugglers, who could be found leading packhorses laden with tea or brandy up the narrow Devon lanes. The new custom house was constructed of brick. It is the oldest surviving brick building in Exeter, and dates from a time when most buildings were still erected using stone or cob or a mixture of the two. The architect was Richard Allen, and the cost of building was £3,000, paid by the City Chamber. The arcades along the front were designed to be left open to allow goods to be unloaded out of the rain. They were filled in during the 18th century, and the building was extended eastwards at the same time. It has a hipped roof and a small pediment in the centre of the front, with royal arms from 1820. Inside on the ground

54 In 1680 the wharfage reverted to the city chamber; they dredged the river, extended the stone quay, built a covered unloading bay and a brick custom house where contraband tobacco was burned in the stove known as the 'King's Pipe'. The pool was enlarged: '100 sail of ship may safely ride therein'. The custom house originally had an open arcade.

55 Canon by Custom House, Wharfinger's Office, Quay House and warehouses.

floor there was the 'king's pipe', where contraband tobacco was burned, and a sluice, where contraband brandy was poured away. There were sharp steel rods to plunge into suspect bales of goods. On the first floor, above a massive staircase, is the glory of the building, ornate Baroque plaster ceilings by the North Devon master John Abbot of Frithelstock, decorated with oak leaves and acorns, eels, flowers and fruit.

A less showy building on the quay is the quay house. It was nearly demolished when it was apparently just a tumble-down DIY timber warehouse, but luckily was recognised as dating from the same year as the custom house and was retained as a tourist centre.

In 1680 James Duke of Monmouth toured the West Country to raise support for his cause; he came through Exeter with 500 horsemen and 900 young men in white uniform. After his defeat in 1685 Judge Jeffreys held one of his 'Bloody Assizes' in the Guildhall, sending 80 rebels to the Heavitree gallows. Hanged, drawn and quartered, the mangled remains were exposed on trees on the public roads 'to the great annoyance and terror of passers-by'.

Assizes were held at the castle twice a year, spring and summer. Two judges were appointed to each circuit to travel to the principal towns and to deal with prisoners held in gaol who were accused of murder, robbery, burglary, grand larceny, rape, coining and witchcraft. Their coach was met at Livery Dole and they were escorted to their lodgings. After the assizes the coach was escorted to the western city limits at St John's Cross at the top of Dunsford Road.

At the summer assizes of 1682 three 'decrepit and impotent' friendless old women, Temperance Lloyd, Susannah Edwards and Mary Trembles, who appeared weary of their lives after being hounded in their hometown of Bideford, and then languishing in gaol, came to trial for witchcraft. The judge advised them to plead not guilty, but in the end decided to sacrifice them to the rioting mob for the sake of civil peace. They were sent to the gallows at Heavitree, having confessed to consorting with the devil in the shape of a small black man, having cats as familiars and causing pain and illness in suffering neighbours by such actions as giving them pains in their knees by pricking a piece of leather. They were almost the last victims of the witch-hunting craze.

Jonathan Trelawny, Bishop of Bristol, was one of the seven bishops sent to the Tower for refusing to read out King James's 1687 Declaration of Indulgence. 20,000 Cornishmen began marching to London 'to know the reason why'. They had reached Exeter when they heard that all the bishops had been released, and the demonstrators went home.

On 5 November 1688 William of Orange landed at Brixham. His troops marched through mud and mist, needing a change of clothes when they reached Exeter. Some needed nursing and were cared for in the Blue Maids' Hospital. The citizens sent in a bill to the king, and invoiced Queen Anne in 1706 to say the £345 4s. 2½d. was still outstanding. On the following day William came riding up Stepcote Hill with an impressive entourage, which included '200 Blacks brought from the Plantations of the Netherlands in America, in Imbroyder'd Caps lined with white Fur ... 200 Finlanders in bear skins taken from the Wild Beasts they had slain ... pages to support the prince's Banner, GOD AND THE PROTESTANT RELIGION ... and the Prince on a Milk White Palfrey, all in bright armour, and 42 footmen running by him'. He did not think much of the state of the walls – 'I could take this city with baked apples' – and he

56   Rear view of the custom house from Quay Hill, showing the roof.

lodged at the deanery, waiting for assurances that it was safe to ride to London. Before William left he had the surrounding heights surveyed to see if it would be possible to fortify the city if he had to retreat. His engineers said it would be impractical 'by the nature of the city's situation'.

Bishop Trelawney was due to transfer to Exeter from the see of Bristol, but there was a delay. As King James crossed from Whitehall to Lambeth on his way to exile in France he had thrown the Great Seal of England into the Thames, so the necessary documents could not be completed.

The following February, when William and Mary were proclaimed king and queen, the conduits again ran with wine. Trade increased. Foreign merchants settled in the town to enjoy the new religious freedom. By 1700 the canal could carry ships of over 100 tons. A sugar house and a glass house joined the paper-mills at Countess Wear, together employing hundreds.

Exeter was now at the height of its prosperity, the third largest city after London, with a population of about 13,000. For centuries the city's prosperity was based for a large part on the wool trade. Uniquely among Exeter's many medieval trade guilds the Company of Weavers, Tuckers and Shearmen, founded in 1471, still exists, although no longer counting craftsmen among its members. The shearmen in the guild's name were not the sheepshearers supplying fleeces to the weavers but skilled workers trimming irregularities in the finished cloth. Tuckers Hall still stands on Fore Street. Its chapel was converted after the Reformation into a meeting hall.

Large quantities of Devon cloth were exported in the 15th century. They were known as kerseys, light in weight, comparatively cheap and dyed in bright colours. Soon after 1600 Exeter changed its production to serge, a heavier hard-wearing cloth. The many flocks of sheep in the surrounding countryside supplied wool to the many weavers in the villages and towns. They carded and spun the wool and then wove it into lengths. Wagonloads of cloth from the loom arrived in the city. Celia Fiennes rode into Exeter in 1698 from Hampshire. She recorded the 'vast trade in serges' and how the woven lengths were treated:

> they lay them to soack in urine, then they soape them and soe put them into the fulling mills and soe work them in the mills drye until they are thick enough, then they turn water into them and so scower them; the mill does draw out and gather in the serges in a sort of huge notch'd timbers like great teeth, one would think it would injure the serges but it does not, the mill draws in with such a great violence, that if one stands neare it and it catch a bit of your garments it would be ready to draw in the person even in a trice; when they are thus scour'd they drye them in racks strained out, which are as thick set out by another as will permit the dresser to pass between, and huge large fields occupy'd this way almost all round the town which is to the river side; then when drye they burle them picking out all the knots, then fold them with a paper between every fold and so sett them on an iron plaite and screw down the press on them, which has another iron plaite on the top under which is a furnace of fire of coales, this is the hot presse; then they fold them exceeding exact and then presse them in a cold presse …

This description makes clear the vital roles played by the many water-driven mills on the river, including those producing paper for the trade, and explains the work of the tuckers and fullers. The rackfields are drawn in on the maps of the time on every clear space on the river-banks. The cloths were hung to dry on tenterhooks on the wooden racks. We still say we are on tenterhooks if we feel stretched in expectation.

57 Stepcote Lane was the steep main road from the river crossing to the city centre until 1778, when a new bridge was aligned with Fore Street and a linking viaduct was pushed through the city wall.

Fiennes describes the dyeing process with equally vivid detail and using her own spelling for words perhaps new to her, such as 'vats':

I saw several fatts they were adying in, of black, yellow, blew and green – which two last coullours are dipp'd in the same fatt, that which makes it differ is what they were dipp'd in before, which makes them either green or blew; they hang the serges on a great beame or greate pole on the top of the fatt and so keep turning it from one to another. As one turns it off into the fatt the other rowles it out of it, soe they do it backwards and forwards till its tinged deep enough of the coullour; their furnace that keeps their dye pans boyling is all under that roome, made of coal fires; there was in a room by it self a fatt for the scarlet, that being a very chargeable dye noe waste must be allow'd in that … the length of these pieces are or should hold out 26 yards.

A large proportion of the local population was kept busy shearing sheep, transporting fleeces, selling at market, carding, spinning, weaving in cottages, collecting urine, working the fulling-mills, dyeing, stretching the cloth on tenterhooks to dry in the rack-fields, raising a nap with teasels, trimming with shears, baling the finished cloth and loading it onto wagons and ships. Daniel Defoe, touring England in 1724-6, saw 'a city famous for two things, that 'tis full of gentry, and good company, and yet full of trade and manufacture also; the serge market, next to the market at Leeds, is the greatest in England; at this market is generally sold … sometimes a hundred thousand pounds value in serges in a week'. Distinctive green baize aprons with red strings were worn 'by almost every other man you meet, all freemen of the Incorporated Company

58 In 1694 a water engine was installed in the New Mill leat below Exe Street. The leat drove a wheel to pump water up through 18in wooden pipes to a reservoir behind the Guildhall (in use until 1833). Steam power was not needed. The huge cistern held 600 hogsheads of water, which was piped to houses in the city centre.

of Weavers, Fullers and Shearmen'. Even at the end of the century the members of this guild were known as the 'Golden Tuckers' – 'from their habit of early clearing the market of their most expensive luxuries'.

Defoe was writing at a time when a weekly six-horse coach service had begun the run to Bath and Bristol, carrying six inside and taking three days. London was still six days distant, travelling non-stop.

The cloth-trade was still flourishing, its manufacturing processes dominating the area round Exebridge – witness Dr William Stukeley in 1724: 'The bridge over the Isca is of great length and has houses on both sides and both ends; a considerable void space in the middle; there is a church upon it with a tower steeple … Woollens are brought here to be dyed, which we saw in passing over the bridge amongst the suburbs, consisting of dye-houses and dry-frames, spread in crowds on the banks of the river.' Izacke's map of 1741 shows these serried racks on 'Shilley' and all the river-banks. For centuries the riverside must have seemed decked for a permanent festival, with the colourful lengths of dyed cloth stretched to dry. The wool trade has left its mark on local surnames – witness today's many Tuckers, Woollacotts, Woolleys, Fullers and Dyers. Even Willey's engineering works developed from woollen mills on Shilhay. The family might have been running them since the days of descriptive surnames, since one of the processes that turns wool into yarn is called willeying.

Mill Lane at Countess Wear runs peacefully along a backwater of the River Exe. Below the whitewashed thatched cottages at the heart of the village are some old lime kilns, at the foot of Lime Kiln Lane. They are completely covered with creeper and give no hint of how important they were for the local economy until 100 years ago. The soils of South Devon are acid and need regular sweetening; tenant farmers were obliged to spread lime regularly on their fields. For example, a farmer in 1694 had to covenant to dress his land with two hogsheads of Topsham lime or 200 horseloads of good stable dung per acre every year. Before it is spread, limestone has to be crushed and burnt to become quicklime. As well as its use in agriculture it makes limewash for painting walls; it makes mortar, stucco and plaster for ceilings. Tanners use it to take the hairs off the skins. In the nearby Countess Wear papermills it was needed to coat satin-white paper. To produce the quicklime a kiln was filled with alternate layers of coal and limestone and left to burn. There is no limestone in South Devon nearer than Babbacombe Quarry in Torquay. A 'stoneboat' or lighter could go there and back in one day. The coal had a longer journey, from South Wales. It was 'culm', that is coal dust or small pieces of anthracite.

Limestone and coal are both heavy cargoes. That is why they were brought in by water, and the kilns stood near the water's edge. Sometimes the large stone boats had to dump their load just off shore and it was retrieved at low tide. These burning kilns were a source of constant warmth. John Swete noted in 1799 that grapes were ripened on the heated walls of Countess Wear limekilns. The Topsham register of deaths for 1670-85 listed four tramps who had stifled from sleeping in the limekilns for warmth.

The Countess Wear lime kilns were not the only ones along the Exe estuary: there were at least 11 between Exeter quay and Lympstone. It has been calculated that together they burnt about 15,000 tons of lime every year. From about 1850 artificial manures began to be marketed, and many lime kilns shut down, including one at St Leonard's. The kilns at Countess Wear continued in use until 1914.

The cathedral preserves a rare autograph letter from the composer Henry Purcell, dated 2 November 1686. He felt obliged to write to the dean to chase up money owed to him for teaching and board.

I have wrote severall times to Mr Webber concerning what was due to me on Hodg's account and rec'd no answer, which has occasion'd this presumption in giving you the trouble of a few lines relating to the matter. It is ever since the beginning of June last that the Money has been due: the sum is £27, *viz* £20 for half a year's teaching and boarding the other a Bill of £7 which I laid out for him; the Bill Mr Webber has. Compassion moves me to acquaint you of a great many debts Mr Hodg contracted while in London and to some who are so poor 'were an act of Charity as well as Justice to pay 'em. I hope you will be so kind as to take it into your consideration and also pardon this boldness from

Sir, your most obliged

humble servant

Henry Purcell

7

Georgian Exeter

A violent storm one night in November 1703 wrecked ships at sea, and in the city ripped the roofs off houses and blew chimney-stacks down. In the cathedral yard many of the elms that had stood there for nearly a century were torn up by the roots. The Dean and Chapter cleared away all the elms and made a fresh start with young lime trees, but these did not thrive and were replaced with elms again. Meanwhile, just as a growing tree is continually adding another outer ring, the living city itself was about to develop a surrounding zone of brick-built crescents, terraces, meeting-houses, prisons, barracks, theatres and a hospital, reflecting changes in society and in fashion.

Pince's Gardens and the Pince's Field allotments have inherited rich soil and mature trees from the Exeter Nursery (founded in 1720 by William Lucombe), birthplace of the Exeter or Lucombe Oak. Thomas Lucombe found that an acorn from a Turkey Oak pollinated by an adjacent Cork Oak grew so straight and rapidly, with such handsome, glossy, over-wintering leaves, that he could sell thousands of cuttings in the first seven years of availability, 1765-72. They grew as tall in 20-30 years as a common oak in a century. An Exeter Oak at Cowley Place in 1957 was the tallest oak recorded in Britain, at 126ft. William had the first one felled to provide planks for his coffin and kept them seasoning under his bed; but as the years went by they were used for something else, and a younger Lucombe Oak was used when he died a centenarian.

The firm later added the name of Pince from a grandson, and by 1884 the nursery was one of the sights of Exeter, taking up more than six pages in Besley's *Guide*:

> All respectable persons are freely admitted by merely leaving their cards and addresses in the office at the entrance… There is a little town of glass … Palms, Camellias 20 ft. high, Orchids, Grape Vines … A Rock Garden where nearly every jutting crag or rounded boulder affords root-hold or shelter to some distinctive kind of vegetation. The walks wind mysteriously under sombre yews and other evergreens, and here and there open spaces, trickling rills and limpid pools afford room for the more hardy exotic plants … Bambus, Pampas Grass, Yuccas … A quarter-mile Coniferous walk intersects the nursery, with views

of the city, cathedral and spires. In the centre of the Italian garden is a wire-covered walk, over which climbing Roses, Clematises, Wistarias and other suitable plants are trained.

The nursery-ground is now a public park but still boasts the elegant pergola covered with wistaria and the coniferous walk. The land was auctioned in 1912, but only a small corner was built on, just after the First World War, the delightful Pince's Gardens, with cottagey terraces round a village-green.

A reputable grocer in the city expected his son to follow him in the trade and educated him accordingly. But the son, Peter King, was ambitious. He read and studied independently and managed to get to university to study divinity. Realising that as a dissenter he would not be able to pursue a career in the Church of England, he switched his attention to law. He managed to get called to the Bar and rose through the ranks to become Lord Chief Justice of the Common Pleas, and afterwards Lord Chancellor and a baron, Lord King. His father decided to visit his eminent son and went on foot to London. He found the house, but the porter shut the gate against him. After a scuffle his son came and fell on his knees to ask his father's blessing. The porter fell on his knees and begged their pardon.

Another example of diligence and perseverance leading to success is John Baring, posthumous son of a Lutheran minister, who came from Bremen in 1717 to learn the woollen trade. He lodged in Palace Gate and attended the dissenters' services in James's Meeting nearby. He studied well and married well, picking the daughter of a wealthy local grocer. By 1737 he could afford to move into Larkbeare; he filled the grounds with large press-shops, packing-rooms and rackfields. Robert Dymond wrote of these times that 'only three persons in Exeter possessed private carriages: Mr Baring the wealthy cloth merchant, the Recorder and the Bishop'. There was only one wheeled conveyance for hire in the city then, otherwise it was horseback or sedan-chair – or one walked. Municipal regulations governed the charges for sedan chairs. By 1805, 300yds from Eastgate to Bedford theatre cost 6d., but 9d. after midnight.

59 The Barings and the Bowrings were among the wealthy Unitarians who built George's Meeting in South Street in 1760, naming it after the new king, George III. The carved pulpit was brought from their older meeting-house in James Street. The building was used for worship until 1987. Until then it remained a rare unspoilt Georgian meeting-house.

In 1748 Baring's three sons inherited the flourishing manufacturing and export business. Two of them founded a bank in 1768, which became the London merchant bank Baring Bros. It has been claimed that the Baring family virtually ran the country during the reign of the four Georges, and helped to finance the British empire. In 1770 the eldest son returned to Exeter, bought the manor of Heavitree, a large area that included Mount Radford, the hill above Larkbeare, and built himself a mansion there. The middle son left £6 million when he died in 1810. This was the kind of money to be made from merchandise and merchant-banking.

Workhouses are sometimes remembered as places of humiliation and cruelty, but when Exeter pioneered the idea in 1670 (shortly after Bristol) it was with the best of intentions. Local Christians and leading citizens were determined to help the sick and destitute – but at the same time the workhouse was never meant to be a soft option for malingerers. Canon John Bury was one of the benefactors who put a roof over the head of the desperate poor.

In the reign of William III an Act was passed for the creation of hospitals and workhouses 'for the better employing and maintaining of the poor in Exeter'. The city's first workhouse stood at the foot of Heavitree Road, where the Triangle car park is now. This building, on the bank of the Chute brook, is portrayed in a vignette on Roque's 1744 map of the city. It is labelled City Hospital and is shown standing among trees and grazing cattle. After the new workhouse was built this old one became a bridewell (prison), before being used as an infirmary, then a factory for weaving tapestry under the protection of the then Prince of Wales – an enterprise that failed. The building was finally let out to poor tenants. Exeter's experiences with this workhouse were found to be useful when the government drew up revised poor laws a few decades later. By 1700 Exeter was building new workhouse accommodation a little higher up Heavitree Road, on a site that later became the Royal Devon and Exeter Hospital (Heavitree) or City Hospital (RD&E). The authorities had learned from experience 'that the poor in the city of Exon do daily multiply, and Idleness and Debauchery amongst the meaner sort doth greatly increase, for want of workhouses to set them to work'. Land for the new workhouse was given by Philip Andrew and others. The central block was erected in 1700 and wings by 1707. The main entrance opened into the chapel, where men sat on one side, women on the other, lunatics and the sick separately. There was a pretty carved stone front for christening babies. Upstairs was the boardroom, where officers were elected. It held portraits of William III and such patrons as Dr John Bury, Dr Arthur Bury, Col. John Bury, Sir Thomas Bury, architect Ralph Mitchell and a view of the workhouse before the plantings. On one side the windows of the boardroom overlooked the interior of the chapel.

The workhouse was described by a visitor in 1868:

Unlike others, the structure on Heavitree Road is absolutely attractive. Constructed of common red brick but with a bold portal dressed with white quoins, standing in picturesque perspective at the end of a splendid avenue of tall elms. A high red boundary wall surrounds it but somehow not pauperesque in character [some of this wall still stands], there is nothing ostentatiously cheap in the turn of the coping. It breaks into a fine semi-circular sweep at the gateway. The gates are hung on respectable massive piers. A fine broad centre path, flanked with shrubberies, leads straight up to the great entrance, intercepted halfway by interior gates and a lodge. The great elms more than half hide the plain red walls and slated roofs of the wings of the building, and the part of the structure visible from the road – the pedimented portal adorned with classical figures in sable and surmounted by a clock and campanile, is quite unsuggestive of the melancholy purpose of the establishment.

From five o'clock onwards each evening vagrants came along with little bundles on their back and a walking-stick. They were not allowed in until half past five or six, at which time they would go in and have a meal and a doss for the night. Vagrants were treated differently from long-term residents. Tramps were provided with a rug in a sleeping box and were not compelled to take a bath. Breakfast was bread and gruel, then they were obliged to break 3 bushels of stone into small pieces or pick apart 1lb weight of oakum (old tarred rope from ships) before being allowed to leave.

The 285 'indoor paupers' had bedsteads in dormitories. Each had a sheet, three blankets and a red and black woollen rug. There were wide landings furnished with Bibles and other books, and with fine views over the city. There were cages of canaries and strips of carpet down the middle of each dormitory. Although there were rooms for married paupers over the age of 60 to sleep together, married paupers under 60 were separated and had to sleep in the men's and women's dormitories. A master and a matron kept order. Rations were 7oz of bread and 1½ pints of gruel for breakfast, while dinner at noon consisted of ¾lb of meat each and ¾lb of potatoes and 3oz of bread – that was on three days a week. On one day there was meat pudding and on two days soup, then 7oz of bread for supper. All the bread consumed was baked on the premises in 7lb loaves. There were a schoolmaster and a schoolmistress for the children. Girls were taught laundering and ironing: their playground was fitted with clothes-lines for drying linen. The children were taught gardening in the grounds. Bedding and clothing were all made in-house, including the men's suits, shoes and stockings. The beer cellar was supplied with ale from Burton-on-Trent: 70 gallons was needed every week. The poor rates were reduced by £1,000 per annum by establishing a pottery, which made tiles and bricks, in a field adjacent to the workhouse. Under kindly and efficient management the system did a good job.

St Thomas had a separate workhouse: the union workhouse at Redhills was the poor law hospital for 30 parishes. As far as vagrants were concerned, those coming to Exeter from the east were directed to the Exeter workhouse on Heavitree Road; those coming from the west had to use Redhills. As at the Exeter establishment, they were not admitted until the evening. Residents of Buddle Lane remember tramps begging hot water for their tea cans as they sat in the hedge and waited for the workhouse to open. Buddle Lane also saw nurses from the workhouse walking toddlers and wheeling prams full of babies in the fresh air. The St Thomas workhouse replaced an earlier one on the south side of Cowick Street, and the splendid building was constructed in 1837 to satisfy the new Poor Law. It could house 450 paupers and stood on rising ground at the higher end of Okehampton Road. It had three storeys of dark red Pocombe stone, and the building was crowned by a three-sided cupola holding a bell.

Redhills was cleverly designed to cater for all the different groups needing care. It was laid out like a wheel with a six-sided rim, each spoke housing a different ward. The tramps had a separate entrance. There was an isolated 'itch ward' and an ivy-covered chapel in one of the courtyards. The chaplain's wife painted the lancet windows in watercolours. A schoolmaster was employed for the 35 resident boys, whose dormitory was in an attic above the master's sitting-room: he popped up through a trap door to see what they were doing. There was room for 25 girls, who were trained to enter domestic service when they left at 16. Men worked in the tailoring and cobblers' shops, grew all the vegetables needed and tended the dozen pigs, as well as pumping water up to tanks in the attic, while the women worked at sewing. A visitor in 1868 praised the orderly and cheerful regime: he was impressed by the fact that the knives and forks were cleaned every day. Here too there were separate bedrooms for old married couples, although they usually preferred the wards with the company of their own sex. This workhouse became a hospital under the NHS, and continued to care for the chronically ill, the sick elderly and maternity cases. It shut in 1989-90 and the site was developed for housing.

In the 1720s Exeter would not license travelling players within the city, and once again the first inn beyond the bridge was the venue for something banned in the city. Performances took place in an upper room, or occasionally in the garden. In 1721 citizens flocked over the bridge to see 'Punch's theatre, with artificial actors, also many wonderful Fancies as dancing with swords by a girl but ten years old, who turns many 100 times round with so swift a motion that it's scarce possible to distinguish her Face from the hinder part of her Head'. In 1726 the Duke of Grafton's company of comedians advertised 'a Diverting Comedy, called *The Busie Body,* at the Seven Stars at the Bridge foot in St Thomas'. John Gay's *Beggar's Opera* opened in London in January 1728, and the original company gave the last performance of the season on 15 November at the Seven Stars: 'before the Play, at the earnest Request of divers of the Gentry, Mr Radford will perform his Agility, which is the last time he proposes ever to do it in Public'. The Seven Stars continued to serve as Exeter's oldest theatre even when proper stages were opened in the city.

The headmaster of Blundell's School in Tiverton, Samuel Wesley, died in 1739. His brothers John and Charles rode to Devon to comfort his widow, and John was invited to preach in Exeter. On the Sunday morning he spoke in Mary Arches on the text 'The kingdom of God is not meat and drink; but righteousness, and peace, and joy in the Holy Ghost'. The rector could not find anything undoctrinal in the sermon, but he asked Wesley not to preach in the afternoon: 'It is not guarded; it is dangerous. It may lead people into enthusiasm or despair.' Four years later Charles Wesley preached in the open air in Exeter 'to about a thousand sinners, mostly gentlemen and ladies with some clergy'. Other dissenters had their meeting-houses by now, but the new Wesleyan Methodists were mobbed and assaulted when they gathered for worship. The established church was less fervent; the satirist Andrew Brice describes 'sleepy maids sent to early service at the cathedral for the good of their lie-abed mistresses' souls'.

By 1682 about 28 acres at the top of the former Polsloe demesne had been leased to an Exeter butcher called John Rowe, and he built a barn; from the early 18th century the lane leading to it was known as Rowe's Barn Lane. In 1730 the Tuckers' Guild bought the estate as an investment, three-quarters of the price having been bequeathed with the stipulation, among others, that the income should be expended 'in providing coats, hats, shirts, stockings and shoes for 14 poor freemen of the company …' The estate failed to bring in as much as had been hoped, and the Tuckers had to cut down on the quality of the cloth and the number of coats distributed.

In 1754 an attempt to mine coal on Exwick Hill, on the Cleave estate, was abandoned when the drill broke on a sledgehammer-head thrown in by a saboteur. The only other coal-mining venture in this county was in North Devon.

An important Georgian building tucked away off Mary Arches Street is the Jewish synagogue. It is the third oldest in the United Kingdom and one of the oldest active Jewish places of worship in the country. It also has one of the most important interiors. The first mention of Jews living in Exeter was in 1181, but in the Middle Ages the community probably worshipped in their own houses. In 1290 all Jews were expelled from England, but they returned in the 16th century, many from Germany, in the shipping trade or as artisans. Exeter's Jewish congregation built their synagogue in

1763 and it was dedicated on 10 August 1764. They had bought a burial plot outside the city walls by Bull Meadow in 1757, which is still in use and well maintained. The synagogue has a plain exterior for security reasons. It is lit by a roof lantern, a glass cupola. The building is oriented to the Wailing Wall, the western wall of the Temple in Jerusalem. There is a box under each pew for books and prayer shawls. Women sit separately. There was a ritual bath upstairs, and an adjacent caretaker's house. Hedgeland's model of the city's buildings shows a garden around the synagogue. The building was extended and remodelled in 1835 and 1905 and again in 1963, to repair war damage inflicted in the blitz of 1942. Refurbishment in 1997 dislodged part of an oak beam from the roof, thought to have been re-used from a sea-going galleon, a man of war: it is on display. West Quarter children remembered playing on a grassy patch next to the synagogue in the 1920s. The congregation went in on Saturdays, the men in black top hats, and when they came out they threw pennies to the children.

60   The synagogue of 1763, the third oldest in the United Kingdom.

8

A Hospital for Devon and Exeter

When the monasteries were closed in the 1540s, their physick gardens and hospices were also lost. For the next two centuries the sick could not expect any public care. From the 1670s Exeter's destitute could find shelter in the workhouse on the east bank of the Chute brook at the foot of Paris Street, while the rich could afford to send for a doctor and hire a nurse; but the majority fell between these two extremes: they had to depend on folk remedies, quack doctors and the kindness of family and neighbours.

Towards the middle of the 18th century the new concept of 'voluntary hospitals' was seen as the way to help the sick poor, to funnel the charitable impulse more effectively than merely carrying soup to cottagers. The invalid could be offered rest and perhaps a cure. The doctors could practise on a steady supply of cases. They gladly gave their services for nothing, knowing that the honorary attachment to a hospital would enhance their reputations so they could charge their private patients more.

Dr Alured Clarke was appointed Dean of Exeter Cathedral in January 1740/1 (what we would call 1741 but regarded then as still in 1740: before 1752 each year ran until 25 March). He had established a voluntary hospital in Winchester in 1736, and although he himself was not well, indeed was to die aged 46 on 3 May 1742, he was determined 'not to give sleep to his eyes nor slumber to his eyelids, until he had secured the same blessings for the County of Devon and its Metropolis'. Dean Clarke's wish became reality with such incredible speed that part of the hospital was up and equipped to admit patients by 1 January 1742/3. He held the first meeting of subscribers in the cathedral chapter house on 23 July 1741, the site was offered on 6 August, and the builder had prepared the plan by 27 August when the foundation stone was laid, little more than a month from the launch. Sites had been inspected in both Northernhay and Southernhay, which were equally elevated and airy, and both outside the city walls. Southernhay was virtually undeveloped at this time: it was still used for horse fairs and the annual Lammas Fair, and the Georgian terraces

on either side were not built until 1795-1824. John Tuckfield (future Tory MP for
Exeter) provided the plot, facing Trinity burial ground and the wall of the Bishop's
Palace, while county gentry donated cartloads of timber, sand, stone and slate. A
local builder, John Richards, gave his services free, offering to design the hospital and
supervise its erection. It was to be 'as plain and frugal as possible', and indeed the only
decorations are the rusticated quoins, dentil band under the eaves and central cupola.
The roof is hipped and covered with large slates. It still graces Southernhay 250 years
later, while its 1970s replacement had to be demolished after less than 25 years. As
the site slopes, the cellars are below street level but not underground. The basement
of the central block housed laboratory, bake-house and baths, while the south wing
cellars held the wash-house, brewhouse, laundry, and stores for coal and provisions.
On the ground floor of the main block was an elegantly proportioned boardroom,
where the governors met every Thursday. It would benefit from many legacies over
the years, which added Chippendale chairs and panelling, and a growing collection
of portraits of benefactors and eminent doctors, by equally eminent artists.

In September 1741 the dean sent an appeal to every church and chapel in Devon.
Every subscriber or contributing congregation would be entitled to recommend one
patient at a time. The target was £3,000, which would help 2,000 of Devon's sick poor
every year. 160 beds would accommodate 1,000 patients a year with lodging, diet,
advice and medicine. A similar number of out-patients would have just the advice
and medicine, but also gratis. Dean Clarke's adviser on the medical arrangements
was Dr Michael Lee Dicker. Also in September 1741 the governors approved Dicker's
election as physician, together with five others (Drs Andrew, Bent, Glass, Hallett and
Walrond) and five surgeons (Messrs Parr, Patch senior and junior, Pillett and Walker).

61 The Devon and
Exeter Hospital. This
building served for 250
years from 1742.

In attracting doctors, the county was in competition with the city, for the guardians of the poor had a rival scheme for a hospital in the old workhouse. Indeed, the city opened a hospital with 40 beds a few months before the one in Southernhay, but it closed from lack of funds in 1754.

The Devon and Exeter Hospital fared better. A matron and two nurses were appointed before it opened, and they were joined in February by a resident apothecary, who was instructed to do a daily ward round and to remain on call at all times. The statutes also required 'That the Clergy of Exeter be desired to attend, by Weekly Rotation, to visit the Sick, and to read Prayers every Day in the Wards, and to give the Communion at proper times'. The category of persons who could be helped was strictly controlled: 'No children under seven Years of Age; no Woman big with Child; no Person disordered in the Senses, or suspected to have the Small-Pox, Itch, or any other infectious Disease; nor any that are apprehended to be in a consumptive or dying condition ...' That certainly made for a better success rate.

There were 30 beds to start with, arranged sideways along the walls, feet meeting at the centre of each window but divided by partitions. Patients were admitted on Thursdays; the rules were read out to them on Friday morning. Rule Six may have come as a shock to anyone looking forward to a rest: 'That such of the Patients, as are able to work, do assist the Nurses and other Servants, in nursing the Patients, washing and ironing the Linnen, washing and cleaning the Wards; and in doing such other Business as the Matron shall require.' Until 1815, when mains water was brought in, patients had to take shifts pumping water from the well in the basement to the cistern in the roof. Matron herself was to call the register morning and evening in each ward and lock the gates at night. Rule Seventeen for In-Patients stated: 'That when the Patients are cured, they be enjoined by the Chairman to return thanks to ALMIGHTY GOD in their respective place of publick Worship.' Of the rules for out-patients, the first was 'That they attend exactly at the Time appointed by the Apothecary.' The possibility of waiting-lists was foreseen: 'Provision is made by the Rules of the Hospital, that they can never stay more than a Week before they are received into the House, if all the Beds should happen to be full at the Time of their coming.'

Annual expenditure in the first 10 years averaged £608 (wages, provisions, candles, coal – and trees and plants for the physick garden). In the yard pigs ate the leftovers and provided protein for the kitchen, until they were declared a health hazard in 1793.

The north wing was completed in 1748. The earliest wards, in the south wing and the central block, had been named Devon, Exeter, Bristol and Winchester. Later additions were also named after places: Gloucester, Plymouth, Cornish, Northampton, Bath, Somerset, London. In 1756 an operating theatre, a casualty department and surgical wards were added. By then the staff consisted of the apothecary, matron, secretary, eight nurses, cook, housemaid, laundry-maid and porter/messenger. From the start the Exeter doctors were at the forefront of medical practice: John Blackall's book on dropsy (1813) anticipated Bright; John Patch senior was the first surgeon in the West Country to remove stones from the bladder; Bartholomew Parr, 54 years a surgeon at the hospital, was a skilled obstetrician; Dr Thomas Glass developed the treatment of 'continual fevers' and 'military fever', pioneered the therapeutic use of baths, and was concerned about the dangers of smallpox inoculation. (From 1807 the safer cowpox inoculation was offered free on Tuesdays and Wednesdays.) Many Devonians were cured of longstanding complaints. Funds continued to flow into the strongbox: Exeter had no banks until 1769.

In 1780 an extra dozen beds were provided, and it was minuted by the governors that 'It is detrimental both to the interest and the credit of the Hospital to put two patients in one bed, and it be recommended by this Court to the Committee to put an entire stop to the practice.' In the same year it was agreed that 'a leaping-stock or upping-block be erected near the entrance for the better accommodation of country patients in alighting from and remounting their horses'.

In September 1789 the manager of the Bedford Circus Theatre handed over £30 from a benefit performance by Mrs Sarah Siddons. In June 1796 there came the first cash crisis. Five wards had to close for several months, leaving only 43 beds in use. One ward re-opened in 1798, one in 1799, but there followed two bad harvests, and 64 beds were taken out of service in 1805. The board of governors stated that they entertained 'too high an opinion of the wisdom and humanity of the Nobility, Gentry, Clergy and Yeomanry of the County of Devon and its Neighbourhood to think for a moment that they will suffer to sink into decay an Establishment which has restored to health 41,500 of our indigent fellow creatures …'

In 1808 an eye hospital with six beds opened in Holloway Street, moving in 1813 to Magdalen Street. Its first oculists, John Saunders and William Adams, had been pupils of the same Barnstaple GP before studying at Guy's and St Thomas's hospitals. Saunders founded Moorfields in 1804 and taught the new method of removing cataracts there; he then helped Adams set up the Exeter hospital. A notable early success was the gift of sight to a 30 year old who had been born blind; and 28 cataract cases were cured in the first year. Patients were admitted for stays of up to 10 weeks. The West of England Eye Infirmary, as it became known, was financed by subscriptions and donations, but any clergyman – subscriber or not – could send a poor parishioner for free treatment.

One Thursday in July 1809 an actor, Joseph Wilde, who had torn a knee ligament performing in pantomime at Devonport, was admitted to the Southernhay hospital for rest. He composed a long poem expressing gratitude to:

> This hospital, this noble monument
> of human worth;
> Where now I lie, struck by the awful
> hand of Providence,
> To punish my mistreadings …

On his first morning in the ward he was amazed to see Rule Six in action:

> All who can wield an instrument
> of labour,
> Are busily employed on cleanliness;
> Till the whole ward,
> for neatness might compare
> and wholesome sweetness,
> with a monarch's palace.

By then the apothecary and individual physicians and surgeons in Southernhay were taking on paying apprentices. One of many excellent teachers was the notable anatomist

John Sheldon, appointed to the hospital staff in 1797. In 1819 two of Sheldon's pupils, John Haddy James (after service as a surgeon at Waterloo) and Samuel Barnes, began giving anatomy classes that attracted students from all over Devon and Cornwall. A properly organised medical school developed and flourished until 1858. A Medical Act of that year put a stop to provincial medical schools, and thereafter doctors at the Devon and Exeter reverted to the system of taking on individual pupils. This continued until the 1890s.

In 1821 beds were arranged feet to the wall instead of sideways on. Four years later they tried head to the wall, and this has remained the accepted practice. In 1828 Haddy James pioneered the use of weights and pulleys to apply safe traction to a broken femur. In 1848 he introduced the use of a sucker on the baby's head during delivery. He was also a founder member of the British Medical Association.

In 1832 Exeter was ravaged by cholera. When the hospital staff began to fall ill the laundry room and carpenter's shop became emergency isolation wards.

At about this time surgeons were beginning to have misgivings about leaving post-operative patients in the hands of kindly but untrained nurses. In 1835 a special operations nurse was appointed to care for them.

Cathedral services were held on each anniversary of the dean's foundation, with the collection going towards repair of the hospital. In 1836 a larger sum than usual was needed, and ladies in pretty hats were mustered to take the collection plates round, to good effect. Until 1847 the apothecary was the resident in charge of the patients, but in that year the post was changed to one of house surgeon. In 1852 a vast legacy of over £70,000 from Mrs Halford, daughter of Mr Cresswell of New Court, solved the financial problems, indeed paid for a new multi-storey wing, with gas lighting, sanitary facilities and a modern kitchen. During the Crimean War a Scotswoman asked to train here before joining Florence Nightingale at Scutari. She was allowed to help for the month of June 1855. Ten years later the hospital began a proper training scheme for pupil nurses. A surgeon at the hospital, William Budd, was far ahead of his time when he declared in 1856 that typhoid was spread by faecal contamination of water and milk. Ward names now commemorated benefactors: Dean Clarke, Tuckfield, Cresswell, Rolle. Rolle was formerly Somerset, and in 1860 became Bowring when a legacy from Sir John Bowring was used to adapt one ward for children, 'to relieve the general wards of wailing children and disturbed nights'. A chapel was added in 1868-9 at the expense of one of the surgeons, Arthur Kempe (who also provided the fountain in Exeter at the top of Sidwell Street). The chapel was Victorian-Gothic in style with a frontage on Southernhay, and it played a central part in life at the hospital. Photographs of some of its stained-glass windows used to be displayed in the lobby of the present chapel at the RD&E, together with one of the six sanctuary lamps, converted from gas to electricity.

The matron was still nominally in overall command of the tired nurses, rebellious patients and unrestricted numbers of visitors. The house surgeon reported in 1871 'that almost all the entire work of the hospital is at present done by the patients … to their serious hurt'.

Mrs Halford's legacy kept the hospital in funds until 1874, when the bishop had to be asked to reinstitute appeals to all of Devon's Sunday congregations. After the terrible fire at the Theatre Royal in 1887 most of the 200 injured were taken to the hospital, which was later allocated £250 from the disaster fund.

Exeter doctors continued to remain abreast, or slightly ahead, of the latest developments. In 1872 a new surgeon, Mr Roper, surprised everyone by washing his hands before operating. Cocaine drops were used as a local anaesthetic for cataract surgery on 29 November 1884, only 10 weeks after this practice had been discussed in Heidelberg. An X-ray was used in Southernhay as early as 1898.

9

Late Eighteenth Century

In 1769 the Exeter Turnpike Act authorised a new Exe Bridge. The marshes had been drained and built on, the river was narrower and deeper, and the new bridge could be shorter. However, a public meeting in 1773 protested that the new design was 'extravagant in its dimensions, of partial use, ill-chosen in site, a bridge that must prove a lasting subject of ridicule'. It went ahead, and was nearly complete when a flood brought it down. The stones were recovered, a new architect was appointed and 'a handsome three-arch bridge' was completed in 1778. Halfway across, a stone marked the border between Exeter and the County of Devon. New Bridge Street was constructed, in line with the new crossing. Gervase's bridge was demolished, except for the landward half, bearing St Edmund's Church and other buildings.

Catholicism in Exeter went underground after the Dissolution of the Monasteries. A small chapel was built in 1688 but immediately burned and destroyed. By 1743 Catholics were meeting in great secrecy in the upper back room of King John's Tavern in South Street. By Christmas 1775 they had more legitimacy and leased part of the St Nicholas's Priory site for a chapel, later purchasing it. In 1789-92 they built the church, which still stands, converted into apartments; it was used until replaced by the Sacred Heart Church in South Street in 1883. In 1807 George Oliver began his long service as priest here, which continued until his death in 1861 and endeared him to his growing congregation and the city as a whole. A wall plaque at 21 The Mint, opposite St Nicholas's Priory, commemorates his 'lifelong services to his fellow citizens'.

Joanna Southcott, born to a Devonshire farming family in 1750, became known as 'The Prophetess of Exeter' and attracted thousands of followers. She worked for many years in Exeter as an upholsterer and servant, and sued her first employer in January 1784 for sexual harassment, probably the first woman in England to do such a thing. She conducted her own defence – successfully – at the trial in the Guildhall, which gave her a taste for public speaking. She was intensely religious, studying the Bible,

attending services in the cathedral several times a week and Methodists meetings in the evenings. She believed God spoke to her personally. Joanna preached and published and prophesied; for example, that grain prices would rise, that the French would invade Italy, that George III would go mad, that the prime ministers William Pitt and Charles James Fox would die. All came to pass. She also foresaw the deaths of the King of Sweden and Louis XVI. Andrew Brice printed a booklet for her, but refused to include the names of respectable people and royalty. Nevertheless the cryptic and slanderous references helped the booklets sell in thousands.

Feeling that Exeter was ungrateful, Joanna moved to London. Followers flocked to her in great numbers, being assured of a place in heaven. Joanna gradually developed a deluded belief that she was the woman mentioned in the Book of Revelations, 'clothed in the sun', who would give birth to a male child destined to rule all the nations. She picked a name for him from the Bible, Shiloh, not realising that this is a place-name rather than a personal name. Her enthusiastic followers prepared for the appearance of the Second Coming. This baby would not be laid in a straw-filled manger but in a splendid crib: 'Pillars on each of its sides were tapered with ribbons of gold entwining them. The head cloth was of blue satin with a celestial crown of gold embroidered on it, underneath which appeared in gold the word Shiloh in Hebrew.' There was also a pair of baby shoes embroidered in silver with the words 'Prince of Salem' and 'Priest

62 Built in 1768, this establishment was the first in England to be called an *hôtel* when its French owner advertised in September 1770. It has been called the Royal Clarence Hotel since the Duchess of Clarence, wife of the future William IV, slept here in July 1827. It could accommodate balls, assemblies and concerts. Franz Liszt performed here in 1840.

of God'. At the end of her life, late in 1814, as she lay in Marylebone with distended stomach and breasts filled with artificially induced milk, bulletins in the *Daily Telegraph* and *The Times* pushed news of the Napoleonic wars off the front page. The baby did not appear – and Joanna died. Her followers persisted in promoting her writings and campaigning for her Box of Prophesies to be opened. She had stipulated that this was to be in the presence of 24 Church of England bishops accompanied by 24 virgins dressed in white. The contents would supply solutions to the world's problems and explain what would happen when the final millennium begins.

Successive custodians of the Box took their duty seriously. The Rev. Thomas Foley was rumoured to keep a white thoroughbred horse saddled in his stables, ready for the Holy Child to ride off to the new Jerusalem. In the 1920s sandwich-board men paraded London with the message 'The bishops must open Joanna's Box to save England from ruin'; and the same message was plastered on the walls of the underground, while a petition bearing 10,000 signatures was delivered to Lambeth Palace. It is not certain where Joanna's Box is now. Precious relics were given to the Royal Albert Memorial Museum in Exeter: two engraved communion chalices, the gold-embroidered bejewelled banner to be laid on the box before the bishops open it (it depicts the woman clothed with the sun), and the patchwork quilt that laid a curse on George III.

In 1789 John Swete had 'past before Franklin, a seat of Counsellor Fanshawes, embosomed in groves of noble Elms'. This is a handsome, square, two-storey, William and Mary house with a hipped slate roof. The ornate doorway has Corinthian pilasters, scrolled pediment and cartouche. There is one excellent ceiling and a fine staircase, with carved vases and flowers on the newel caps (boarded in at present). The house was named from its first owner, but passed by marriage to Jasper Radcliffe and then to his son Walter (d. 1751). In 1757 rainwater gutters were added. From about 1825 to 1925 a branch of the ubiquitous Snow family lived here; from 1928 to 1957 the house was the Home of the Holy Innocents; then it was Franklyn House Hospital. It was altered and extended in 1972.

Cowley Place is a handsome building with an interesting history. It stands concealed by trees in parkland just beyond Cowley Bridge. It was built in 1788 for one William Jackson, returning to Exeter after a successful career in India in the diplomatic service. Exeter was a popular retirement place for such people, but here there were also family connections. The house was designed for him by his father, the more famous William Jackson, the multi-talented composer, writer, organist and painter, who was organist at Exeter Cathedral and master of the choristers from 1777 until his death in 1803. He trained there himself as a boy. The builder of Cowley House (as it was called at first) was Mr Hicks, who was to erect many of the houses in Southernhay during the next few years. Cowley Place has an impressive staircase with scrolled balusters. Externally what makes it so distinctive and charming are the two bow windows running the full height of the four storeys. Pevsner suggests that it was Jackson who had the bow windows added to Rougemont House at about this time. When it was built, Cowley Place stood in 140 acres of meadowland between the banks of the Exe and the Creedy. The estate has since diminished to 12 acres but is still the haunt of otters, herons, green woodpeckers, squirrels, rabbits, owls, buzzards, foxes and deer. In 1968 it was refurbished for office use and became the regional headquarters of the Midland Bank; then in 1986 it became the NatWest's administrative centre for Devon and Cornwall. In 1997 the house was turned back into private residential accommodation, being divided into 14 apartments. The graceful white edifice is a reminder of a cultural age 200 years ago.

William Jackson senior was a friend of the writers Goldsmith and Sheridan and the painters Gainsborough and Reynolds; his own paintings were in the style of Gainsborough's landscapes. Jackson was one of the founders of the Exeter Literary Society, and he composed comic operas as well as church music. Such talent often attracted envy, and a bitter insult has been recorded: 'His genius, judgment and taste were alloyed by selfishness, arrogance and an insatiable rage for superiority.'

Until the late 18th century Exeter did not sprawl outside the walls. The grassy area running from Eastgate to Southgate was originally called the Croulleditch: it was a rough muddy stretch of common land, churned up by attackers during sieges, grazed by cattle in times of peace. By the 13th century it had been hedged in, to stop the cattle straying. Since Hay means enclosure it began to be called Southyngehay. In 1792 it was the venue for 'earth bathing', a practice advocated by a Dr Graham, who toured England lecturing about it. He 'exhibited himself naked in the earth for three hours on several following days', 14 patients joining him on the first day and more than 20 subsequently. Unfortunately the doctor died soon afterwards, and the fad was forgotten.

Matthew Nosworthy began to build the Georgian terraces of Southernhay in the 1790s. These were spacious houses for well-to-do families, with basement kitchens and cellars. Servants had bedrooms in the attics. Dymond reported in 1804 that the road was 'literally a mud pit' and the Green was partly railed with iron 'for the elegant purpose of exercising sick horses'. The regular horse fairs, with as many as 300 beasts awaiting new

63   The terraces of Southernhay West and East were built from the 1790s on.

owners (people took them for test rides to try out their speed and action) were tolerated until 1821; the Lammas Fair had already found another site. Soon the greens were raised to the pavement levels of Southernhay West, and by March 1815 many of the terraces were complete. The upper part of Southernhay was levelled and sown with grass seed. In the 1820s the green was still an open space where children played, and was used by visiting fairs and menageries, but the gardens were then railed in and planted with shrubs and trees: an Exeter oak was put at the corner of each section. Young surgeons bowled along the sandy carriageway to reach the hospital. By now the houses of Southernhay were occupied by the families of professional men, several of them doctors.

In June 1834 a fountain was installed on the Upper Green – a *jet d'eau* supplied from the water company's works at Danes Castle. It was soon vandalised: on 7 November a cannon was fired at it, shattering one side and breaking windows in the surrounding houses.

The Blitz of 1942 took out the easternmost block of Southernhay West. The space was used for car parking until it was replaced in 1974 by Broadwalk House. The Georgian terraces were gradually vacated by families over the next 40 years, making way for council offices, estate agencies and legal practices. In 1950 the middle green in Southernhay was still the responsibility of residents with frontages onto it – and at this time there were still a few domestic households. The frontagers agreed to the council taking over the middle green as a public open space.

At the top of Southernhay there stands a rough rock of Heavitree stone, commemorating a Civic Trust award in 1960: 'The above award was received by the Exeter City Council in respect of the improvement of Southernhay which scheme was completed in 1954 and was designed by J. Brierley, City Engineer and Surveyor.' Brierley's scheme treated Southernhay as one road, with traffic in one direction only in Southernhay East and West. This allowed parking spaces along all the carriageways.

Barton Place near Cowley Bridge is a handsome square Georgian house of three storeys, built by a builder called Coffin in the 1790s for John Merivale. Merivale was a well-to-do Exeter merchant who brought his wife to the new house, and they proceeded to fill it with children. The couple persuaded the artist Frances Towne to move to Exeter to become drawing master to their children. Their youngest daughter, Laura, sadly died aged 5½, and like many other members of the Merivale family lies in the churchyard of the parish church of St David's. Their only son, John Herman Merivale (1779-1844) was a friend of Byron and wrote these lines, inspired by the lovely view over the valley from his home:

Yet poets too by Isca dream
Rich meadows kiss her sparkling face,
And ancient walls o'erhang her stream,
And peopled town her borders grace.

Barton House (as it was called at first) was described in the rate valuation of 1838 as having gardens, stables, yard, coach-house, plantation, woods and lodge. Large households in those days were usually self-sufficient in vegetables, fruit, eggs and sometimes even pigs. On its land was a farmhouse called Barton Place, predating the mansion. The farmhouse was occupied by William Wreyford, who probably gave his name to Wreford's Lane. It is this farmhouse that may have been 'the cottage in Devonshire' which features in Jane Austen's *Sense and Sensibility*, published in 1811. It has four bedrooms and two garrets, just enough accommodation for Elinor, Marianne and Margaret Dashwood and their mother, who were downsizing from Sussex, bringing only three servants (two maids and a man). The house is rented for a year from 'Sir John Middleton of Barton Park'. The Dashwoods felt that Exeter was rather remote after Sussex, but found that the valley was pleasant and fertile, well wooded and rich in pasture: 'High hills rose immediately behind. In front, the valley branched out between two of the steepest hills.' Was Jane Austen herself ever a guest there, as she describes the scenery so accurately and lovingly?

Barton House remained in the ownership of the Merivale family until 1911. Its first owner, John Merivale, who had had it built, greatly enjoyed the view over the River Exe to the hills near Exwick. He designed Weircliffe House as a focal point in the view. Jenkins described it in 1806 as 'a neat cottage, built on the edge of a cliff, hanging over the river; underneath are waving walks cut out of the rock, and beautifully overhung by trees and coppice wood, in a neat romantic manner; the roaring of the river below, over an artificial weir, the hanging cliffs etc. are very pleasing'.

In 1916 Barton Place was bought by Lord William Cecil, Bishop of Exeter 1916-36. He chose to live there rather than in the Bishop's Palace next to the cathedral, and was often seen pedalling to and fro along Cowley Bridge Road on his distinctive yellow bicycle, his long flowing hair streaming in the wind. On other occasions he could be seen sitting in the back seat of an open-top chauffeur-driven motor car. The next occupant was the principal of the University College of the South West, John Murray. During the Second World War the house and grounds were used for a school and a nursery run by the Save the Children Fund: the sunny lawns were ideal for children's play. In 1948 the university college acquired the premises for use as a

64   The Quadrangle, Higher Barracks.

65   Colleton Crescent was built on the cliff above the Quay in 1802-14, one of many terraces designed and built by the brothers Matthew and Thomas Nosworthy, mostly in brick, with round-headed doors ornamented with Coade keystones. The Nosworthys built the New London Inn (1790s), Barnfield Crescent (1792), most of Southernhay and Dix's Field, where they chose to live themselves.

residence for women postgraduates. There were 27 rooms and seven bathrooms. Space was found in the grounds for a hockey pitch. These students planted a tree in 1953 to commemorate the coronation of Queen Elizabeth II. The tree has disappeared, but when the owner of the present nursing home, Henry Davey, was having a patio laid 40 years later a lemonade bottle was dug up containing a message about the tree and signed by 20 female students. In 1965 Barton Place became a residence for male students.

Higher Barracks, the cavalry barracks, were built above Howell Road (thereafter called Barrack Road) in 1794. The brick buildings were put up by James Fentiman and Son. A guard house stood inside the gate by the road, and at the top of the site they built two large barrack blocks and separate officers' quarters, forming three sides of a quadrangle. The barrack blocks were divided at ground level into eight stables, each containing up to 16 stalls. Three stone staircases led to the first floor in each block, where the soldiers' quarters consisted of shared dormitories approached by a central corridor running the length of the building. The top storey held the quartermaster's stores, the cobbler's shop and the saddler's shop, in one continuous roof-space. The officers occupied a prominent brick building overlooking the parade ground, with the royal coat of arms fixed in a central pediment. In 1868 the eastern block was destroyed by fire, flames spreading quickly through the open roof-space. This block was rebuilt to a distinctive galleried design, the horses still stabled on the ground floor and their riders now enjoying balconies on the first floor. The officers' quarters burnt down in 1879

and were replaced in 1880-1. The original royal coat of arms was saved and reaffixed. After 1945 the buildings were used for the Army Pay and Record Office, and in 1998 the whole site was sold to be developed for housing. Extra blocks were inserted among the 200-year-old buildings, which comprised the oldest surviving complete cavalry barracks of its time. Converted buildings include the original riding school, bath house, granary store, straw store, coal store, forage store for animal feed, wash house, latrine, morgue, hospital, funeral carriage shed, veterinary stables, blacksmith's shop, pensions office, suttling house or canteen and (after 1870) some married quarters.

66 The cedar tree towering over St Sidwell's School.

Between 1700 and 1703 the city council sold off the Duryard estate to private citizens, but it and the adjacent hills remained farming land until the turn of the 19th century, when large country residences were being built, many by the non-conformist banking families of Exeter.

In 1794 Stoke House was already the seat of Joseph Sanders, co-founder of the Exeter bank in 1769. In a superb position on a hill-crest, a possibly 16th-century farmhouse was extended and embellished, to remain the home of the Sanders dynasty for four generations. It was frequented by friends and relations who were writers, artists and musicians, part of the lively crowd who helped to make late 18th-century Exeter into the 'Athens of the West'. Joseph's son, Edward Lloyd Sanders, married the pretty Isabella Andrew (1775-1851), related to the Powderham Courtenays; their son Edward Andrew Sanders (1813-1905) married Marianne (1828-1925), daughter of the Rev. James Ford and niece of Richard Ford, and sister-in-law to the author of *Tom Brown's School Days*. Her daughter, also long-lived, Isabella Jane Sanders (1850-1936), remained a spinster and inherited the house. As a girl she would have walked across fields to her grandfather and great-uncle near Heavitree Church.

A carriage-sweep from Stoke Hill led to the wide two-storey front of Stoke Hill House with its two splayed bays. A Georgian wing faced south. Stable-yards, camelia-houses and walled gardens reached back as far as Rosebarn Lane. The surrounding lanes, like sunken ha-has, left the view clear across to Exmouth. The site was sheltered by tall exotic trees, Monterey cypresses and Cedars of Lebanon. The children of St Sidwell's School were allowed to hold their summer treats in the grounds of Stoke House. In 1875, 800 children marched up the hill led by a band. They enjoyed tea, cake and buns and games of cricket and races. Then they assembled in front of the house, sang songs

67 Eleanor Coade grew up in Exeter but developed her flourishing business in London.

and the evening hymn and gave hearty cheers 'for the worthy squire and his lady'. Mrs Sanders was impressed by their good behaviour: 'Not a *leaf* was injured.'

The last heiress to the estate died in 1964 aged 90. The house was left empty, was vandalised and deteriorated. Although it was a listed building the council issued a compulsory purchase order, demolished it and used the land for Stoke Hill School and a housing estate. What survives from its golden days? A stone gatepost and curved wall from the entrance to the carriage drive can still be seen by the road on Stoke Hill. The giant exotic trees still fringe the estate and have provided the street names for Lebanon Close and Monterey Gardens. Neatly squared limestone blocks still form the wall where Rosebarn Lane forks off from Stoke Hill.

10

Early Nineteenth Century

In 1804 the chief magistrate proposed that the city needed more public lamps. He also said that the names of each street and lane should be painted at the corner and the houses numbered 'after the manner of London and other improved cities', and that a regular nightly watch should be established. Some parishes took up the suggestions and some did not.

The St Thomas Hospital for Lunatics moved into Bowhill House on 1 July 1803. This stood below the Bowhill mansion, on the north-west corner of the crossroads, just outside the turnpike. The hospital's hope was cure rather than incarceration, by forbidding contact with razors, scissors, beer, sugar and tea. There were six 'airing grounds' (three spacious walled courts and three gardens) and five indoor galleries. The inmates, some quite well-to-do, were encouraged to seek amusement, visit friends and take drives; and in the winter months they had their feet rubbed night and morning. By 1869 this caring establishment had proved so successful that it moved to grander accommodation at Wonford. The huge building was demolished and the bricks were used to build houses at Edgerton Park in Pennsylvania.

Bowhill House stood just above the flood-plain. On 9 November 1800 there had been 'a prodigious flood; all the streets in St Thomas were inundated, the water reaching up to the windows'. A boat was rowed up Cowick Street, dragged by horse-drawn sledge to Okehampton Street and re-launched. In January 1809 floods carried away the centre of Cowley Bridge, and all the tenter-racks on Bonhay and Shilhay. The following winter brought an even greater flood (greater even than the one in 1960): on 9 November 1810 the remaining arches of Cowley Bridge were washed away and three large ships were thrown onto the quay. St Thomas's Vicarage had been rebuilt just after the floods of 1800-1 with its floor 3in higher, but the 1810 flood rose just enough to meet the challenge.

In the same years that the river wrought such destruction, its power was being harnessed for more and more industrial development. For centuries the fulling mills and grist mills at Exwick had used the strong combined flow of Exe, Creedy and Culm. In the small peaceful settlement tucked in the creases between humpy green hills, Jenkins (1806) says that 'Edmund Granger and Samuel Banfill have established a large woollen manufactory and erected spinning machines, workshops, dye-houses, tenter-grounds etc. Also dwelling-houses for the manufacturers.' When these mills were advertised for sale in 1830, the description read: 'Upon a very powerful stream of water, with a Factory, Fulling Mills, Gig Mills, Warehouse, Dye Houses, Drying Houses, Picking Shops, Spinning Rooms, Drying Lofts, Stabling, Weaving and Press Shops; 15 cottages and gardens for workmen.' Granger's main interest was his wine-business in the city, and the refurbishment of Rougemont House. Banfill, however, lived close to his workforce and their worries. His letters on the subject survive, as do the sturdy brick cottages he built.

If we struggle up the punishing incline of Isleworth Road, we shall understand why General Fairfax chose to garrison the Barley House of his time during his siege of Exeter in 1646. Few positions were so impregnable, with such a commanding view of the city. Charles II granted the estate to Thomas Carew, with Bowhill. A Carew heiress married John Pinnock, who rebuilt Barley House early in the 18th century. It was inherited by his nephew Richard Sawle. Richard's daughters sold Bowhill and Higher Barley in 1792, but kept the rights of carriage access to Barley. Bowhay Lane is a modern road at the Dunsford Road end and a grassy bridleway at the Barley Lane end, and the middle section, so indispensable for carriage-horses tackling the steep contours, survives as back alleys between High Meadows and Charnley Avenue. Elizabeth Sawle married John Graves (one of four brothers who all became admirals). She occupied Barley at the beginning of the 19th century, when the Doric portico and curving stairs were added. A century later a distant cousin lived there, blind old Walter King. He attended church in a smart carriage pulled by chestnut horses, his dalmatians running underneath. The family sold the house in the 1930s. Devon County Council purchased it in 1938, and it became the administrative centre of Devon Library Services. A two-storey brick and glass extension was built at the south side in the mid-1960s. Today white doves flutter by the green-washed walls of the main house.

When the United States became independent, England began transporting convicts to Australia instead. Penal colonies were established in Tasmania and at Port Phillip, a settlement on the Australian mainland that later developed into Melbourne. Colonel David Collins, first Lieutenant Governor of Tasmania (1804-10) and George Harris his Deputy Surveyor General (also 1804-10) were chatting one evening on the shore at Port Phillip when they discovered that they had both grown up in Exeter, in the very same street, Gandy Street, but 20 years apart. The Royal Over-Seas League put up a commemorative plaque to the two men in 1999. It may be compared with the one commemorating John Graves Simcoe, which may be seen in the cathedral close, near the New Cut. Simcoe was First Lieutenant Governor of Upper Canada, present-day Ontario. He attended Exeter Grammar School, commanded a regiment in the American Revolution, then laid the foundation for the orderly growth of Ontario and died in a house near this site.

Willey's engineering works shut down in 1980 after a long and proud history. Henry Frederick Willey had been bound apprentice in 1844 to William Canute Bodley: the name Bodley was then synonymous with kitchen ranges, since George Bodley had patented 'a portable stove or kitchen for dressing victuals' in 1805. H.F. Willey built up his own engineering firm to one of the largest in the west of England. In 1860 he moved it from Shilhay to Water Lane. He died in 1894, and his son Henry Alfred took over. He was a benevolent employer, believing in profit-sharing, workmen-directors, educational trips to America, a works' band, pensions, gardens and dwellings for his men, anything 'which should make a straightforward workman's life a pleasure'. He had one of the first motor-cars seen in Exeter, and would have liked to start a car factory. One of the many things Willey's made was gas-meters, and when Stephen Simpson invented the coin-in-the-slot gas meter he was taken on as a director.

Next to Willey's on Tan Lane was another famous iron foundry: the name Garton & King can be read on countless manhole covers and pavement gutters. The firm started in 1661 with a foundry in Waterbeer Street. In 1847 they made the radiators for the tropical house in Kew Gardens. They later incorporated Taylor & Bodley and made gear-wheels up to 9ft in diameter, and aluminium bodies for ice-cream machines.

Lieutenant John Richards Lapenotière, commanding officer of HM schooner *Pickle*, the smallest British ship present at the Battle of Trafalgar on 21 October 1805, was entrusted by Vice-Admiral Collingwood to carry the news of victory to London and the king. Lapenotière was born in Ilfracombe. His father had probably come with other Huguenots from Holland with William of Orange in 1688. There followed a speedy race against one Captain Sykes to win the £500 promised by the Admiralty for the first person to arrive with the despatches. The news was shouted from the *Pickle* to a fishing crew off Penzance before Lapenotière landed at Falmouth on 4 November. There was then a 271-mile dash to London in 36 hours, with 21 stops to change horses and post-chaises. One stop was as Lapenotière travelled through Exeter High Street. The epic journey was commemorated on the bicentenary by a re-enactment, naming part of the route through Devon the Trafalgar Way and putting up plaques at each stopping place. Exeter's plaque is not on the High Street but tucked away in Dix's Field. The king was at Windsor, so after a further ride Lapenotière was able to tell him that the battle had been won but Nelson had been killed. He demonstrated the layout of the battle on the breakfast table, a silver sugar-shaker representing the *Victory*.

Cowley Bridge stands at a very ancient crossing-point, where the Creedy and Exe run close together to pass between the hills into the same valley. A bridge is recorded in 1286. After the floods of 1809 and 1810 brought down the stone bridge, James Green, the county surveyor, designed the present handsome structure, with its three segmental arches and niched piers; it was built in 1813-14. As it straddles the boundary between Exeter and Devon, it took five years for the two bodies to collaborate over the rebuilding.

Tablets on the bridge read:

The first stone of this bridge was laid on the 22nd day of June MDCCCXIII by James Buller of Downes Esq. Member of Parliament for the City of Exeter and John Quicke of Newton House Esq. Magistrates for the County of Devon.

Cowley Bridge. Built in the years MDCCCXIII and MDCCCXIV at the joint expense of the County of Devon and the Chamber of Exeter in the Mayoralties of B.W.Johnson, Burnet Patch and John Hart Esq. for the County of Devon by James Green Civil Engineer and Surveyor of Bridges for the County of Devon.

In 1814 the road was cut through to Marypole Head, presumably replacing a farm-track, and in 1815 Waterloo Cottage was built by John Cooke (1765-1840), a wealthy Exeter

68 John Cooke, captain of the Javelin Men, a uniformed ceremonial troupe that attended the assizes in March and July.

saddler, a loyal Tory and Captain of the Javelin Men, a uniformed ceremonial troupe which attended the assizes in March and July. His passion for reflected glory made him travel to London to see Nelson lying in state, to Torbay to see Napoleon on the *Bellerophon* and to London again to set eyes on Wellington. He was affectionately regarded as a local character for such pranks as scrawling slogans at night on the walls of the city's principal buildings, and constantly posting up placards. In those days the High Street and Fore Street were regarded as one main street running from Eastgate to Exe Bridge, and John Cooke felt the need for the shops to be numbered. He got up early one morning, took a piece of chalk and wrote numbers all the way down one side of the street and up the other. Someone pointed out that he had started at the wrong end, and he patiently did them all again. To this day the numbers run unbroken from High Street down Fore Street and up again. Cooke's new house had its back to the hill and its front windows overlooking the city to Haldon and the estuary. It had a thatched roof, two parlours, four bedrooms, a veranda with trellis supports, and a tablet over the door reading 'Waterloo Cottage in memory of Europe's victory Sunday, 18th June 1815.'

On 1 October 1817 the Cookes were subjected to a Grand Skimmington Riding (as depicted in chapter 9 of Thomas Hardy's *The Mayor of Casterbridge*). A procession formed in front of the Black Horse in Longbrook Street:

> 8 men bearing poles, on which were placards affixed, of various inscriptions, appropriate mottoes, etc. – a head painted and affixed on a pole, with a motto over, 'Where are my honours now' surmounted with a huge pair of gilded horns … Ahab and Jezebel on donkies, belabouring each other, 24 asses respectably mounted … 4 cocklemen on donkies bearing flags, 6 boys with handbells, a Full Band of Music … parading through the principal streets of the city and St. Thomas for nearly three hours, repaired at 5 in the evening (followed by thousands) to Waterloo Cottage, where the gallant Captain and his Wife, seated in their parlour with a few *select* friends, over a bottle of wine, boldly awaited their approach; – after a *delicate serenade*, a few exhibitions of fun, and some *polite* salutations, which were *graciously* returned from within, the motley group returned down the hill, to the spot where they first assembled.

After this, the Cookes rented the cottage out to the iron-founder Mr. Coldridge and moved back to Longbrook Street, where they owned 'two neat small houses and gardens, with Apple Trees, north of Howell Road'.

In 1817 gas-lighting was installed in High Street and Fore Street, the first place in Devon to use gas for public lighting. By 1819 the Bedford Theatre was lit by gas,

69   In 1817-24 Caleb Hedgeland made a wooden scale model (10ft by 6ft) showing the city's streets and buildings before the many changes that had been made shortly before. The Treasurer's House stood against the north tower of the cathedral until 1798. St Michael's Gate can be seen at Broadgate (removed 1819). Behind old St Mary Major the post office stands alongside the cathedral's west front.

which caused it to burn down two years later in the small hours. The theatre was rebuilt in 1821.

The sheriff's ward, the county prison for debtors, was rebuilt on the north side of Cowick Street in 1818, 'strong and capacious, in every way calculated for health and convenience'. Only the entrance block has been kept: brick with vermiculated quoins, segmental granite arch and brick arch above. In January 1855 the debtors were moved to the county gaol, and the building became militia barracks: soldiers in pill-box hats paraded in the yard at the rear. In this century the building was divided into rented flats, and it was demolished in the early 1970s.

In the 1820s the vicar John Coplestone and lay rector Buller decided to enlarge St Thomas's Church. The north aisle and porch were added in 1821; in 1828-30 the chancel was rebuilt, and lofty transepts with extra gallery seats were added. The odd roof-line shows where the new taller parts awkwardly abut the old. The churchyard was also extended by half an acre in 1830. From 1838 to 1845 the vicar was John Medley, promoter of Pugin's Gothic revival. He redesigned the sanctuary and begged the eagle lectern from the cathedral, where it had been put aside as old fashioned. Rightly: its elaborate base from about 1320 is the oldest surviving cathedral lectern. In 1841 Medley's wife Christina died aged 34. Her father was the sculptor John Bacon junior (1777-1859), who came out of retirement to carve a loving likeness of her sleeping form, and a memorial in medieval style was placed north of the altar.

The large churchyard is shaded by tall deciduous trees as well as funereal cedars and yews. Church almshouses formerly bordered the road. Most of the gravestones have been cleared to provide lawns. The Snow family tomb still stands near the south wall, near the stone listing John Stocker's services to his community. Here, in 1848, a 61-year-old man from Leeds called Thomas Gray was buried. In 1818 he had tried to interest the government in a railway network, to transport soldiers, goods, passengers and letters 'without the necessity of horses'. The inscription on his vault read: 'The original projector of Grand Trunk Railways throughout Great Britain and Ireland with Direct and Level Lines.' He died in poverty in a house in Alphington Road, within sight of Brunel's railway.

For centuries the main road out of Exeter had been Magdalen Road: traffic left from the great Southgate. As coach traffic built up Paris Street was improved and Heavitree Road was widened to become the Great London Road. About 24 coaches passed this way every day.

Midway Terrace on Heavitree Road consists of 10 houses in five pairs. They were built in 1822 by William Hooper, who kept one (now no. 138) for himself and his family. No provision was made for garages or coach-houses. The name Midway Terrace comes from its position halfway between Exeter and Heavitree. At the time when it was built there was nothing but market garden land between Livery Dole at the top of the road and the workhouse at the bottom. William Hooper (1751-1831) was a leading Exeter builder: his firm had put up the county gaol in 1794, Higher and Lower Summerlands in 1804-12 and then the brick terrace in Magdalen Road called Baring Place. He then switched to stucco for Midway Terrace and in 1825 built Chichester Place in Southernhay, with a Classical portico. The situation of Midway Terrace is elevated and healthy. Well-to-do families in the city had begun to decamp to Heavitree in the summer for the more salubrious country air.

Later in the 19th century the artist George Rowe lived at 3 Midway Terrace. He produced many engravings of English scenes but was particularly acclaimed for his paintings of gold-rush Australia. It was on his return to Exeter that he rented no. 3. He died there in 1864 and was buried in Heavitree churchyard. His wife stayed on for another 24 years and was buried in the same grave. Their daughter Philippa, also a painter, also a widow, lived with her mother at no. 3 for many years. Her husband was a surgeon in the India Medical Service: he was sent to India a month after their marriage, contracted dysentery and dispatched home – but died at sea.

In 1817 James Pearce, wine and brandy merchant, went bankrupt and had to relinquish a 10-acre field of rich pasture-land. 'In this field is a most beautiful and extensive view, and a more desirable situation for building in the vicinity of Exeter is not to be found.' In 1818 Joseph Sparkes took over the lease of this field, called Whitley or Craddock, and commissioned a row of houses, including one for himself. The architect was John Brown of Exeter (who had just designed Baring Crescent); he now designed Exeter's first completely stuccoed terrace. Joseph Hyde Rowe of Paris Street began building in about 1821, and completed six houses in all (although the print by his brother George shows eight, without verandas, said to be 'drawn from nature'). The row could have been named Bank Buildings, or even Craddock, but it was called Pennsylvania, or Pennsylvania Buildings, later Pennsylvania Terrace and now Pennsylvania Park. The name of Pennsylvania originally applied only to the terrace of six white houses on the hillside, which are clearly visible from most parts of Exeter. Nearly 60 years after they were built, '5 Pennsylvania, Exeter' was sufficient address to reach Mrs Halloran's school for young ladies at the terrace, although Pennsylvania

70 In the 1820s the Quaker banker Joseph Sparkes put up a stuccoed terrace of six handsome houses commanding an unparalleled view of the estuary. Called Pennsylvania after the settlement in America, it has since given its name to the entire hillside suburb that has gradually crept up the surrounding slopes.

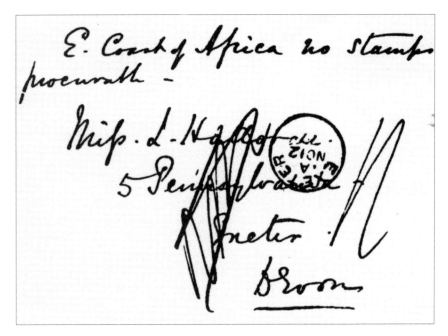

71   Even 60 years after it was built, '5 Pennsylvania, Exeter' was sufficient address to reach Mrs Halloran's school for young ladies at the terrace, although Pennsylvania had begun to be used for the whole desirable district.

begun to be used for the whole desirable district by the middle of the 19th century. Pennsylvania is not a parish but a residential area. Its boundaries are primarily of interest to estate agents, who like to refer to ever wider areas below Union Road as Lower Pennsylvania, and the new estates to the north as Higher Pennsylvania and even Sylvania.

In 1818 Sparkes & Co. had taken over control of Exeter's General Bank, of which all the partners were members of the Society of Friends. Joseph Sparkes settled on the name Pennsylvania at a time when his bank was issuing £1 banknotes (between 1819 and 1822) decorated with a vignette showing William Penn under the elm at Shakumaxon, making a treaty of friendship with the Indians: 'This transaction afforded a proof to the world of the singular honour and uprightness of those members of the Society' (Thomas Clarkson, 1806). Prints of Benjamin West's painting were proudly displayed in Quaker homes, sometimes together with a print of a crowded slave-ship, on walls otherwise kept free of frivolous decoration. The treaty with the Indians, never ratified by an oath and never broken, symbolised fair dealing, a very suitable motif for a banknote. The name Pennsylvania for the houses would likewise suggest solid worth, and also the quietness and good order associated with Quakerism.

The spacious promenade and carriageway in front of the houses was approached by a carriage-sweep from the Lower Lodge (now Beech Avenue) or through iron gates opened by the gate-keeper at the Higher Lodge (now demolished, along with the gates.)

Nos 1 and 2 were put up for auction in July 1824, and euphemistically described thus:

> a few minutes' walk from the New London Inn, seated on the ascent of an easy hill, and commanding the richest scenery in the county, having the city (with a grand view of the cathedral) in the near ground, the Sidmouth and Exmouth hills, the whole estuary of the Exe, and some miles of ocean, on the south-east; the romantic brows of Haldon and Dartmoor on the south and west, at the distance of several miles, and is in the immediate vicinity of some of the richest pasture, and has the purest air in the county of Devon.

The houses have been erected about two years and a half, substantially and gradually, of the very best materials, on the plans and under the inspection of an eminent architect …

Thomas Sharp in *Exeter Phoenix* (1946) says: 'The brief but exquisite terrace of Pennsylvania Park, which sits on the tree-hung slopes of the North-western part of the city, is one of the most beautiful things in Exeter and in England.' Perhaps his hyperbole was due to relief that this at least had survived the war.

There is a narrow entrance to Pennsylvania itself. The terrace was designed to give the appearance of separate houses connected by single-storey Ionic porches, but in fact the break only went halfway back, although far enough to cast a sharp shadow between each. No. 3 filled in the gap with extra rooms before 1838, and No. 1 in about 1927. The low-pitched slate roofs have very wide eaves, which nearly bridge the gaps between the houses. The base of the verandas lines up with the tops of the porches to make another strong horizontal line. The iron balconies, of plainer trellis-work than those at Pennsylvania Crescent, have slender coupled supports. The French windows were glazed with 'best polished British Plate Glass'. Nos 1 and 6 still have their shutters, and all have their area railings.

72   Exeter from Pennsylvania Hill, after G.B. Campion, published in 1832. About 70 passenger coaches left Exeter daily in the 1830s. Pennsylvania Road had just been cut through for wheeled traffic, providing a less precipitous route than the turnpike road over Stoke Hill.

These opulent dwellings with the idealistic name soon became homes for the fashionable rich. An auction of the furnishings of no. 2 in 1853 indicates the lifestyle of the Rev. Mr Jackson, incumbent of the modish Bedford Chapel. There were nearly 50 dozen of rare old port, Schiraz and other wines, while many of the articles originally came from the Palace of Fontainebleau, including ormolu and marble chimney ornaments and an elaborately worked, carved and gilt pier table in Louis XIV style. There was a purple and gold basin of the late Queen Charlotte, a pair of ice pails and an inlaid oak marquetry table showing Alfred burning the cakes. When we reach the inventory for the library, we can clearly visualise Mr Jackson preparing his sermons. He had 'a

mahogany whatnot [a set of shelves on slender legs, popular at the time]; phrenological casts of Thistlewood the conspirator, Queen Charlotte and others; a most convenient mahogany reading and writing chair, on castors; a mahogany reading couch …' A large oil painting of Job and his Friends hung in the master bedroom, and the Triumph of Bacchus, after the manner of Poussin, in the dressing-room.

In about 1890 Henry Willey, head of the Water Lane Foundry, bought nos. 3 and 4 and added the Victorian Gothic portico in Portland stone with solid teak door and

73 The central house in Pennsylvania Crescent has an imposing pediment surmounted by an acroterion and supported by a length of key-patterning (echoed by the iron gates by Garton and King, 1953).

74   In 1750 a 'New Cut' was made through the city wall near the cathedral. In 1814 mayor Burnet Patch had a little iron bridge built over it to facilitate the Muraltie Walk, the perambulation of the walls that followed the mayor-choosing.

oak-panelled hallway. He also fitted out a marble-lined billiard hall, heated by a huge boiler 150ft away in the kitchens. The Drew family lived in no. 5 at the beginning of the 20th century. The banister-rail was studded with wooden acorns after the children slid down three flights without stopping.

William Sandford, who built Portland Villa, also built Pennsylvania Cottage in 1824 above the Pennsylvania Park stables and mews. Now called Moor View Lodge, it has kept its thatched roof, unlike Waterloo Cottage. It has Gothic windows including the dormers, Gothic shutters, some Gothic glazing-bars and an oriel overlooking the road. The original veranda has been altered.

Hoopern Lane, still rural in 1984, was the main road along the side of the cricket field to Streatham Farm, until Prince of Wales Road was cut through in the 1920s.

The hedged triangle at the junction is a pleasure-ground for the five white stucco Regency villas facing south in a shallow crescent above sloping front gardens, called Pennsylvania Crescent from 1905 onwards. Building began in 1823, while Pennsylvania Park was still being developed, but already the fashion for terraces was passing, and the demand was for detached villas. However, these resemble Pennsylvania Park in having basements, verandas and side entrances, so that the rooms have the best of the front view. Although comparable in proportions to the houses in Baring Crescent, these are in a tighter grouping and have kept more of their original rural charm. The central house, Crescent House, has an imposing pediment surmounted by an acroterion (an ornament on a plinth) and supported by a length of key-patterning (echoed by the iron gates and railing by Garton & King, 1953). There are three sets of windows flanked by four pilasters, and a round attic window encircled by a garland. The pairs of houses to left and right have wide-eaved hipped roofs, two sets of windows, elaborate iron-trellis verandas with canopies and quoin pilasters with the garland decoration. The porches have fluted Tuscan supports or peaked canopies. The end house to the west, Sungum Villa, later Copeland Villa, has a two-storey bow at the side. The house at the Pennsylvania road end, Marypole Villa, has special treatment of the porch: it is recessed between two extra pilasters. The coach-houses and stables belonging to these properties have become a builder's yard and a car-repair works.

When Joseph Rowe had finished building Pennsylvania he remodelled the interior of St Stephen's Church, rendering it light and airy with two rows of narrow pillars. The church has a tablet commemorating William Jackson, the famous composer of anthems who died in 1803. It reads: 'His genius united elegant expression, pure and original melody with peculiar delicacy of harmonic combination.' The monument was

75 Longbrook Valley is pictured in 1831, between the elms of Northernhay and the prison (rebuilt 1810), with the 'pepperpot' St David's Church (1816) in the distance. Cossins reminisced: 'Before the North Road was cut there was a succession of fields from Barrack Road to St David's Church, a very pleasant walk and a resort for children gathering buttercups and daisies.'

76 While building
Barnfield Crescent the
builders uncovered a
strong spring supplying
an angular bath of grey
bricks, very hard burnt,
strongly cemented, with
steps leading down to it.
The discovery inspired
the erection of the Public
Hot and Cold Baths in
Southernhay, making
use of the abundant
water. It stood above
Chichester Place.

put up by his daughter Mary, who was also buried nearby, along with his sons Charles, Frederick, Romulus and Remus.

Between the entrance to Mowbray House and the busy main road through Heavitree there is a driveway to a secluded development among tall trees, called Heavitree Park. This should not be confused with the large public Heavitree Pleasure Ground opened 80 years later on the other side of Heavitree Road.

In 1825, 10 years after Captain Blunt had built Wonford Hill (later Mowbray House) on the green hillside, a merchant called Edward Eardley was granted a lease on the adjacent field, with the condition that he would put up houses and outbuildings of brick and stone (not cob) to the value of £3,000 each. The resulting residences built in 1825-9 were more solid, grander in design and more expensive than most houses in the Exeter area. Later, Eardley was involved in developing the impressive houses on Mont-le-Grand. All of these houses, those in Heavitree Park and those on Mont-le-Grand, are faced with fashionable white stucco and display classical detailing.

Former mayor Bill Hallett's early memories included living in Heavitree Park in the 1920s, as a schoolboy attending Bramdean and the Maynard School. He recalled the lodge at the entrance to Heavitree Park, which was 'manned by a dapper little man in a bow tie and a snappy round hat' who was leader of the trio that played in Deller's café. The grand houses at the top of the carriageway were already divided into flats. In no. 1 was a Miss Vanbrugh, a kindly motherly woman who taught at the Maynard School. In no. 2 was a retired butcher, who must have done well in business since he owned all the houses. He wore a panama hat and had a beard. Mr Hallett recalled that the butcher's wife was the image of Queen Mary and their son was exactly like the Prince of Wales. The son's hobby was jumping, and he practised on three or four jumps erected on the big grassy area that is still there. There was also a large vegetable garden backing onto the walls of Mowbray House. This area has been concreted over and now holds garages and modern blocks of flats.

The county ground has been a fixture behind St Thomas's Church for more than 100 years, but even before that it was an important sporting venue – a useful flat open space known as the wrestling field. Competitive wrestling was a crowd-puller on public holidays such as Easter Monday and Whitsun. Sabine Baring-Gould records that the competitions mostly took place between the hay harvest and the corn harvest, presumably after the grass had been safely stored, leaving a clear field. The bare field was covered with tan, which was oak bark left over after it had been used in the process of tanning leather. The wrestlers vied for a champion's belt or a hat, or a purse of money. In late July 1841 there was a great match for a prize of 100 sovereigns: 'An area of an acre and a quarter, in a circular form, in a fine and level field, near St Thomas Church, was enclosed by boarded work, one half having raised seats covered with tarpaulins, the other half a bench running round, and a gallery with a band of music.' In 1888 W.H. Commins put the wrestling field up for sale: 'Important to Capitalists, Builders, Speculators and others …' either for houses or a 'much-needed Recreation Ground'. In 1882 a butcher took possession of the 'Pasture called the Wrestling Field near Cowick Street, eight acres'. Speculative builders were fought off for 100 years, and the ground was dedicated to a great variety of sports. According to Pollard's *Guide to Exeter* of 1894:

> The old St Thomas Cricket-field, for many years famous as the venue of a flourishing cricket club but since re-christened as the County Grounds has for many years been the battle-field of County and local matches and the H Q of the Devon Rugby Football Union and the Exeter Football club. On 14 May 1894 these grounds were opened by the Devon County Athletic Co Ltd as general athletic grounds, replete with an excellent four-lap track. Its elliptical circle with two straight runs of 100yds each was a fast and wonderfully safe track with a limestone surface laid in burnt clay. There was a commodious grandstand to seat 700. Inside the cycling track the ground has been laid out as a football and cricket ground. Outside there would be accommodation for rackets, tennis, archery and other games.

The novelist Thomas Hardy pictured rural life in the West Country in the early 19th century. A notebook has recently come to light which shows that he copied items from local papers and drew on them for ideas or for authentic details. An account of a coach crash is used in *Tess of the D'Urbervilles* and a wife sale figures in *The Mayor of Casterbridge*. Also in *The Mayor of Casterbridge* Hardy used the newspaper report of a wrestling match in St Thomas on Easter Monday 1829. The account went into as much detail as a football commentator would give today: 'Hill began, using his right hand only, firmly grappling Jem's left collar. Hill planted the first toe, and made free use of the right, whilst Cann crossed him with his left … A fine rally ended at the end of 15 minutes in Jem's going down on his knees. At the end of 29 minutes Jem delivered his man by the left fore hip as fine a turn as ever was seen. Hill instantly complained of injury of the shoulder …' In the next contest 'Webber turned Esworthy a complete "somerset" and put him down spinning on his head like a top.' It is fascinating to see these events transformed by a creative novelist. Hardy describes a more desperate fight than the rounds on St Thomas wrestling field, but it follows the pattern of the newspaper account: 'At the outset Henchard's hold by his only free hand, the right, was on the left side of Farfrae's collar, which he firmly grappled … Henchard planted the first toe forward, Farfrae crossing him with his … Henchard contrived to turn Farfrae a complete somersault [and] delivered the younger man an annihilating turn by the left fore-hip …' Hardy asked for his notebook of newspaper cuttings to be destroyed after his death, but his wishes were disregarded and we are able to marvel at his genius.

Exeter became a popular destination for men retiring from colonial service. The climate suited them, and access by turnpike roads led families of fortune and distinction to settle here. Lieutenant-Colonel John Godfrey served in India for 36 years and nine of his children were born there. On retirement, some time after 1830, he settled the large family in the recently built terrace of Pennsylvania. His fourth child, Henry, attended Exeter School and sailed to Australia in 1843 to make his fortune as a sheep-farmer. He was advised not to settle in Tasmania, which was already fairly comprehensively developed, so he crossed to Port Phillip and prospered as a sheep-farmer, with a little gold-prospecting on the side. He visited Devon again in 1850 and three years later took an 18-year-old bride, Mary, back to Melbourne. Less than six months later he indulged her wish to make the long voyage home – three months at sea – for her first child to be born in Exeter. The couple stayed on for a year (Henry joined the South Devon Militia), so that their second son could also

77 Here houses of the Elizabethan period at Cricklepit abut the town wall. There is a fulling-mill to the left. The mill-leat is being used for laundering.

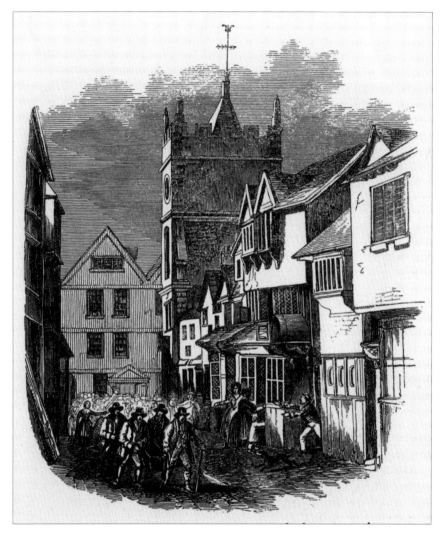

78 Cholera raged through the poorer quarters in 1832, sometimes taking whole families in the space of a few hours. Here a coffin is being carried along Goldsmith Street, past St Paul's Church.

be born in Exeter. Henry's parents had moved from 5 Pennsylvania to Northernhay House by then. Although Mary was pregnant again they sailed back to Australia with their two-year-old, leaving the 11-month-old second son with his Cornish grandparents for the next eight years.

The Hermitage on Exwick Hill is a charming, rambling *cottage orné*, thatched, its two wings forming a V-shape. The east wing was a 16th-century cottage, of which the front section was even older, with cruck structure and a bulging bread oven. This part may have been the chamber which the priory could not afford to repair in the early 15th century. Banfill retired to this cottage in 1830, and had it knocked through to the neighbouring cottage, forming the Hermitage as it is now – its architecture ranging from the low-ceilinged, heavily beamed room in the east to the late Regency drawing room at the west end, with its 19th-century leaded Gothic casements. Samuel Banfill died here in 1843 aged 81.

Anthony Trollope's older brother, Thomas Adolphus, remembered travel in the 1830s: 'A journey on the box of the Mail was a great delight to me. One journey frequently performed by me with infinite delight was to Exeter. My business was to visit two old ladies living there, Miss Mary and Miss Fanny Bent.' These were cousins of his mother. 'A new and accelerated mail service had been recently established under the title of the "Devonport Mail". It was at that time, I believe, the fastest in England. Its performance caused somewhat of a sensation in the coaching world, and it was known in those circles as the "Quicksilver Mail" … The guard sat on a little seat made for one, with his pistols and blunderbuss in a box in front of him.' There were three outside and four inside passengers. Over smooth macadamised roads the coach reached 12mph. When the four horses needed changing it was achieved in less than 50 seconds.

Thomas remembered strawberry and cream parties in Hoopern Fields and excursions to Marypole Head and Haldon Down. On a later visit he was sorry to find that 'Marypole Head has been nearly swallowed up by the advancing tide of "villas". People no longer walked down the High Street nodding right and left to acquaintants. Everybody knew everybody no longer. The leisurely gossipy ways of the shopkeepers had been exchanged for the sharp promptitude of London habits.'

Exeter did not escape the cholera epidemic that spread from Asia across Europe and into Britain in the 1830s. The city authorities realised that infection would spread quickly in the crowded unhygienic streets of the lower city. The Corporation of the

79 The streets and gutters were washed down. The fire plugs were opened to build up a good puddle, then men threw the water over the cobbles with wooden shovels.

Poor and the Commissioners for Improvement collaborated in the new Board of Health
to introduce preventative measures. Dr Thomas Shapter published a detailed history
of the epidemic. He described the thorough cleaning of Exeter's streets brought in as
an emergency measure:

> The water being turned on from the fire plug ran down the gutters in a full stream, and,
> being dammed up at short distances by coils of straw and tarpaulin, was collected in
> considerable quantities. Men with large wooden shovels then threw it plentifully over the
> neighbouring surface. This mode was not only effectual as a means of watering the streets
> but was most useful in cleaning the gutters … three or four powerful men, jackbooted,
> or naked as to their arms and legs, took possession of the street, and stream after stream
> of water flowed from their well-plied shovels.

Other urgent measures recommended were to whitewash walls, issue thousands of
flannel belts and warm stockings, supply nutritious food and stockpile lime to throw on
corpses. Extra nurses were engaged. The clergy called on wrongdoers to repent. Cholera
was said to be more likely to infect drinkers of spirits and 'those who indulged in irregular
and sensuous habits'. The population was loath to change their ways. The first deaths
came in North Street in mid-July when a woman came home from Plymouth. Despite

80 Every effort was
made to combat infection.
Here Butchers' Row is
being fumigated.

81 Bedding and clothing was incinerated at Lion's Holt and on the river bank, near the drying racks of the cloth industry.

the urgent measures taken and prompt attention from doctors and nurses the cholera victims died quickly and in large numbers. The Corporation of the Poor bought a closed horse-drawn hearse to carry the dead to lime-filled graves. A second hearse was soon needed. The Board of Health had to find more burial space for those dying in St. Sidwell's parish. Joseph Sparkes offered the higher corner of his field on Mary-Pole Head near the Tiverton turnpike-gate, but only on condition that the bodies should be carried along St Sidwell Street, through the turnpike-gate, and up the Back-Lane to the spot. The Board preferred a lower field, 150ft by 60ft, belonging to St. John's, just west of Rosebarn Lane and 60ft north of Union Road, with no stipulation against carrying the infectious corpses up Longbrook Street. Thirteen were buried that summer, and 33 in the autumn of 1834, including three in midnight funerals. The name Charingthay on the Sylvan Road flats, built in the grounds of a Victorian house of that name, commemorates the cholera burials.

There were riots at the burial grounds in Southernhay and at the new burial grounds that were hastily consecrated in Berry Meadow and Rowe's Barn Lane. The coffin-makers worked day and night to meet demand. The grave-diggers had to be bribed with increased payments and frequent draughts of beer and brandy. Shapter describes a typical burial: 'Two men without coats, their shirt sleeves turned up to the elbows, with short tobacco pipes in their mouths, carrying a coffin "underhand" towards the grave;

at a good distance off from the grave was the surpliced clergyman performing the last solemn duty of religion. If this were by night, as frequently was the case, there was also the flickering light of one or two lanterns.' Infected bedding and clothing was burned or buried, and compensation was paid for it. There were 181 deaths by 15 August and 17 more on that day. Out of a population of 32,000, 1,400 had sickened and 440 died. The epidemic suddenly came to an end, and Thursday 11 October was set aside for a day of solemn public thanksgiving. Bishop Philpotts deserted the city during the cholera epidemic, returning only for the service. This added to his unpopularity. There was a possibility that the consecration of Bedford Chapel set for August 1832 would not go ahead but it was not postponed, and neither were the summer assizes. They were accompanied by the usual theatre performances.

In 1849 cholera returned with 26 deaths, and in 1853-4 with 10 deaths. In 1865-6 there were again 247 deaths from cholera.

A hero of the cholera epidemic was a young Irish doctor, Peter Hennis. He came to Exeter in 1830 and was appointed physician to the Exeter Dispensary, a charitable institution set up in 1818 to give advice 'to such suffering and industrious people as were unable to procure it for themselves'. Hennis was active in the campaign for better hygiene, improved water supplies, street cleaning and sewage treatment. When cholera reached Exeter in July 1832 Hennis was a medical officer responsible for the southern district, an area of slums. One tiny house there had 15 families crowded into airless rooms. Another had 31 pig sties in the basement and another had 13 years' accumulation of dung piled in the kitchen, while poultry was kept in the cellars. Hennis worked tirelessly throughout the epidemic, earning the lasting respect and affection of the citizens. He became engaged to the daughter of the rector of Moreton Hampstead and enjoyed attending the theatre and musical evenings with his fiancée. However, his happiness was to be cruelly cut short.

In May 1833 Sir John Jeffcott had recently been appointed as Chief Justice of the Admiralty Court in Sierra Leone. His sailing was delayed and he lodged in Exeter at the Clarence Hotel. Jeffcott hoped to marry Flora Macdonald's granddaughter (living in Higher Summerlands), but there were rumours in the city, possibly about a medical condition, possibly about whether he had lied about travelling to Dublin when he had gone only as far as Bristol. Hennis was falsely named as one of the people spreading the rumours, and Jeffcott accused him of being 'a calumniating scoundrel'. Hennis denied it, but felt he had to challenge Jeffcott to a duel, though he stated he would not return his opponent's fire. They met on Haldon racecourse at 4.30pm on 10 May, supported by seconds, to face each other 14 paces apart. The commands were 'Prepare' and 'Fire'. At 'Prepare' Jeffcott fired and wounded Hennis, then ran to him and begged his forgiveness. Hennis repeated that he had never done anything to harm Jeffcott's reputation, and forgave him. Jeffcott travelled on by postchaise to Plymouth and his ship, while Hennis was carried to his lodgings at the corner of High Street and Castle Street. Badly wounded, he lived until 18 May. The church bells were silenced as he lay on his deathbed; 20,000 people lined High Street and Sidwell Street as his funeral procession passed. His tomb can still be seen in St Sidwell's churchyard. A man was heard to say that 'In him the sick poor have indeed lost a friend.' Jeffcott returned from Sierra Leone a year later, but was acquitted of murder at the Assizes for lack of evidence.' In 1838 he was drowned off the coast of South Australia while visiting a prison ship.

Healthy improvements after the lessons of the cholera epidemic included covering all the open drains, including the Longbrook and Chutebrook streams. The water company

82 Blackboy Road looks towards the cathedral, St Sidwell's and leafy Rougemont, but in the foreground are the 100ft-high cones of the brick kilns built in 1834 to give employment to the inmates of the workhouse on Heavitree Road. Exeter gardeners know how suitable the clay soil is for brick-making.

built a new reservoir between 1833 and 1840 at Danes Castle, 150ft above the river.

In December 1834 'Robert Harvey of Waterbeer Street, mason and bricklayer, completed the erection of a cone in the Brickfield in rear of the Workhouse, at the instance of the Corporation of the Poor of this city. This circular chimney is of considerable magnitude, and its situation being lofty, is a very prominent object. Its diameter at the foot is 59 feet, at the top 7ft. 6ins. The height from the bed of the kiln is 100ft. 6ins. 220,000 bricks were used.' Clay for bricks had been excavated from Polsloe Ridge for many years; in 1674 the area was already named Round Pitts. The cliffs left by quarrying served as the dry ski slope in Clifton Hill and the rockery at the top of Belmont Park.

By the end of the cholera epidemic the St Bartholomew burial ground was full. The steep slopes below the Roman wall were consecrated for extra space just 200 years after the first cemetery, in 1833. Egyptian-style catacombs were built against the city wall and first used in 1837; one end was for Anglicans and the other end for Dissenters (the burial ground was similarly divided), and coffins could be lowered into the catacombs from the pavement above. Exeter was ahead of the fashion here, two years ahead of a similar enterprise in London's Highgate Cemetery. However, the catacombs proved too expensive for Exeter families and very few niches were taken up. The sloping graveyard holds several interesting memorials. Andrew Brice the printer was buried here, and David Evans, a supporter of Tom Paine, who was commemorated with an obelisk, although much of the inscription is illegible now:

He was a Man who dared to be honest in the worst of times.

THIS MONUMENT is erected by One Hundred and Seventy of his Fellow Citizens who think that his honest character and political consistency should not pass unrecorded.

He possessed and through a long life had the courage to avow strong liberal principles. For the intrepid and honest advocacy of his opinions he suffered imprisonment in the great conflict of 1791. It was his privilege not only to survive the age of direct persecution but to witness the adoption of his political opinions by the party who had oppressed him.

A whitesmith, Evans lived in St Bartholomews Yard, and in 1791 was arrested for sedition, his crime being support of Tom Paine's call for universal suffrage. At one

time his house was attacked by a drunken mob, and local butchers vowed 'to do for' the hated Jacobin if they ever caught him in Butchers Row. For a long time he never ventured into any of the many city inns. In 1808 one of his sons died while helping firemen fight the fire at the Covent Garden Theatre, London, and in 1815 two other sons rescued a boy from drowning in the River Exe.

83 Napier Terrace alongside the Old Cemetery.

Besley's 1831 directory tells us that 'Pester-road has been widened for a walk or a drive, and a carriage way is now made through this circuit to Heavitree'. In 1835 the name changed from Pester Lane to the 'more attractive appellation' of Union Road. This new name applied all the way, so 'Union' may describe this new road-link between Pennsylvania and Heavitree, not, as has been suggested, commemorating the union of parishes for poor law purposes in 1834. By 1836 Pennsylvania Buildings were also served by a new private carriage-road, rather steep for the horses, running from 'the higher parts of St. Sidwell's'. This is now Sylvan Road.

Samuel Sebastian Wesley (grandson of Charles Wesley), the finest composer of church music of his time, was organist and Master of Music at the cathedral from 1835 to 1841. His nine-week-old daughter is buried in the Lower Cemetery alongside the catacombs, and when he himself died in Gloucester in 1876 he chose to be laid beside her.

In 1830 the St German's area level with Victoria Terrace was called 'Hoopern-place a most delightful spot for air and scenery. There are three houses, with the grounds around fancifully laid out, which present a novel appearance. At the upper end of these stands the beautiful villa of Wm. Kendall Esq., built and laid out under his own directions; and when this is known, it is unnecessary to add that the exterior prospects, together with the interior decorations, display all the charms of an accomplished taste.' This was Elliot

Cottage, now called Spreytonway, a stucco villa with a Gothic porch. The other two were Ibsley Cottage, now Montefiore (stucco, with an ornate iron porch, a tower, and dormers protruding from a – now shortened – spire) and Swiss Cottage, since demolished.

St Olave's Hotel is a quiet haven in the midst of the city. The elegant building stands between Mint Lane and Mary Arches Street, facing the back wall of the restored refectory of St Nicholas's Priory. The beautiful Georgian house – at first called Priory Place – was built in the 1830s in the grounds of the priory by James Golsworthy, manager and later owner of the city's waterworks. He overhauled the water supply, which was pumped up from the river to a tank behind the Guildhall, putting in a more powerful pump and replacing the leaky wooden pipes with iron ones. Two inscribed stones here relate to the history of Exeter's water supply. A stone by the garden wall where it backs onto Mint Lane came from the waterworks at Engine Bridge in Exe Street: 'This Water Work was contrived by Amb. Crowley and Dan Dannell A.D. 1694. Improved and rebuilt by James Golsworthy A.D. 1811.' Dannell was a carpenter so it was probably he who made the wooden pipes. The outside wall of the hotel, on Mary Arches Street, has been rebuilt, but it still incorporates Golsworthy's stone marking a public conduit, which brought water from the Longbrook for his household and the garden fountain: 'The water brought here and this conduit erected for the public use at the sole expense of James Golsworthy with the consent of the Mayor and Council 1839.' He charged 30s. a year 'for a first-rate private house' but only 400 out of 4,000 houses in the city chose to be connected to his supply.

84   New housing in Exe Street in the 1980s.

Golsworthy's house became the rectory for St Olave's Church on Fore Street. In 1962 it was a listed building but derelict and run down, and was advertised for sale. There were four bedrooms in the rectory and seven in the adjacent church house. Donald Clarke bought it at auction, retained the outer walls and the lovely curving staircase, but replaced every interior wall and ceiling. He kept the Georgian style throughout and opened it as a 17-bed hotel in June 1984.

Richard Ford, author and traveller, boasted to his friends that Exeter was 'quite a capital, abounding in all that London has, except for its fog and smoke'. Born in London in 1796, he lived 30 years in Heavitree, died on 31 August 1858 and was buried in the south-west corner of St Michael's churchyard. After the Napoleonic wars had ended, allowing travel in Europe again, Ford and his delicate wife had sailed to Spain and spent three years there. Travelling by diligence and on horseback, Ford crisscrossed the whole country, amassing information for the book he wrote on his return to England, *A Hand-Book for Travellers in Spain and Readers at Home*. This was the first travel book of its kind and was published in 1845; it was followed by *Gatherings from Spain* in 1846. Notable events of these years included the christening in St Sidwell's of little Sabine Baring Gould, who had been born in 1 Dix's Field, Southernhay, on 28 January 1834. He grew up to become parson, squire, antiquarian, folklorist, father of a large family and author of many historical novels, but is perhaps best remembered for his hymns, which include 'Onward Christian Soldiers'.

Ford purchased a cob cottage and 12 acres of land next to St Michael's Church and transformed it into a Moorish estate in the style of the Alhambra, the former Moorish capital of Granada. He filled the house with antiquities, majolica, ceramics and actual tiles from the Alhambra. The garden was also modelled on the Alhambra, with terraces, rows of cypresses and a Moorish-style tower with horseshoe-shaped arches. He invited John Gendall to stay to teach him to paint, and the Royal Albert Memorial Museum has a painting by Gendall of Ford walking in his garden with a macaw on his arm. Often seen striding through Heavitree in a Spanish cape, Ford appreciated the resources of the Devon and Exeter Institution – but he told Gendall that he considered Exeter women ugly. Ford was not a religious man, but his brother James was a vicar in Exeter: he hoped to get to heaven 'on the coat-tails of my brother'.

11

Mid-Nineteenth Century

For centuries packhorses and carts coming in and out of Northgate faced a steep downward slope to the Longbrook and up again. The Romans made a cobbled ford across the stream; and later generations filled in the hollow with a stone causeway to form Lower North Street. However, the way between Northgate and St David's Hill was still very much up and down until the Iron Bridge was built in 1834. The arches were made of cast iron in Wales and sent round by sea and up the canal. The foundry's name is embossed on the curve of the arches at each end of the bridge: 'RUSSELL & BROWN'S BLAINA IRON WORKS'. The bridge has lasted well because each arch is made of several sections pinned together: solid cast arches would have cracked by now.

The 1830s saw other solutions to the problem of access to Crediton and North Devon. In 1833 the New North Road provided level access round to Eastgate. Soon afterwards, in 1835-40, the city wall was knocked through at the end of Queen Street, and this thoroughfare was continued over a viaduct to join New North Road.

Exwick's population, both agricultural and manufacturing was expanding fast. The hamlet was considered large enough and far enough from the parish church to require a chapel of ease. St Andrew's looks unexceptional to us, accustomed as we are to Victorian Gothic, but in 1832 it was hailed by the Camden Society as 'the best example of a modern church we have yet seen'. It has a chancel, nave, south porch and bell-gablet; a north-west spire was designed but never built. The stone altar, reredos and font were small versions of those in St Thomas's, reflecting the enthusiasm of the Rev. John Medley for Pugin's Gothic revival. Medley founded the Exeter Diocesan Architectural Society in 1841, the first of its kind outside Oxbridge, and his new chapel could incorporate all the latest ideas about Christian socialism and the sacredness of pointed arches. Medley appointed a young architect, John Hayward (whose later career would provide such local landmarks as St Luke's College, the Royal Albert Memorial Museum and New Blundell's), James Buller, lord of the manor and patron of the parish, donated £100

and the site, and on 30 July 1841 laid St Andrew's foundation stone. Medley expressed his joy that the equality of all in the eyes of God would be mirrored in the seating arrangements: open benches, all free, all of equal height. The builder was Moore, of St Thomas, and the vicar asked the workmen not to desecrate their work by any profane swearing or immoral conduct. A bottle, containing a parchment scroll recording the event, and three small silver coins, were sealed inside the foundation stone. At 11am on Monday 26 September 1842 the chapel was filled to overflowing for the consecration. Afterwards the bishop's party took lunch at Medley's house, and in a tent near the chapel 250 poor children from the St Thomas Schools 'were regaled with roast beef and plum pudding through the kindness of the Revd. J. Ford of Barley House'.

Another determined man left his mark on the building 30 years later. William Gibbs of Tyntesfield, who had a family fortune based on the import of guano for fertiliser, begged Buller to sell him the Exwick living, and make it independent of St Thomas's. In 1873 he brought back the original architect, Hayward, to lengthen the chancel and add a north aisle, behind polished marble pillars crowned with lilies and passion flowers. Panels illustrating the Benedicite were stencilled on the chancel ceiling, and there was a dado of musicians along the wall. William Gibbs also paid for a substantial stone house for the new vicar, William Cobham Gibbs. This stands high above Exwick

86 Before the Queen Street viaduct bridged the Longbrook valley, horse-drawn carts and carriages from the north had no choice but the steep climbs and descents over St David's Hill. This view by P.V. Pitman also shows the older road, and the weather vane marking the site of Northgate.

87 When the improvement commissioners were considering a bridge, an iron-founder called Russell from Blaina in Monmouthshire was in town selling iron lamp-posts, and won the contract to design and supply the cast-iron arches. They came by sea in 1835.

Road, and was the diocesan training centre after 1983, renamed Mercer House after Bishop Eric Mercer (1973-85). It made a huge vicarage, with a private chapel, a dairy with cool slate shelves and stables on Exwick Hill.

St Luke's School of Education, Heavitree Road, was founded in 1840, one of the earliest diocesan training colleges in England.

In the middle of the 19th century St Sidwell's parish was twice disrupted by 'surplice riots'. By now the local population was fervently Protestant. The bishop had tried to standardise practices, including the wearing of the surplice in the pulpit, but in

88 The Queen Street façade of the Higher Market, shown here in an etching by P.V. Pitman, was designed by George Dymond, finished by Charles Fowler (famous as the architect of London's Covent Garden) and opened in 1838. It was saved from demolition in the 1960s and incorporated into a new shopping centre.

89 The main hall of the Higher Market, where local farmers and fishmongers rented trestle tables.

Diocesan Training College, Heavitree Road, Exeter.

90 St Luke's teacher-training college, founded in 1840, was one of the earliest in England. New premises on the Heavitree Road were opened in 1855, two years after Besley had published this print. The tramp in the foreground is waiting for the nearby workhouse to open for the night.

December 1844 he relented and allowed each parish to choose whether to conform. Parish meetings in St Sidwell's and St James's came out strongly against the surplice, but a curate preaching in St Sidwell's on 19 January 1845 insisted on obeying Church regulations. On this occasion, and again in 1848, the result was a disgraceful display of bad behaviour: the young curate was assailed with hisses and groans; the rector was pelted with mud and rotten eggs; his hat was beaten in; coarse jokes and laughter filled the air. The *Illustrated London News* of 11 November 1848 featured these 'surplice riots':

> After the church had been wrecked in the morning, the Rev. F. Courtenay felt bound to close the church in the evening, in consequence of a 'State of Dissoluteness and Disorder,' which he described as the usual state of things at this Church on a Sunday Evening. In a part that he designated the Ante-church, a young man had been known to light his cigar at the gas. Parties talked, and young girls flirted there; young people had been seen making signals to each other across the gallery, and many young females had been ruined by their attendance at these Sunday evening lectures.

Bishop Philpotts did not oppose the Tractarian Movement, but changed his mind often enough on the Catholic question for some to regard him as a traitor. Sidney Smith was quoted with glee by many when he said: 'I must believe in the Apostolic Succession, there being no other accounting for the descent of the Bishop of Exeter from Judas Iscariot.'

In 1808 James Kemp had written *Northernhay*, a poem addressed to Solitude, where the evening silence was broken only by the curfew's solemn sound, the screech-owl and the distant river. Later in the century '*Musopolus*' (servant of the Muses) also sang of the evening, the curfew and the cawing of rooks, but now:

> … from out the valley broke
> Snowy whirls of shrieking smoke!
> 'Tis the form and 'tis the scream
> of the great familiar, Steam.

The Bristol & Exeter Railway reached St David's in 1844, and the London & South Western line was to disturb the peace of Northernhay from 1860. At midday on 1 May 1844 the first passenger train from Paddington arrived at the station at Red Cow, called St David's for greater dignity. Sir Thomas Acland travelled back on it that evening, and went to the Houses of Parliament at 10pm to announce that he had still been in Exeter at 5.20pm. As Exeter time was still local time, the journey had been even shorter than it sounded, by 14 minutes.

The whole country went by local time until the spread of the railways and wireless telegraphy – but these innovations made it essential to agree on a standard time. Until then, each quarter degree of latitude that a place lay west of Greenwich meant that midday happened one minute later than in London. Exeter is 3.31 degrees to the west, so there is a 14-minute delay in the arrival of the sun overhead. The Astronomer Royal objected to imposing one standard time on the whole country but it was made law in 1880 by the Definition of Time Act. However, the dean was persuaded to put the cathedral clock forward 14 minutes as early as 2 November 1852. Exeter had one clock that showed the two times, standard and local. This was at St John's Church in Fore Street, just below the present City Arcade, where until 1937 there was a large illuminated dial projecting over the street. This was affectionately known as 'the moon of Fore Street', and it had twin minute hands, one golden, one silver.

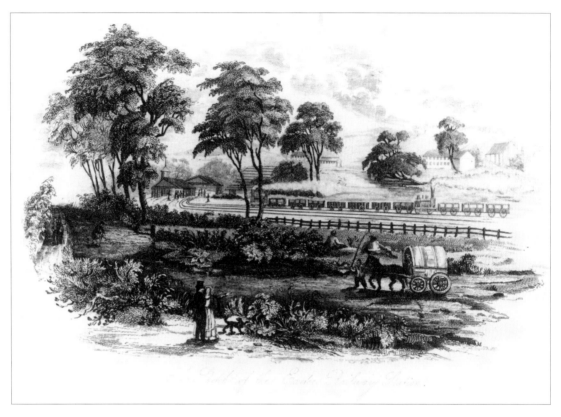

A hook on a wall in Exwick is a reminder of the turnpike roads that used to lead out from Exeter in all directions. Unlike congestion charges, which are intended to limit the amount of traffic inside towns, turnpike tolls paid for the upkeep of privately financed roads between towns. And it was not a question of cutting down on fumes from petrol-driven traffic: turnpikes served travellers of the 100 years or so before motor cars were invented. It was horses' hoofs and the wheels of carts and carriages that churned up road surfaces, causing damage that had to be paid for. Turnpike tolls can be viewed as more like road tax.

91 Two steam locos speeding towards the passengers waiting at the Exeter railway station in 1850, seen from Cowley Bridge Road.

The Buller family of Downes near Crediton were the lords of the manor in St Thomas and Exwick, and also patrons of the parish church of St Thomas. They built the toll house that still stands at the corner of Exwick Road and Station Road, and gave the land for the school that stands next to the toll house, built in 1859 and serving as the school for Exwick until 1971. The Bullers also provided the site for St Andrew's Church, built as a chapel of ease in 1841 across the road from the toll-house; and after the First World War they gave the site for the parish hall beside the church.

The function of the hook in the wall of the toll-house was to carry a chain, which barred the way until the toll had been paid. Luckily it did not block the route for Exwick village's inhabitants to their church- althoough it did lie across the road for the parson who rode in from St Thomas to conduct the services. The solution was for him to cut across the field behind the school and enter the church by a door on that side.

All the turnpikes around Exeter were removed in October 1884. The Bullers still owned Exwick's toll-house, and Art Daymond, one of their gamekeepers, was given it rent free as part of his pension. The house was sold in 1988 by the Buller estate – the last of the Buller property in Exwick. It is not a listed property, but it has an interesting history and the hook survives as a reminder of its past function.

In the middle decades of the 19th century food prices were high in Exeter, and poor families were hungry and restless. There were food riots in May 1847 and January 1854. On the first occasion the mayor had been in London attending the lord mayor's banquet, but he dashed back by express train. The mob tried to free prisoners from the Guildhall, but the mayor called out the Third Light Dragoon Guards from the barracks with a display of bayonets to disperse the crowds.

In January 1855 it was so cold that the Exe froze – and Mr Vickary roasted a joint of meat on the ice at the back of the Seven Stars Hotel. In November 1867 there was such unrest that the usual cathedral yard bonfire was cancelled, and the Riot Act was read to the hungry crowd. The militia tried to hold the bridge with fixed bayonets, but the mob stormed into St Thomas to fetch the timber-wagons, and to attack food-shops and smash windows.

In such times it was as well to be self-sufficient. John Stocker described Cowick Street in the 1860s: there were 'many thatched houses and any number of courts. The kitchens were floored with pebbles. Nearly all the houses had tiny gardens and nearly every cottage kept pigs. In Reed's Court there were 20 houses and about 100 pigs.'

Wippell's is an old Exeter family firm, established about 200 years ago and specialising for the last 150 years in clerical outfitting and church furnishings. The factory was built for Heathcote's Lace Company but never used by them. The alley opposite, behind the St Thomas shopping centre, is on the line of the old rope walk, where ropes were

92   HM Prison, New North Road.

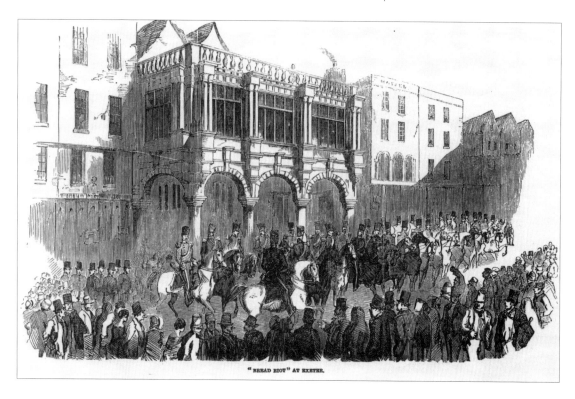

"BREAD RIOT" AT EXETER.

twisted by hand. Bell-ropes had coloured wool twisted into them. Apple trees grew here in living memory. In 1853 there was a potato patch by the viaduct, into which a traveller fell unharmed when he stepped out of the train too soon.

Argyll and Belvidere Roads were laid out on the Duryard estate in the 1850s by Copplestone Cross, Esq., in the belief that 'so healthy and delightful is the situation that an immense revenue may be raised by indulging the wealthy merchants of its neighbouring city with sites for the erection of villas in a district which has long claimed to be pre-eminent for the respectability of its inhabitants'. Provision was made for a church to be sited in the centre of this respectable development. The villas were never built. After Copplestone's death, tax problems led to the estate being sold off quickly and split into smallholdings and orchards.

Until 1850 Lion's Holt and Hill's Court were separate little hamlets set among fields, a quarter of a mile outside the Eastgate. Pennsylvania Road was a leafy lane leading up to a few white-stuccoed mansions on the hillside. Between Hill's Court and Lion's Holt there was a green pasture, called the Cistern Field because it held the well and spring that supplied water to the city via the Underground Passages.

In 1848 the London & South Western Railway Co. was planning a line from Yeovil to a proposed central station. York Road and Blackall Road did not yet exist but were planned as approach roads to the new station. In 1857 the engineers cut through the lands of Polsloe Priory, tunnelled under the ridge of Mount Pleasant (pick and shovel, horse and cart) and slashed through the peaceful hamlet of Hill's Court, demolishing at least one property there and displacing the turn-off to Hoopern. Train services began on 19 July 1860, one to and from Yeovil each day, and two to and from Waterloo.

93 From the *Illustrated London News*: dragoons guarding the Guildhall during the bread riots of January 1851.

Twenty years later the Cistern Field was sold for development. A thoroughfare was laid out across the meadow and named Powderham Crescent. The first four houses were built on the northern side and occupied by 1881. An oval pleasure garden was railed in for the use of residents. Over the next 20 years builders completed the double crescent and the terraces at each end. There were strict guidelines to ensure uniformity: 'The front fences shall consist of a dwarf wall with piers and iron railings and gates of uniform pattern and the ground in front shall be used as a garden with grass, flowers or shrubs only and such shrubs shall not be allowed to attain a height to obstruct the view of any dwelling house adjacent or near thereto.' The massive piers guarding each front path would be more appropriate at the entrance of a substantial estate. This is probably why Robert Newton called the crescent 'a monument to pretentious architecture'. Residents could exit via Pennsylvania Road in their carriages, and the railway halt at the other end of Powderham Crescent was convenient for commuting to Queen Street; but they felt the need for protection from the riff-raff who lived in Well Street. Each resident was obliged 'to bear a fair proportion of the expense of keeping the Gates at the Lion's Holt end of the Crescent in repair'. During the Second World War the iron railings were taken for the war effort and a cistern was sited in the pleasure garden, to hold water for firefighting – a reminder of the days when this was the Cistern Field.

Franz Liszt, the Hungarian composer and virtuoso pianist, performed in two concerts at the Royal Clarence in Exeter in 1840, when he was 29. He had 'an excessively tall and thin figure. A pale face with sea-green eyes, which shone with rapid flashes like waves in flames.' His unusually long fingers gave him an enormous reach over the keys. Liszt was touring to raise funds for the Beethoven monument in Bonn, and there were six other musicians with him. He complained in letters home to his mistress that these others were extremely boring company. They bypassed Exeter on the outward leg of the tour. After performing in Weymouth they drove in a hired carriage to Exmouth, where they had a cream tea. A plaque commemorating this visit was put on the Manor Hotel in 1983. The carriage then took them along the sands to Teignmouth. Was the sandbar across the Exe safe at low tide? The party planned to give two concerts in Plymouth, but cancelled the second when they found that everyone had gone down to the docks to watch the launch of a ship. From Plymouth they set out at 8am for Exeter, skirting Dartmoor and stopping at Ivybridge for a cream breakfast. The group performed at the Royal Clarence Assembly Rooms, Exeter's only available venue for balls, assemblies and concerts, at 8pm on Friday 28 August and again at 2pm the next day. Tickets were available from Mr Pilbrow's Pianoforte and Harp Warehouse. Liszt performed some of his own compositions, interspersed with songs and piano duets.

He did see something of Exeter while he was here: the party 'walked and visited the cemetery'. This was probably Bartholomew Yard, with its splendid outlook over the river to the western hills. On Sunday they passed the time playing cribbage and whist, and strolled around the cathedral close. Liszt wrote to his mistress that English cathedrals were superior to French ones because there was a good clear view of them. They were surrounded by grass and trees, not glimpsed between crowded streets. At 5 p.m. the performers caught the coach to Taunton, arriving there at 10. They went on to perform at Bath, but found that everyone had gone to watch the opening of Brunel's railway. Making the best of it, they treated themselves to a train ride to Bristol at half a crown a ticket.

The clock-tower in the New North Road (now a major landmark) was not built until 1897, replacing a simple obelisk and horse-trough. It commemorated the queen's

94 William Miles was an authority on the care of animals, particularly horses' feet. He built a simple obelisk and horse-trough in 1877. His widow incorporated it in the elaborate clock tower built to mark Victoria's diamond jubilee in 1897.

jubilee and stood at the head of Queen Street, named at the time of her coronation 60 years earlier.

The directories from 1791 to 1839 list Mrs Hill and then James Hill as resident near Rope Walk Lane and carrying on the trade of ropemaker. From 1847 to 1871 the entry is 'James Hill, Ropemaker and Beer House'. In 1881 and 1899 Mrs Susannah Hill, ropemaker, and the Ropemakers Arms are listed. Thus the property belonged to the same family for over 100 years, and they continued their trade when the house became licensed. It was customary for men of one trade to drink together. In 1880 Robert Dymond composed an Exeter version of Harwood's poem about this:

The Farmer to the Oatsheaf
The Sailor to the Ship
The Student to the Oxford Inn
Hastens with Spur and Whip.
The Churchman to the Cross Keys
Or the Mitre hurries on …

The Great Western Railway leased the Bristol to Exeter line for five years, then took it over. Their chief engineer, Isambard Kingdom Brunel, approved the adoption of a new system for the next undertaking, the South Devon Railway extension to Plymouth: the atmospheric system, which had been patented by Samuda Brothers and Clegg. It moved trains by suction, like the cash capsules once used in banks. Pumping stations 3 miles apart created a vacuum in a pipe lying between the lines. The train inserted a piston in a slit in the pipe and flew along at up to 68mph without any of the noise, soot or judder of a steam locomotive. A pump-house was built next to the station at Red Cow, and another by the estuary at Star Cross. The three roads just west of Exebridge would have needed so many level crossings that a 62-arch viaduct was built instead. By early 1845 a number of humble cottagers who had been in the way of this grand project had been ruthlessly unhoused. The first trains to Teignmouth on this line were pulled by locomotives after all, but the atmospheric system was used for 12 months from September 1847. It was then abandoned, because either rats or the salty sea air had damaged the leather flaps that maintained the vacuum.

By 1851 visitors could travel by train from Plymouth to London for the Great Exhibition. The Vivian family, travelling up from Cornwall, made a game of it from Plymouth as far as Exeter, wagering that Papa would go faster across Dartmoor in his carriage than Mama and the children on the South Devon Railway. It was a tie. Queen Victoria praised an unusual exhibit in the Crystal Palace, a model of the west front of Exeter Cathedral, 9ft high, made by Mrs Kingdon from the pith of rushes from the canal, using only a gum-pot and a pair of scissors. Mrs Kingdon had been born a Bodley and married into another well-known Exeter family. Among the visitors to the

95 'A General View of the Pump and Passenger Stations at Exeter.' The Italian-style pumping station is on the left, and the simpler barn-like structure of St David's station on the right.

96 Two men out rabbiting in 1848 on the slopes above Exwick chapel (of 1842) look across to the city on its cliffs. St David's station lies below them, but to the right, echoing the tower of Allhallows, is the campanile-like chimney of the pump-house of the atmospheric railway.

Exhibition was her six-year-old grandson, William Kingdon Clifford, of Longbrook Street, whose father was a High Street bookseller. William attended Dr Templeton's Academy in Bedford Circus. At his aunt's house in London he was looking worried at bedtime, having been trying to calculate how many times the width of his penknife blade would go into the rim of their carriage-wheel. Uncle was able to reassure him that he had got it right. William was to become second wrangler at Cambridge, professor of applied mathematics at University College London. He was a brilliant and inspiring lecturer, swinging around a lamppost to illustrate one theory, and he developed a system of algebra that came into prominence in the 'Space Age' of the 1970s. He wrote that 'Space has little hills of curvature like ripples in a wave'. In 1879 the British Association met in Exeter, and their programme included a discussion of Clifford's theory of curvature of space. Sadly, by then he had died of tuberculosis. George Bernard Shaw wrote to his widow: 'You were lucky enough to be married to a very clever man – cleverer than anyone except Einstein – even cleverer than me.' It is said that William was so far ahead of his time that Clifford Algebra has had to be reinvented time and time again by physicists.

Tractarian ideals were embodied in a new church built on Mount Dinham in 1865-8 and described in a newspaper report as 'the finest church in Exeter next to the cathedral'. The inspiration came from Augustus Pugin, who had written that pointed arches and soaring lines were a truer representation of Christian belief than designs modelled on pagan Greek temples. The finance came from a man with local connections, the aforementioned William Gibbs. He commissioned the architect Rhode Hawkins to design a chapel of ease for almshouses and a blind school in this part of St David's parish. The site lay high above the Longbrook valley, and the new church of St Michael and All Angels was given a spire that was 220ft tall, reputedly the fourth tallest in the kingdom.

Several events in Victoria's reign inspired elaborate street decorations. When the Royal Agricultural Society met in Exeter in 1850 a baron of beef was roasted on gas jets in the castle yard, then carried shoulder-high along a leafy Queen Street to a marquee below Northernhay. The wedding in March 1863 between Princess Alexandra of Denmark and the Prince of Wales (the future King Edward VII) was marked in Exeter by naming Denmark Road, which runs from Heavitree Road to Magdalen Road. There were also popular jollifications in the form of a great donkey race on Sidwell Street, races by women for skirt pieces and scrambling for red hot pennies thrown from the upstairs window of the Buller Arms.

Exeter is a centre of excellence for the education of the blind and the partially sighted. A Mrs Friend was the driving force in 1838 to set up in South Street the West of England Institute for the Instruction and Employment of the Blind. After fundraising it was able to move to premises in Paul Street in 1840. The curriculum included basket-making and knitting stockings. When it outgrew the Paul Street accommodation it removed to St David's Hill, and remained there (in what became the community centre) until 1965. Some pupils trained as piano tuners. The Education Act of 1944 ruled that blind children should be educated separately from the partially sighted and they were sent to Bristol. In 1965 the school moved to its present site in Countess Wear as the West of England School for Children with Little or No Sight. Today it includes St David's House for young people with additional complex needs. In Bartholomew Street the site of the former Paradise School became Andlaw House for the deaf-blind.

97 A portrait of William Kingdon Clifford in the National Portrait Gallery (courtesy of the Royal Society).

A benefactor, Mrs Hippisley Tuckfield (was she related to the Exeter MP who donated the site for the Devon and Exeter Hospital?), saw the need for a school for deaf children. She set up the West of England School for the Deaf in a house on Alphington Causeway and admitted six children from Devon and Cornwall, four boys and two girls. Soon larger premises were needed and the builder William Hooper erected a fine house on Topsham Road 'just within the tollgate on a site which was open, dry and healthy' – where the school is still sited today. The building was in use from 1828, though often extended. The little boys were taught knitting; older boys, staying until they were 18 or 20 years of age, became proficient in printing, tailoring, cabinet-making and wood-engraving; girls learned domestic skills – so they all qualified for useful employment. The school was particularly proud in 1865 when a former pupil exhibited a painting in the Royal Academy and it sold for 50 guineas on the first day of the exhibition. In 1902 King Edward VII visited and allowed the school to add Royal to its name. In 1912 the school purchased Mount Radford Lawn on the other side of Topsham Road for a playing field, but the outbreak of war two years later meant it had to be dug up to grow potatoes.

Western Way takes a sharp corner as it bends into Magdalen Street; it runs on a viaduct above the valley of the Chute brook. The block of flats between the Jewish cemetery and the dissenters' burial ground is called Magdalen Bridge Court. A stone parapet along the pavement overlooking Bull Meadow used to be matched by one on the other side before Western Way cut into it in the 1950s. The surviving parapet would have been breached in 1973 if the plan had gone ahead to build a flyover across Bull Meadow, to lead to a new bridge across the Exe. The steep slopes of Bull Meadow

98 The Community Centre on St David's Hill, formerly the Institute for the Blind.

and the approach to the Jewish cemetery from Bull Meadow Road show how deeply Magdalen Street used to dip to cross this valley. This was the main road from London, running from Livery Dole to Southgate, the entrance to the city used for royal visits and other important occasions.

In the middle of the 19th century a family of builders and property developers called Hooper dominated the council and changed the face of Exeter. They built Lower Summerlands, the stucco houses of St Leonard's Road, Magdalen Road and Baring Crescent, the Higher and Lower Markets, St David's station and the ornate post office in Queen Street. In the 1840s and '50s one Hooper or another served three times as sheriff and three times as mayor. In 1825 they had bought most of the Baring estate in St Leonard's – which remained outside the municipal area until 1877. Henry Hooper was one of the improvement commissioners, and managed to get hold of £4,000 of city money for improving the access to No Man's Land near Fair Park, claiming it was part of the municipal area. But in 1857, wearing another hat as overseer for St Leonard's, he claimed that the land did not have to pay municipal rates as it was outside the city. Historian Robert Newton records: 'Mayor Henry Hooper was charged with improving his own property at the public expense and then evading rates. He achieved the distinction of being the only mayor who was never thanked, even perfunctorily, for his services to the city.' The *Gazette* reported: 'Mr Hooper will retire from the chair without enabling us to say a single word in favour of the mode in which he performed the duties of his office.'

In May 1856 Sidwell Street celebrated the end of the Crimean War:

> The appearance of nearly 2,500 persons, all dining in the open air, and deporting themselves in the most orderly manner, was a sight as novel as it was gratifying. Viewed from either end of the street the effect was almost magical; it seemed as though the wand of the enchanter had converted the busy thoroughfare into a continuous woodland. The tables were profusely supplied with beef, mutton and lamb, and plum pudding, together with hot vegetables and a liberal supply of bread and beer. During the dinner a vast number of the influential residents of the neighbourhood, together with the wives and families of respectable citizens, either promenaded the avenues between the tables, or rode past in vehicles gaily attired, thus imparting unusual animation to a scene in itself remarkable. Many of the young men wore laurel leaves on which were imprinted in gilt letters the suggestive motto 'Peace and Plenty'. The musical peal of bells poured forth its joyous strains, the band performed, and everything that was calculated in any way to promote the rational enjoyment of the people was most cheerfully and liberally provided. The bones and scraps were distributed among the most needy parishioners, by whom they appeared to be most gratefully received.

In 1857 the London & South Western Railway Company, building the Exeter Extension from Yeovil, cut deep into the upper Longbrook valley, deeper than the surface of the red sandstone, disturbing the spring which filled the cathedral well and leaving the Bishop's Palace and the other cathedral residences without water until September 1860. The well had been partly rebuilt in 1836 but now it was completely dismantled. The standpipe was found to rise through a lead disc 10ft across which covered a circular platform of two layers of Killerton stone laid in five concentric circles, closely jointed but without cement; the stones were channelled underneath to guide the water towards the pipe. Immediately under the stones lay a copper coin, scarcely worn, of Nero (Roman emperor A.D. 54-68). Another very ancient well was found on the opposite side of the cutting.

Exeter Central is such a familiar sight below Northernhay that it is hard to believe that the plan in 1836 was to run the railway along the Chutebrook valley to the quay, with the main station in the Barnfield. However, the Longbrook valley was used instead, the London & South Western Railway reached Queen Street in 1860, and on 19 July at 3pm, during a violent cloudburst, the first passenger train from Waterloo brought the railway's directors to a celebration dinner in a leaky marquee. On 1 February 1862 the Queen Street station was linked to St David's via a tunnel under St David's Hill. The gradient is 1 in 37; there is no steeper slope between Exeter and London. The Rougemont Hotel was built opposite Queen Street station in 1876 to cater for rail passengers, at a cost of £30,000.

99 In the winter months of 1857-8 the navvies levelling the bed for the London and South Western Railway cut off the cathedral's water supply, which had been piped from an ancient well at Lion's Holt for over 600 years. With pick and wheelbarrow they dug through the clay and into the underlying red sandstone.

100 The cathedral was left without water for nearly three years. The brickwork of the well had been renewed in 1836, but this was the first time that it had been completely excavated.

101   On 10 February 1858 the standpipe was found to rise through a lead disc 10ft across, resting on channelled stone slabs. Lying on the bedrock and under the stones was a shiny copper coin of Nero (Roman emperor A.D. 54-68, when the legionary bath house was being built).

102   Cathedral well on St James' Halt, which replaced the one cut through in 1857 and was in use until 1904.

Stoke Hill overlooks Exmouth Junction Railway Carriage and Wagon Shops, established in 1861. Nearly 2,000 men worked here on repairs; shunting on 12 'roads' went on 22 hours a day, stopping only between 2 and 4am. The red-brick building with high-arched doorways was the stable for the shunting-horses who pulled the engines into the loco sheds and out onto the turntable.

Exeter's Episcopal Schools were founded by Bishop Blackall. He was born in London in 1654 and was christened Offspring. He was ordained in 1690, and became chaplain to Queen Mary, the consort of William of Orange, from 1694 to 1708. After that he became Bishop of Exeter, until he died in 1716 after falling off his horse. The bishop was keen to set up Church of England charity schools for the

EXETER.

local children. He quickly founded four free schools and also planned a girls' school for the middle class, who would be expected to pay. The little boys were taught reading, writing, arithmetic and accounts, which was intended to qualify them for 'the middling ranks of life'. The girls learned to sew and knit. All the children had religious instruction on Sundays.

Impressive large-windowed classrooms were built on Mount Dinham 150 years later. The foundation stone recorded the date: 17 April 1861. After the Education Act of 1870 the Episcopal Schools became public elementary schools, eligible for parliamentary grants but still run on Church of England principles.

In 1876 the Middle Class School for Girls was finally built at Hill's Court on Pennsylvania Road. Postcard views named it as the Middle Class School or the Middle School or the Episcopal Modern School, until it was renamed Bishop Blackall School in 1934.

Bill Hoskins was born above his grandparents' bakery on St David's Hill, entered the Episcopal Boys' School on Mount Dinham in 1914 when he was six and a half and left in 1918, when he won a scholarship to Hele's School at the early age of 10. From Hele's he progressed to the University College of the South West, eventually becoming the ground-breaking local historian of the English landscape, Professor W.G. Hoskins.

Dorothy Gardner was a contemporary of Bill Hoskins at Episcopal School. She remembered that parents paid a certain fee for their first child, a little less for a second, less for a third, while a fourth went free.

The 1938 re-organisation of schools set up the Episcopal Senior Boys' School and Episcopal Senior Girls' School. After the war they became secondary moderns. John Meredith remembers that the boys' school was divided into four houses called after bishops

103   By 1870 Townsend's etching of 1848 had been updated to emphasise Mount Dinham cliff and to include the new spires of St Michael's and St Mary Major, but above all to add the large train-shed of St David's station and the track climbing steeply through a tunnel to Queen Street.

of Exeter: Temple, Philpotts, Blackall and Curzon. Exeter College eventually took over the building for many years, until it was sold to be redeveloped into residential housing.

Bishop Blackall Girls' School was amalgamated with Hele's Boys School to form St Peter's in Heavitree. Both of their vacated buildings were used by Exeter College, but in 2010 Bishop Blackall was sold for university student accommodation.

Reed Hall was built by a millionaire as a private residence. Richard Thornton West inherited a fortune, increasing it by trading in spices and coffee in Java. On retirement he moved from Streatham to Devon for its climate, purchasing Duryard Lodge on the death of ironmonger Samuel Kingdon. The old house was demolished except for its walled kitchen gardens and greenhouses. In November 1865 Richard's two-and-a-half-year-old son laid the foundation stone of Streatham Hall. The architect and builder, William Moore of Exeter, proudly inscribed his own name over a window near the front door, and the Bowerman West coat of arms in a loggia on the south-east corner is dwarfed by supporting cherubs holding the tools of the architect's trade, set square, quill and trowel. The mansion is Italianate in style, with a campanile and terraced gardens with sets of stone steps and balustrades. £80,000 was spent on the house and £70,000 on the gardens. The local firm of Veitch supplied the arboretum with trees from every temperate zone in the world. A heated palm-house 72ft long stood south of the house. Pollard's *Guide to Exeter* (1894) listed Streatham Hall among 'famous Parks and Gardens' in the area and it had national coverage in *Country Life* in 1899. But Richard had died in 1878. His son died in 1901 and his widow in 1903. The gardens were neglected and

104 Stables at Exmouth Junction for the shunting-horses, who pulled engines needing repair into the loco shed and on to the turntable.

the house lay empty. It served as a military hospital during the First World War, and was eventually sold for a fraction of what it had cost to build. The University College of the South West had been striving for official recognition, and the acquisition of the Streatham estate tilted the balance. Paper manufacturer Alderman William H. Reed donated the cost of the house and gardens, and Principal Hetherington persuaded the college to buy the undulating fields of Streatham Farm. Streatham Hall was renamed Reed Hall in the benefactor's honour and opened as a men's hall of residence in 1925, with several students sharing each spacious bedroom. There is a persistent rumour that President Nasser of Egypt lived here as a student, attending one of the college's prestigious holiday courses. The huge iron-framed conservatory was moved down the hill to the Imperial Hotel. During the Second World War Reed Hall housed drama and then medical students, relocated from London. The university's staff club now occupies the building. The mews, which once housed six coaches and the horses to pull them, now houses student careers and health services and the University of Exeter Press. The spacious restaurant with views of green lawns and trees is often booked for wedding receptions. A particular delight is the formal parterre garden with its little wistaria trees.

105 Bishop Blackall School, by architect James Jerman. The pointed cupola on the roof was lost in a fire in 1979.

12

Later Nineteenth Century

The death in 1861 of the prince consort, who had done so much for science and the arts, inspired fund-raising for a museum to be founded in his honour, which was to incorporate a free library, reading room, science classes and a school of art. In 1868 J.B. Goodrich celebrated its opening:

> Here's the Museum of fair design,
> Carved and polished superbly fine …
> Inwardly all is nicely plann'd,
> Corridors branching on either hand …
> Students of Art and Literature
> Will draw, and read, and look demure,
> While others will information gain,
> Or just 'pop in' to dodge the rain.

Cambridge supported university extension lectures, and the basis was set up for the eventual birth of the University College of the South West in 1922.

The long-term favourite exhibit, Gerald the Giraffe, was shot on the slopes of Mount Kilimanjaro in Kenya by big-game hunter C.V.A. Peel. He offered it to the museum in 1920 when he moved to Umberleigh.

On 15 July 1874 Exeter's chief constable reported to the city council that he needed to appoint a member of the police force to regulate street traffic. The force would be increased by one man for the purpose, and the constable selected would wear a badge on his arm marked 'Traffic Regulator': he would judge how long a vehicle needed for loading and unloading. The councillors remarked that the city's prosperity depended on goods coming in and out. This was, of course, before motorised lorries and vans.

The striking red-brick hall at the lowest part of Longbrook Street runs east to west from the pavement, but it is not a church; it is a workshop built in 1881-2 for

the ecclesiastical and architectural sculptor and carver Harry Hems, and enlarged in 1884. An inscription on the front, commemorating William the Conqueror's crossing of the Longbrook in 1069, is typical of Hems's enthusiasm for local history, and his desire to share it with one and all. Harry Hems was born in Islington, apprenticed to the Sheffield cutlery trade, but escaped to study drawing and sculpture. He worked as a journeyman carver in London, then 'in nearly every other part of England, also in Ireland and Scotland'. He went to France and Italy, and walked home from Florence, crossing the Alps on foot in mid-winter. He came to Exeter in 1866, with only half a crown in his pocket, to do the carved and sculptural work for the Royal Albert Memorial Museum. He found a lucky horseshoe as he walked up from the station, fixed it over his doorway and announced that one day it would be fixed in front of one of the best buildings in Exeter. At first the Sign of Ye Luckie Horseshoe was in Paris Street, but now it is set here, in the middle of a tablet and standing on a detached pillar of polished Aberdeen granite, below a statue of Art personified. Teak casements with stained glass, decorative brickwork and hung tiles fill in the tall frontal arches of a building that is nearly all red: warm-coloured bricks, dressings in red Dumfries stone and high-pitched roofs of strawberry-tinted tiles, surmounted with a red ridge. The architect of this monument to a self-made man was R. Medley Fulford, who subsequently went to Australia, where he took holy orders. The style was known as 'domesticated'

106   The museum's Queen Street façade, in early French Gothic style, uses a variety of local different coloured stones. The architect, John Hayward, also designed several other important buildings in Exeter, including St Luke's College and the Devon county prison.

107   Harry Hems's workshop in Longbrook Street, still sporting his lucky horseshoe.

or modified Queen Anne Flemish. The chimney-stacks are prominent features; two arch together to form a bell-turret. The apprentices and employees had to come running when the bell rang, and woe betide any who did not share Hems's extraordinary vitality and capacity for work. If jobs were some miles away, say at Topsham, nothing was paid for travel time. An Italian employee found that his mates were being paid more than him and went upstairs to Hems's office to ask for a rise. A metal plaque fixed to one of the stairs marks the spot where he hit the ground when he was kicked downstairs, an example to others.

From this workshop, said to be the most extensive of its kind in England, carved stonework for churches and town halls was sent out by rail all over Britain, including nearly 100 statues for the high altar screen at St Albans' Abbey, the colossal equestrian statue of William of Orange in Belfast, and copies of Hems's own 'Safe in the Arms of Jesus'. His personal motto 'I excel' is expressed cryptically on the front and on the north wall of the building. He is said to have employed one person just to paste in his press cuttings, of which 20 fat volumes survive. He was a churchwarden for St Sidwell's, a local councillor, the 'working man's representative' on local charity committees and provided splendid Christmas dinners for the aged poor. Hems lived in the end house of Park Place, with its weathercock and fairy-tale window turret on the corner. After his death in 1916 his family built the adjacent, less flamboyant, Hemsley (architects Ellis, Son and Bowden). A piece of the medieval wood-carving that Hems collected in the course of his church restoration work is inserted over the front porch. Hemsley is now a reading room for the Church of Christ Scientist, which was built in its front garden in 1938. The massive stone wall along the side of the garden could be the original boundary between Park Place and the brook.

On 7 July 1869 the opening ceremony for Wonford House Hospital was delayed for an hour because the Earl of Devon, who was to give the speech, was 'detained by the lateness of the train'. The patients moved into the new accommodation on 17 August, vacating the St Thomas Asylum on Buddle Lane. French doctors were recommending that mental illness should be treated not with strait jackets and locked doors but with exercise in fresh air, cheerful surroundings and useful occupations. The new site above the village of Wonford faced south with a view of the Haldon Hills, and the hospital had spacious grounds laid out by John Veitch. It had its own farm to supply fresh produce to the kitchens, and surplus produce was sent to the higher market by horse and cart. The architect of the new hospital, W.F. Cross of Queen Street, sadly died before the grand opening. His design in mock-Tudor style was built by Moass and Sons in Westleigh limestone with dressings of Bath stone. The roof line was varied, with pointed gables and corner turrets. Steep steps led up to a central porch. There were open fireplaces in all the rooms and corridors. It was called a retreat rather than an asylum and resembled a large country house, with suites of rooms for the richer patients who brought their own staff. Patients were not simply assigned males to the left, females to the right, but were divided into three classes, rather like the system on the railways, where there

108 Harry Hems, 'Ecclesiastical and Architectural Sculptor and Carver'.

were first-class, second-class and third-class carriages. In each wing, the one for men and the one for women, there were 'first and second classes of the quiet and orderly, but separated by their condition and station in life', i.e. the upper-class patients lived apart from the middle-classes. The third-class accommodation was for 'the violent, who were not suitable to mingle with the others from the infirmity of their malady'. The building was funded by donations and by the sale of Bowhill House. Anyone contributing 20 guineas could sit on the committee. Appeals were started for the erection of a chapel and the purchase of a billiard table. Patients paid for their care according to their means. Today the extensive grounds have mostly been lost to the re-sited RD&E Hospital.

In 1872 a field to the north of Union Road was purchased to erect a 'Benevolent Asylum for decayed licensed victuallers'. For the stone-laying ceremony on 8 August flags floated from almost every hotel and public house in the city. A procession from the Guildhall included the Lord Mayor of London, and 300 lunched in a marquee (although only 200 had been catered for.)

St Thomas First School was built in 1872, the first school built in the St Thomas district from public monies. R.M. Fulford designed the soaring polychrome Gothic walls with plate tracery windows and it was opened on 21 July 1873 by Bishop Temple. In 1987 the building was modernised, and children's safety was safeguarded by blocking off two adjacent roads. Queen's Road has also been shut to traffic at its eastern end.

The Improved Industrial Dwellings Company was founded in Blackboy Road in 1873 to 'provide commodious and healthy dwellings for the poorer classes'. In 1876 the company erected Kendall Buildings, two blocks, one close behind the other.

Newtown Community Centre uses the old low buildings of the church schools, built in 1874 as a ragged or free school for the many 'Arabs' infesting the streets who could not afford the penny a week for St Sidwell's School.

Exwick Cemetery was opened at Landhayes in 1877. Bishop Temple consecrated two identical chapels to cater for non-conformists and churchgoers, then led a procession over the burial ground, reciting the 49th psalm. The first interment was given a free tombstone. The melancholy inscription records that Elizabeth Curry, dying at 29, was joined a year later by her small son, and in 1880 by her young husband. A nearby stone was erected in memory of Robert Hodges 'by the son of his wife James Blackmore of Kobie, Japan'. The path was bordered with yews and firs, but the yews were rooted out after a stray bullock ate a twig and died. During the Second World War a landmine exploded here and threw a tall tree across the main road. The cemetery has been extended several times, taking in hillside fields named Higher Barnclose, Lower Barnclose, Long Meadow, Water Park and Wheatley.

In Blackboy Road, among the rose-beds, stands a shell-shaped monument to Arthur Kempe (1812-71). This is The Fountain, which gives its name to the area. It was a drinking-trough placed in front of the gate of St Anne's Almshouses for the horses on the Sidwell Street cab-rank, and was paid for in 1879 by the ladies of Exeter RSPCA in memory of the senior surgeon of the RD&E in Southernhay. The shell was replaced in 1930 after a bus smashed into it in the fog.

Hoopern House is an imposing mansion standing high on Pennsylvania Road. It was built in 1829, complete with fashionable 'plantation', intended for the residence of one E.P. Lyon. However, he died, and it was acquired by a member of the Kennaway

family, who were well-to-do and prominent in the city's trading and political life. Mark Kennaway was a leading Liberal, who believed that 'the election of councillors is a political act' and should be 'pure and disinterested'. He was a solicitor, co-founder of the Western Bank, and served as clerk to the improvement commissioners when they were tackling the problems of cholera and the water supply. After Mark Kennaway's death in 1875 Hoopern Mansion House was advertised for sale. The description at the time stated that the house had:

> … ample and beautifully planted grounds, well suited for a family of distinction. One mile from the High-street of Exeter, it has a southern aspect, stands 350ft above the sea level and commands a charming prospect over the city, and a wide extent of rich and varied scenery, including the estuary of the Exe and a glimpse of the English Channel. The ground-floor apartments are 12.5ft high, there are circulating hot water pipes. The stable has three stalls and another has three loose boxes. The coach house is large enough for three carriages. The large yard is well supplied with hard and soft water and there is a brewhouse, piggeries and other convenient accessories.

An auction of effects in 1877 included a Broadwood semi-grand piano, orange trees and a wagonette. The university used the property for some years after 1962, including as a store for the mattresses that had been delivered early for the Duryard halls of residence then being built. These were piled up under the high ceilings, and a young lecturer found he could save rent by sleeping undetected on top of the pile.

Henry Arthur Jones was a commercial traveller who taught himself to write plays. He eventually became successful enough to give up the day job. The turn in his fortunes came while he was living in Exwick, and it was Exeter's Theatre Royal that gave him the chance to see his plays staged. Jones was born in 1851, left

109 The Arcade ran from Eastgate to Southernhay. Built in 1882, it was an elegant shopping precinct sheltered from traffic and the weather. The grand officer would usher the public out at 6pm, pull on white gloves and make a ceremony of lowering the iron gates.

school aged 12 and worked as a draper's assistant. He was promoted to travelling salesman, married in 1875 and rented The Hermitage on Exwick Hill for the next six years. It was conveniently near St David's station, from where he could cover his area by train. In 1878 the Shakespeare season at the Theatre Royal was proving disastrous. In exchange for buying half the seats in the dress circle Jones was allowed to put on one of his plays, *It's Only Around the Corner*. The following summer the Theatre Royal staged another play by Jones, *Hearts of Oak*. By then he had decided to give up 'bagmanship' to become a full-time playwright. It was the right decision: he went on to make his fortune. The family moved nearer to London, and in 1892 *The Silver King* was an instant success. Jones wrote many comedies, but like his friend Pinero he treated social and moral issues, such as the double standards applied to men and women. Jones received encouragement from Max Beerbohm and George Bernard Shaw. The latter wrote to Jones in 1898: 'The missus thinks you vastly inferior to me as a dramatist (Shakespeare also), but she appreciates you as a man.' Perhaps Oscar Wilde was jealous of Jones's success. He published three rules for writing plays: 'The first rule is not to write like Henry Arthur Jones, the second and third rules are the same.'

   The Silver King was revived at the Chichester Festival Theatre in 1990. The director found that the melodramatic repetition and asides could be cut: they had been necessary when played by gaslight, which made the air appear to swim. In 1994 *The Case of Rebellious Susan* was put on in Richmond. A wife refuses to hush up her husband's

110   Horse trams ran from the Bude Hotel to Heavitree from 1882, and from St David's station to the top of Blackboy Road from 1883, but the High Street tradesmen would not let them run through the city centre. The High Street is here free from trams but open to carts and carriages. This view looks across London Inn Square to Sidwell Street. The post office of 1885 is on the right. The shop canopies are supported on poles that fit into slots in the kerb-stones.

infidelity or to forgive him: 'I'm going to pay him back in his own coin.' A recent collection of famous last words included those of Henry Arthur Jones. Mischievous to the end, he was asked during his last illness whom he would like to sit with him during the evening, the nurse or his niece. He said he would like the prettier one: 'Now fight for it.'

Tennis was a popular local sport. A club, called Victoria Park after its premises in St Leonard's, was founded in 1879. This makes it the second oldest tennis club in Britain, Queen's being the older but Wimbledon and even the Lawn Tennis Association younger.

In 1882 there was a huge fire on the quay. Barrels of oil were stored under the cliffs on the riverside, and a workman lighting his lamp ignited the oil vapours. There followed a series of enormous explosions, blowing the massive oak door right across the Exe, spreading flaming oil over the river's surface as far as Trews Weir. The workman was thrown to one side, dazed but unhurt.

In August 1883 the Exeter Tramways Company extended their horse-drawn service from St David's station all the way to Mount Pleasant, via Sidwell Street and the Bath Road (Blackboy Road). In the summer of 1897 a horse-bus went from the Guildhall to Pennsylvania via the Old Tiverton Road and Union Road, but did not prove popular enough to be continued.

The Theatre Royal stood for nearly 80 years on the site of the Prudential Building at the junction of Longbrook Street and the New North Road. Built in 1886 to replace a city theatre that had been consumed by fire, it was itself burnt down on 5 September 1887. Scenery caught alight and more than 160 members of the audience were unable to escape. Burning beams fell on the horses waiting at the cabstand, and one bolted all the way to Marypole Head. Flames could be seen from Topsham. The victims were interred in a mass grave in the Higher Cemetery, the memorial sculptured by Harry Hems. The repercussions were nationwide, giving rise to a poem by William McGonagall and a tightening up of safety regulations, requiring outward-opening exits in all places of entertainment. The theatre was rebuilt in 1889 and was the first in the country to install a fireproof curtain. Coachloads of theatre-goers travelled in from surrounding areas, and Christmas pantomimes were particularly well supported: from 1889 until 1950 the new theatre put these on every Christmas, the only theatre in the world with an unbroken record of 61 consecutive annual pantomimes.

In February 1888 the city set up a municipal fire brigade. They took over the premises of the West of England Insurance Company right behind the theatre site, and these were used until the new fire station was built in a much less central site in Danes Road in the 1930s, where it remained when rebuilt 75 years later. The old fire station on New North Road, a listed building, stands behind a high brick wall with gate piers that originally held lamps. The building just antedates the road and is set obliquely to it. The new road cut through, leaving most of the fire station's exercise yard on the other side (this was formerly a bowling-green). The station is a three-storey plaster-fronted building with an arched opening, pilasters above, a central niche and pediment. The ground floor contained the large stone-paved engine house; stairs and a trap-door hoist led to two large workshops, from which a trap-door led to the roof and the wooden platform used for drying the hose.

Exwick Mill stands over the leat that powered the Saxon mill mentioned in Domesday, the mills run by St Andrew's monks and later ones that stood until 1886. In that year

Mallett had Banfill's Higher Woollen Mill demolished and replaced with the present five-storey red-brick edifice, and installed huge new machines, including a semolina purifier for all those Victorian milk-puddings. Taylor & Bodley of Exeter made an enormous steel Poncelet water-wheel, the widest in Britain. The mill supplied self-raising flour for the baking trade until 1958. For over 1,000 years it ran mostly on water-power, supplemented occasionally with electricity. The present owner, Dick Pennell, is carefully restoring the building, which is used for storage, as a rehearsal space for rock-bands, and for the Tools for Self-Reliance Group to recycle hand-tools for Africa. Another part of the mill is used by a garden centre, reached by a bridge of stone salvaged from Ide Rectory in 1979.

The Bath and West Show came to Exeter at the beginning of June 1889. Sidwell Street was decorated with green branches; fir trees erected each side of the street 'gave it the appearance of a Parisian boulevard'. Elaborate arches reaching over the whole width of the street bore improving mottoes: 'He that would thrive must rise at five'; 'He that has thriven may lay till seven'; 'Plough deep while sluggards sleep'.

Robert Louis Stevenson visited Thomas Hardy in Dorset, then planned to travel to Dartmoor, but fell ill in Exeter and lay in the New London Hotel for several weeks. He wrote in the visitors' book: 'Should it be your misfortune to fall ill at an inn pray Heaven that it may be the New London.' A memorial pane was placed in the window of the room he had occupied, reading (in Latin): 'In this bedroom Robert Louis Stevenson lay ill in 5 September, 1885. His prison-home, the body, was weak and fragile, but his was the bright spirit. This pane was placed here by two admirers of his books, which are, in very truth, a more enduring monument.'

In the 1890s E.A. Sanders sublet the fields by Rosebarn Lane, called Higher Guilding, to a dairyman. Rowe's Barn became the destination for summer Sunday walks. There were two swings, and a penny would buy a glass of milk and a scone with a dab of jam and cream. Earlier this century factory girls would walk up Rosebarn Lane at six o'clock on May morning to wash their faces in the dew, dance round 'ring-a-roses' and eat their sandwiches with a glass of milk warm from the cow.

In the year of Queen Victoria's Jubilee it was decided to provide a safe playground for local children. Four years later, on 30 March 1891, the St Thomas People's Park was opened, with music from the Post Office Band, and a speech from the chairman of the local Board of Health about not damaging the shrubs. One acre was reserved for adults to use on Saturdays; children could play on the other 3 acres.

In Longbrook Street, on the right-hand slope and well above the stream, a terrace of 'genteel Dwelling houses' grew from about 1815 onwards, named Park Place. The row lay above the ancient 'Mawdlyn Ground', a hedged field belonging to the Magdalen charity, but from 1847 part of this was leased to provide the long front gardens. In 1881 Mr E.H. Shorto, then classical tutor at Hele's School, occupied 7 Park Place, and his wife ran a preparatory school, which became the long-lasting Norwood School. Mr Shorto 'was very particular about tidiness of the person, he himself always wearing the formal dress of tail coat, high collar and red handkerchief'. The Shorto family had a great impact on Exeter in the 19th century. Edward Henry Shorto, son of an Exeter watchmaker and jeweller, taught at Hele's school for 55 years. His brother George was town clerk at a time when the city was organising waterworks, electricity, an asylum, the Albert Memorial Museum and college. George's obituary says that 'he dearly loved to show by the valuable documents which the

Corporation possess that Exeter is one of the most ancient cities of the kingdom'. George's daughter Amy wrote a very readable history of Exeter for schoolchildren. Edward's obituary said that he was one of the best-known and most active Exeter churchmen. He was parish clerk at St Petrock's for 45 years, manager of St Sidwell's Schools and St David's School for 20 years, and a layreader. But he was best known as a teacher at Hele's School.

Elize Hele died in 1635, leaving a fortune for 'godly, pious and charitable use'. His executors died and the money lay unused for 200 years. Finally Queen Victoria directed by royal warrant that it should be spent on education. Hele's School opened in 1850 in the stone building now used as part of Exeter College. It was a middle school, bridging the gap between elementary and grammar schools. Exeter and Bristol were praised at this time for being unusual in catering for every stage of education. Edward became a pupil-teacher at Hele's soon after it opened, then served 26 years as assistant head and headmaster from 1899 to 1905. The school stood halfway between St David's station and Queen Street station, and boys were able to attend from as far away at Tiverton, Teignmouth, Axminster and Seaton.

George Gissing put Park Place undisguised into his novel *Born in Exile*, published in 1892:

> In a by-way which declines from the main thoroughfare of Exeter, and bears the name of Longbrook Street, is a row of small houses placed above long strips of sloping garden. They are old and plain, with no architectural features calling for mention, unless it be the latticed porch which gives the doors an awkward quaintness ... The little terrace may be regarded as urban or rural, according to the tastes and occasions of those who dwell there. In one direction, a walk of five minutes will conduct to the middle of the High Street, and in the other it takes scarcely longer to reach the open country. On the upper floor of one of these cottages, Godwin Peake had made his abode ...

Gissing was born in 1857. He had to leave college when he was imprisoned for stealing to help a prostitute; he married her but she drank herself to death. He then wandered across America, studied in Germany at Jena and returned to England in 1878, determined to earn a living from writing. His best-known book, *New Grub Street*, is about the degrading effects of poverty. He came to Exeter early in 1891 and rented 24 Prospect Park. Before he brought his second wife there from London he began to take long walks into the countryside, sometimes so far that he had to take a train home. He was surprised to find Exeter and its surroundings so pleasant and intellectually stimulating, and enjoyed reading books and journals in the Devon and Exeter Institution. His memoir, *The Private Papers of Henry Ryecroft*, gives glimpses of his happy experience of Exeter: 'I find myself reading with interest all the local news in the Exeter paper. Not that I care about the people ... but the *places* grow ever more dear to me. I like to know of anything that has happened at Heavitree, or Bramford Speke, or Newton St Cyres ... I like to learn the names of the farms and fields.' He thought Bramford Speke was the most beautiful village he had ever seen. In the summer of 1891 Gissing and his bride moved from Prospect Park to 1 St Leonard's Terrace (which would be lost in the 1942 Blitz). A son Walter was born there. Gissing loved St Leonard's, calling it 'a flowery, bowery suburb'. But it was difficult to write in a house with a young baby. He rented a quiet room at 7 Eaton Place and *Denzil Quarier* was written very

111   Looking in the
same direction as the
previous photograph, but
now there are tram-lines.
By 1903 High Street
traders had heard that
Sidwell Street businesses
were benefiting from the
horse-drawn trams passing
their doors, and they lifted
their ban.

quickly between August and November 1891. It is set at the time of the famous
Exeter election of 1880 when there were riots. Exeter is given the pseudonym of
Polterham, made up from Poltimore and Powderham.

Born in Exile is set unambiguously in Exeter as a cathedral town. The love-interest
has the quintessentially Exeter name Sidwell. Godwin Peake walks to her home: 'At
little more than a saunter, he passed out of the High Street into its continuation,
where he soon descried the Church of St Sidwell, and thence walked towards the Old
Tiverton Road. He was now quite beyond the town limits, and few pedestrians came
into sight. An errand boy came along, whistling townward, a big basket over his head.'
Godwin walks up what is clearly Stoke Hill, past Mincinglake: 'He found that the
road descended into a deep hollow, whence between high banks, covered with gorse
and bracken and many a summer flower, it led up a hill thickly planted with firs: at
the lowest point a bridge over a streamlet, offering on either hand a view of soft green
meadows. Aspects of exquisite retirement: happy who lived here in security from the
struggle of life!' Sidwell shows Godwin the view from her garden: 'A few years ago
none of those ugly little houses stood in the mid-distance. A few years hence, I fear,
there will be much more to complain of.' She must be referring to the closely packed
streets of Polsloe Park on the opposite ridge.

At the end of June 1893 Gissing returned to London. His wife became mentally ill and ended up in an asylum; he is said to have spent the rest of his life hiding from her. Gissing travelled to Naples, Rome and Athens. H.G. Wells was one of his few friends. (He taught him to ride a bicycle), they visited Italy together in 1897. Gissing died of pneumonia in France in 1903. His years in Exeter may have been among the happiest of his life.

In 1896 Exeter pioneered a new system of sewage treatment, the septic tank, devised by the city surveyor Donald Cameron. It was said that it would 'spread the name and fame of Exeter to the ends of the earth'.

Belmont Pleasure Ground was opened in 1886 as a public recreation ground under the Public Health Act of 1875. In 1897 Queen Victoria's diamond jubilee was commemorated with 'olde Englishe sportes'. During the Second World War the gravelled part of the park was covered with 'temporary' wooden huts to house the Royal Army Pay Corps. Later these huts were used by the technical college.

Cycling had become so popular by the end of the century that several clubs had been formed: the Exeter Rovers, the YMCA, the Exeter Cycling Club and so forth. In October 1890 there was a cyclists' carnival in aid of the Devon and Exeter Hospital. Clubs were invited from neighbouring towns – and 200 cyclists came from Topsham alone. The procession included fire brigades, the Devon Volunteers Artillery Band and hand-bell ringers. The cyclists were in fancy dress: 'courtiers, clergymen, clowns, princes, costermongers, smugglers, country bumpkins and mashers'. No women took part. One cycle had fairy-lamps along its handles, a tricycle carried 17 large lanterns and a safety machine had 12 lanterns over the rider's head, surmounted by a Japanese parasol. At a rocket signal at 8pm the bands began to play, and the cycles moved off from Bury Meadow along Queen Street, High Street and Sidwell Street until they reached The Fountain, then back through the city to St Thomas, where they turned, across Commercial Road to South Street, along Southernhay, finally ending up in Bury Meadow again. £96 18s. 3½d. was collected.

The Albert Memorial College and the Devon and Exeter Hospital both added 'Royal' to their name on 19 July 1899, when the future George V and Queen Mary opened new wings for them.

In 1899 the Exeter Brick and Tile Company set up a factory on the Polsloe Priory estate with machinery that could turn out 100,000 bricks every week. The band of red clay that runs through Pinhoe to Pennsylvania is particularly suited for brickmaking. It has also been used on many local cricket pitches to make a firm dry underlay for the turf.

In 1899 the works next to the Zoar Chapel in Longbrook Terrace saw a race to manufacture the first Exeter motor-car. A car had been exhibited in a circus at Pinhoe in 1897, and another had been driven to the New London Inn in 1898. William Shepherd and his son managed to design and build their own model at their Albion engineering works by September 1899, narrowly beating their rival, a watchmaker.

From the end of the 19th century terraces of sizeable houses, always with attics for servants, were built on the lower slopes of the hill. Pennsylvania became an exclusive suburb. Mrs K.R. Pollard, remembering a city childhood in *People Talking*, vol. 9, said, 'I do remember my parents saying, "You are never ever to go down Longbrook Street". It was like walking into Buckingham Palace … Pennsylvania was a snob area … if you was a child there, you'd be chased off, otherwise you had to raise your hat to them as you walked through, specially West Avenue. Past the bottom of Longbrook Street, going up Pennsylvania was taboo.' Howell Road children found the same about Mowbray Avenue: they weren't allowed to go round the corner there except on a specific errand.

13

Twentieth Century to the Aftermath of the First World War

By Bury Meadow, where the roads divide (New North Road leading to Crediton, while Hele Road goes down to St David's Hill and St David's station), there stands a magnificent equestrian statue of General the Right Honourable Redvers Buller. Buller was born on 7 December 1839, the second son in a family of seven boys and four girls, at Downes, near Crediton. He was given the name of a distant ancestor, Redvers, Earl of Devon. Redvers lost his mother when he was 16. In December 1855 she went into Exeter to buy Christmas presents, and then went down to St David's station to meet her two eldest sons, one coming home from Cambridge and Redvers coming from Eton for the Christmas holidays. She suddenly broke a blood vessel and was laid on a bed in the waiting room, where she lasted for three days, Redvers fanning her without a break. He took over the care of his two-year-old brother, bathed and dressed him, and also looked after his mother's azaleas. The same doggedness and kindness marked his army career, during which he won the love and respect and personal affection of his men – who were properly fed, clothed and nursed when wounded. In Buller's 10 years at the War Office he set up the Army Service Corps, which brought together supplies and transport under one command. Buller fought in China, Egypt, South Africa and Canada. He was awarded the Victoria Cross for gallantry in the Zulu War, rescuing wounded men from the battlefield. He was thoroughly at home on horseback, galloping cross country at home in Devon and into battle during wars: 'Leading his men at a swinging canter, with his reins in his teeth, a revolver in one hand and knobkerrie he had snatched from a Zulu in the other, his hat blown off in the mêlée, and a large streak of blood across his face … this gallant horseman seemed a devil incarnate to the flying savages …' When Buller was invited to Balmoral Queen Victoria found him clever and intelligent and modest. She was also surprised at his frankness: 'If I am not to tell the truth to my Sovereign, I don't know to whom I am to tell it.' He was attacked in Parliament for indecisiveness and for having considered

114 General Redvers Buller attended the unveiling on 9 September 1905 of his statue. His record in South Africa was controversial but crowds of loyal supporters attended. He died on 2 June 1908 and the statue was draped.

the possibility of surrender at Ladysmith. In fact, he broke the siege at Ladysmith on his fourth attempt on 28 February 1900, relieving 12,000 British troops before their food ran out. He was retired in disgrace on half pay. In retirement he looked after the estate at Downes lovingly and efficiently, served on Devon County Council's Education Committee and Bridges and Roads Committee. He visited schools, promoting independent thought, instructing teachers not to concentrate on the Three Rs, but the Three Hs – Head, Hand and Heart.

On 9 September 1905 Buller attended the unveiling of his statue, an unusual situation. 50,000 admirers had contributed to the cost of the bronze statue, 13ft high on a plinth of granite 11ft high. It was the work of Captain Adrian Jones, one-time army veterinary officer, who also sculpted the Quadriga at Hyde Park Corner. The statue shows the general in full dress uniform wearing a greatcoat. For the unveiling there was a civic procession from the Guildhall. The band of the 4th Battalion of the King's Royal Rifles played. The Lord Lieutenant of Devon, Viscount Ebrington, unveiled the statue, and lunch followed in the Victoria Hall. The band of the 4th Devonshire Regiment played in Northernhay Gardens. Tea in Bury Meadow was laid on for 500 navy and army veterans. In the evening there were illuminated band performances in Northernhay, Belmont Pleasure Grounds and St Thomas Pleasure Grounds. Excursion trains were laid on for crowds wishing to attend the celebrations. The people of Devon also presented Buller with a ceremonial sword, decorated with gold, rubies, diamonds and sapphires. It is kept in the Guildhall. During the First World War it was noticed that soldiers passing the statue constantly saluted the bronze horse and rider, more especially men belonging to overseas contingents. On one Anzac Day Australians in Exeter clubbed together to lay a wreath there, although he never commanded any Australians in South Africa. There is another memorial to Buller in Winchester, the home of his regiment, a recumbent bronze figure.

In 1887 a new parish was carved out of St Thomas to serve the new streets off Okehampton Road. Redvers Buller donated the site, and a little iron church was erected, called Emmanuel. In all 113 designs were submitted for a stone church, and the winner was a Gothic design by Harold Brakspear. The cost was raised within 10 years, thanks to 'a notable contribution' from the vicar's father, Sir George Williams, founder of the YMCA. Redvers Buller laid the foundation stone in mid-October 1897 under 'an awning which just sheltered it from the rays of the setting suns… The bells of the mother church rang out merry peals.' After an open-air service with choir and orchestra, the ladies served tea to over 350 people at the adjacent board schools, with

115 Nursery gardens have surrounded the city for many centuries, supplying flowers, fruit and vegetables. The Sclater family grew tulips and daffodils in the orchards around Bowhill, and stored apples and ripening peaches in the spacious upstairs rooms of the house.

116   Harvesting
sweet-scented Mrs Simkin's
pinks on the hillside below
Hambeer Lane.

more music. The church was built of grey limestone with a tiled roof. The interior is lined with red Pocombe stone. The planned south-west tower was too expensive, but there is a distinctive polygonal vestry at the south-east corner. Bishop Bickersteth consecrated the church on 2 October 1900. From 1924 to 1963 the vicar was the Rev. Ernest Francis Tozer. The church was slightly damaged in the 1942 blitz. In 1988 David Gubbin installed windows depicting St Francis, and the conversion of St Paul, in memory of Mr and Mrs Tozer.

The vicarage, a large house on the other side of the road, had been the residence of old Mr Walton of Walton's drapery store; he set out to business every morning in a carriage and pair. The vicarage faces the turning to the church hall. When the vicar's wife laid the foundation stone in October 1921 it was felt necessary to state that it would be for the parish and Sunday School, and would not be let out in competition with the larger King's Halls. Emmanuel Hall faced demolition in the 1970s, but found a new role as a branch of the Northcott Theatre, for rehearsals and small productions.

In 1904 a new power station was needed for the electric tram system. It was built next to the basin, convenient for the delivery of coal by barge. So much power was needed to carry a laden tram up Fore Street that only one at a time was supposed to attempt it. P.G. Martin, when a small boy, was on a tram when this rule was broken, a fuse blew, and they saw the tram ahead beginning to slip backwards. They got off.

The distinctive dome of Sidwell Street Methodist Church is a landmark on the city's eastern ridge, visible from many directions. There had been a small Wesleyan chapel here since 1836. The wealthy paper-mill owner W.H. Reed helped pay for Sunday School rooms in 1896-7 and wanted to use the same local architect, F.J. Commin, for an imposing new church. Commin's design was Edwardian Baroque with Art Nouveau details. The interior was octagonal, as recommended by John Wesley as best for preaching.

The design could only be built by using the cheapest tender, that of Paul Cottancin of Paris, who was pioneering the use of reinforced concrete. The walls are built of hollow bricks threaded onto steel rods. The galleries and domed roof were made of stout steel netting embedded in concrete; the ornate surrounds of windows and doors were not carved expensively from stone but cast cheaply in concrete. Even so, the contractor went bankrupt when the walls were scarcely started, but it was too late to change the design. What with the foreman speaking French and the materials being delivered late, the church was not finished until 1905. The roof is a shallow copper dome surmounted by a cupola that lights the interior. The stained glass windows were crafted by a local

117 The Guildhall end of the High Street. Horses still outnumber motors by two to one. When the last horse-drawn tram gave way to the first electric tram on 4 April 1905 the Guildhall was the setting for the ceremony.

118 The tramlines and overhead electric wires of the new system dominate the High Street, but there is still room for a bicycle and a horse-drawn cart.

firm, Gubbin of Well Street. The same family firm repaired war damage in the 1940s. The church did not prove watertight. 'Snow' fell on the congregation from the plaster ceiling, and maintenance proved expensive. It was listed Grade II and could not be demolished to be replaced by flats, as happened with the church at Mount Pleasant.

Exeter Cricket Ground is a beautiful level green field near the university with panoramic views of distant hills. The Thornton Wests gave this part of the Streatham estate to the

119 A new Exebridge was opened on 29 March 1905. St Thomas was incorporated into the Exeter municipal area in 1899, Willey's iron-works and the new electricity works brought rush-hour numbers up to 3,000, and 10,000 crossed on Saturday evenings.

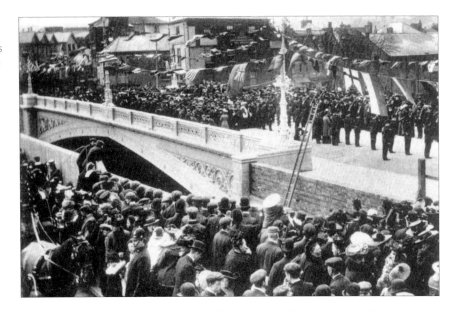

Devon County Club in 1902: they could have the use of it as long as cricket continued to be played on it, otherwise it would revert to the heirs of the family. The ground was inaugurated with a two-day event for which Dr W.G. Grace came to play. The Prince of Wales Road was not cut through until 1925-7, so the main entrance to the cricket ground was by the gate at the top of West Avenue. Thornton Hill and West Avenue were laid out in the same time as the sports ground, taking their names from

120 The 1905 bridge, drawn by P.V. Pitman.

121 The new
single-span steel bridge
opened in 1905 was
designed to accommodate
the new electric trams.
Here the tram proudly
displays the name of its
new destination.

the Thornton West family. Other sports were also accommodated. There was a bowling green, two croquet lawns and tennis courts; the croquet hoops had to be pulled out before cricket matches. Once a year there was a big croquet tournament, which took over the whole field. In 1978 it seemed that Exeter Cricket Club might not be able to ensure that cricket was still played regularly here, and there was an application from the heirs to build town houses along the southern edge. In 1982, however, the Isca Hockey Club stepped in to use the field in winter, and a private squash club and bar was built in one corner of the ground. In the summer spectators enjoy sitting on the pavilion steps watching the white-clad cricketers as the sun sinks over the distant hills.

Exeter City football team turned professional in 1908, joining the Southern league. St James's football field is deeply rooted in Exeter's history. The youngest daughter of the 2nd Earl of Bedford was born in Bedford House and christened Margaret in St Stephen's Church in July 1566. Nearly a century later, in December 1654, a charity was set up in her memory by her daughter, Lady Anne Clifford. The proceeds from renting out a field near St Anne's Chapel, called Mountstephen, were to pay 'yearly to the world's end' for the apprenticeship of 'one poor Child, Boy or Girl, born and residing in the parish of St Stephen'. The field was rented out for fattening pigs, and travelling menageries camped there each year. The old boys of St Sidwell School used it for football, and their team took the name of Exeter City in 1904, taking over the field for football only: the lease stipulated 'no menageries, shows, circuses or steam roundabouts'. In 1908, when the club went professional, the supporters voted for the nickname 'the Grecians'. This was the traditional name for the inhabitants of St Sidwell's, which for centuries had been part of the city but outside the walls. Boys of the parish fought the city boys regularly during the annual ceremony of beating the bounds. The city boys wore blue uniforms and carried blue Tory favours, and the St Sidwell boys wore yellow for the Whigs, perhaps representing the ancient Greeks who had besieged Troy, since like them they were outside the city. Andrew Brice's epic on the elections of

1737 describes fights between the Blues and the Greeks, and he explains in a footnote that the Greeks are 'the rugged inhabitants of St Sidwell's' who contend with the city at football, while the townsmen are like the Trojans defending their ground. The local boys certainly knew the Homeric story of the Trojan war from their schoolbooks, just as their medieval predecessors (including Joseph of Exeter in the 13th century) had known it from medieval romances. In 1346 Robert Noble was mayor and had a beautiful daughter. One of her admirers composed this verse:

> As noble Helen was the cause
> Of ten years' war in Troy,
> So Helen Noble is the cause
> Of this my great annoy.

In July 1726 the Siege of Troy was enacted during the fair on Southernhay by puppets, with a large wooden horse, Troy in flames, and the 'Grecian' fleet sailing home across the sea. In 19th-century court cases plaintiffs from St Sidwell's were referred to as Greeks and people writing to the local paper signed themselves as Grecians. So the name was adopted and a Grecian Gate was put up at the ground. Supporters flocked to games on foot or via the nearby railway halt. The pitch was not quite the regulation length, but the neighbouring landowner refused to part with the necessary extra yards until the MP Henry Duke intervened in 1911 – which explains why Big Bank was known as Duke Bank for some years. In 1921 City raised enough money to purchase the whole field by selling to Bolton their goalkeeper Dick Pym. The 'Cowsheds ' were built in 1925, giving a good view from a raised grassy bank. The main stand was built in 1926. In his book on football grounds, Simon Inglis calls St James's Park 'a picture of warm red and green, although much of it looks ready to fall down, as if a combination of nails, moss, wire and paint keeps it standing'.

122 Magistrates found it necessary to direct the police to control some nursemaids: 'The perambulator in itself is not a nuisance, but becomes so when under the care of gadding females.' Here the decorum of Northernhay is preserved.

In the 1920s the house next to the newsagent's in Well Street sank until its window sill was at pavement level; it had been built on top of the city cistern, St Anne's Well. In 1785 the citizens found that their water was not getting through. If the well's original dedication was to St Agnes (symbol a lamb, *agnus*), it is fascinating to learn that the pipe was found to be blocked by the long-bone of a breast of mutton, blackened with age. The labourers dug a pit 20ft by 20ft by 10ft, and when they moved a stone slab 'such amazing Gush of Water poured out and with such sudden Force that it was with some Difficulty the men that were in the pit could save themselves'. After pumping for four days they found that an arched drain ran from beneath the present football field. One of them, John Pearce, quite naked and with a lighted candle in his hand, crept up it. After 70ft it ended in a perforated stone that let through the spring water but held back the earth. This conduit had not been heard of in living memory – hardly surprising if this was the City Chamber work licensed on 1 May 1444. The spring had now found a different route; in the quiet of lunchtime the surveyor listened carefully and heard the gush at the steep foot of the road. After two days of cutting through solid rock the spring was found and brought back into service. In 2010 the whole field was stripped of turf, drainage was installed and new grass was laid.

Crowds flocked to Whipton in June 1911 – some sleeping out overnight – to wait for the pilots in the 1,010-mile race round England and southern Scotland; they were due to swing round Pinhoe Church and land on the showground. A French pilot came first and the popular Texan-born Wild West showman Sam Cody 24 hours later, stepping out of his plane saying 'I'm sorry I'm late.'

123   Queen Street station before the First World War, viewed from almost the same spot as the view of the Longbrook Valley. The London and South Western Railway had reached Exeter in 1860. Access was from the path below Northernhay Gardens or down the adjacent slope. The station buildings were wooden, with roofs of different lengths sheltering the up and down platforms and track.

124 St David's station was rebuilt in 1912-14. This view from the water tower shows the decorative urns on Fox's façade of 1862-4, the GWR building inside it, the overall train-shed being dismantled and new platform canopies being built. Streatham Hall stands on the hill among its woods.

Up until the First World War a grand cart-horse parade was held every Whit Monday. It started in Bury Meadow or Higher Barracks, and judging took place first. The mounted police or a band headed the procession; next came the heavy draught horses belonging to the council, then timber haulers, railway horses of the Great Western and the South Western, then light van horses and cobs, milk round horses and ponies, and finally privately owned horses. Tails and manes were plaited with coloured ribbons, brasses made to shine, hooves polished. St Anne's Well Brewery had a dray pulled by a popular and well-behaved horse called Acty. Once the band began to play he swayed in time to the music as if he were dancing. There were cups and rosettes to be won and proudly displayed.

P.G. Martin recorded the arrival of automatic traffic lights in Exeter in the late 1920s. They were a novelty, and to warn approaching drivers banners were hung across the main roads and posters were fixed on tram standards. Exeter was one of the first towns, if not the first, to introduce this form of traffic control and to dispense with policemen on point duty. Roger Brien tells how a Taunton family acquired a car in about 1930 and piled in to try it out on a run into Exeter. They had never heard of traffic lights and had never seen any. They arrived in Exeter, took no notice of a red light at London Inn Square and narrowly missed a Parnell's coal cart. The horse reared up and coal was scattered across the entire junction. A policeman came over to speak to the car's driver, and he was so embarrassed that he never visited Exeter again. In January 1939 Councillor Vincent Thompson reported on the Ministry of Transport's experiments with traffic lights in the city. He said the Ministry had paid 60 per cent of the cost but 40 per cent had been borne by the ratepayers. He reported that the experiment had failed, however, and that traffic lights should not be installed at the city's expense.

Poverty in the West Quarter was alleviated by a soup kitchen in the Lower Market, hot dinners from the Exe Island Inland Mission, and the Farthing Breakfast scheme. For the latter, citizens put aside the odd farthings they received at a time when most prices ended in 11¾d., and handed them in at the *Express and Echo* office in High Street. A list of donors and amounts was printed, and rich children looked eagerly to see their name in the paper. Poor children paid a farthing for the subsidised breakfast: 'as much cocoa as you could drink, plus three doorsteps of bread, one spread with butter and the other two with jam': 'A farthing, of all coins the least, helps turn a fast into a feast.'

Heavitree was not such a poor, crowded area. Exeter families went to stay there for healthy summer holidays: after all, it was a good mile away. As a settlement, standing at the crossing of ancient ridgeways, it may be older than Exeter. Its church was the mother church of the three early churches outside Exeter's walls: St Sidwell's, St David's and St Leonard's. Perhaps it was a feeling of superiority that made Heavitree resist annexation by Exeter in 1900 when St Thomas joined the city. It held out for 13 years, then on 24 November 1913 'Sergeant Snell at the stroke of midnight led a posse of police to take over the new area'. This added a population of 11,000 to Exeter's 49,000. Three existing wards (Heavitree, Polsloe and Wonford) were joined by three new creations: St Loye's, St Mark's and Whipton.

Early in the 20th century the area within the city walls was still the main centre of activity. It is true that rows of terraced brick houses had replaced the orchards and fields below Union Road, along Pinhoe Road and west of the river, but shopkeepers still lived over the shop and there were enough inhabited premises on the principal streets and behind Fore Street, Sidwell Street and Paris Street for the pavements to be crowded all week and for the churches to be full on Sundays. People thronged to Northernhay to listen to the band, to Queen Street for concerts in the Civic Hall, or to London Inn Square for the Theatre Royal or the Hippodrome.

Henry Wood conducted a matinée concert at the Hippodrome in 1909. During the midday rehearsal he noticed an appalling smell. The manager explained that a visiting menagerie had made way for the orchestra, but he had not been able to move the sea-lion's tank, which was under the stage. A large supply of rotting fish kept the animal quiet, but the audience had to put up with the stench, and the sound of splashing water during the softer passages.

Fred Karno, the impresario, was born in Waterbeer Street in 1866, the son of a cabinet-maker called Westcott. Karno took over the lease of the Hippodrome and brought Marie Lloyd there, as well as the then unknown Charlie Chaplin. The Karno Company took Chaplin and young Stan Laurel on tour in this country and as far as America in 1910. Their knockabout comedy led to the use of the term 'Karno' for any botched-up jobs. When war broke out the drill-sergeants used it as sarcastic abuse. A marching song (coincidentally using a hymn-tune by Exeter's Samuel Sebastian Wesley) went like this:

We are Fred Karno's army,
The ragtime infantry,
We cannot shoot, we cannot fight,
What ruddy use are we?
But when we get to Berlin
The Kaiser he will say,
'Hoch, hoch, mein Gott, what a ruddy fine lot
Are the ragtime infantry'.

The *Echo* headline of 31 July 1914 was 'Europe Under Arms, Great Powers Ready to Fight'. On Sunday 2 August there was a War Special Edition: 'Europe Ablaze, War Declared by Germany'. The well-to-do rushed to stockpile food and coal, clearing the stores. Prices rose. Flower shows, regattas and cricket matches were cancelled. There were no Sunday School treats because the trains were needed to carry men and guns to the ports for France.

In December 1914 volunteers enlisted in 'Exeter's Own' regiment at the Guildhall, receiving rosettes in the city's colours. Canadian troops passed through *en route* from Plymouth to Salisbury. At St David's station passing troops were given hot tea, buns and good luck cards by the mayoress and her committee. The Devonshire Regiment crossed to France and fought in 63 battles, with huge losses of life. A battalion of the Black Watch was camped at St Sidwell's School: the children had never seen Scotsmen with kilts before. The soldiers left late one night to go over to France, and the children were allowed to stay up to watch them marching off playing their bagpipes. In battle they won some VCs, but they were nearly all slaughtered.

In September 1915 the king and queen visited the war-wounded in the RD&E. It was the first time that distinguished visitors used 'mechanical traction', and onlookers used to clattering hooves and tossing manes found that motor cars glided surprisingly softly and steadily over the tarred wooden blocks of the main thoroughfares. In November 1915 German guns captured at Halluch were exhibited near the castle gatehouse. Several schools, including St Sidwell's and Bishop Blackall, were turned into hospitals for the wounded. Hospital trains came into Queen Street station and the casualties who could walk went on foot. When Germany started using gas in 1917 soldiers blinded by the gas went along in file, each holding onto the man in front. The wounded soldiers

125 In 1916 the Devonshire Regiment had one battalion of mounted infantry which trained not on horseback but on bicycles, with rifles carried as smartly as possible. The bicycles did not accompany them to France or Mesopotamia.

wore bright blue serge uniforms and red ties; little dolls dressed like this were sold to raise funds for them.

Most traffic was still horse-propelled and benefactors remembered that they needed water to refresh them. A drinking fountain at the junction of New North Road and Bonhay Road was erected in 1915 'in memory of Q.R. Kay of this city and his wife, brothers and sister ... by their daughter E.S. Strong', while a trough for cattle and horses on Topsham Road opposite the gate of the artillery barracks was the bequest of Mary Heathfield in 1917.

In 1917 there was a severe frost, with skating under Exe Bridge. A bicycle was ridden from Cowley Bridge to the fish quay, and an ox was roasted on the ice. Also in 1917 there were food shortages, with no potatoes to be had.

128 Between
St David's Church and the
Attwyll-Palmer almshouses
are the buildings of Hele's
School, which range
from the small limestone
school-house of 1850 to
the redbrick extensions of
1909 and 1932, and army
huts for the overspill. The
planned move to a larger
site on the bypass was to
be delayed by 20 years,
until 1959.

Willey's made aeroplane parts and shell cases for the war. For years the company was Exeter's largest employer. When the hooter went at knocking-off time, 1,000 bikes would stream past the bridge.

At 11am on 11 November 1918 the war came to an end. Church bells rang. Crowds filled the cathedral and the overspill stood outside the west front. The bishop, mayor and Corporation gave thanks to God. The cathedral choir led the crowds in the singing of 'All People That on Earth Do Dwell'.

Once, in about 1920, the Devon County Show was held in Mr Littlejohn's field off Buddle Lane. Bulls, cows, sheep and horses came from St David's station, together with a great crowd of farmers, carts, stock and traps. The lane remained rural until about

129 In 1907-8 it was thought that there would never be another war, and that the rows of houses off Thornton Hill could be extended across the redundant barracks. But the barracks are still there in this postcard of the early 1920s. The county cricket ground at the top of the picture had been inaugurated in 1902 with a match against a team headed by Dr W.G. Grace.

1923, when the council built 64 houses for people moving from back-to-back slums in the city. The present occupants have the benefit of the Buddle Lane Family Unit nursery centre in Merrivale Road, where the King of Spain's daughter helped teach in 1988 as part of her child-psychology course at Exeter University.

The City Basin was fairly quiet in the 1920s, only three ships visiting regularly. A small tanker, the *Ben Johnson*, came from Southampton every month to fill BP's storage-tank. A Swedish ship supplied the large timber mill. Salt cod from Newfoundland was brought to a warehouse; the fish was tasty but generally known as 'toe-rag'.

Exeter has two war memorials – one on Northernhay for the city and one for the county on the cathedral green. When the latter was erected in 1921 to honour the dead of the First World War there was a lot of discussion about where it should be sited. The Victorian church of St Mary Major still stood in front of the cathedral's west front,

130 County War Memorial, Cathedral Yard.

131 At the top of this picture from the early 1920s St James's School and Church can be seen next to the Grecians' football field. Sidwell Street Methodist church is as yet unchallenged by any massive cinema auditorium. The Acland Hotel stands on York Road, Acland Terrace has six houses and Summerland Street is a residential area.

occupying much of the grassy area. It was decided to place the cross in a prominent position to be seen when approached from High Street through Broadgate. It faces east, standing on a hypothetical line drawn from the high altar through the nave of the cathedral. The memorial was designed by Sir Edwin Lutyens, who was well known for having recently designed India's new capital at Delhi. He was also the architect of Castle Drogo at Drewsteignton and also designed the national memorial, the Cenotaph in Whitehall. Sir Edwin attended the unveiling of Exeter's memorial by the Prince of Wales (later Edward VIII) on Whit Monday 1921. To make the cross a large block of Dartmoor granite was specially hewn from a quarry at Haytor that had not been used for many years. Sir Edwin said, 'It is out of one stone, the biggest I could get. It should endure for ever.' The cross is 30ft tall, standing on a plinth approached by three broad steps. The arms of the cross are no wider than the plinth. The names of Devon's war dead were inscribed on parchment in a roll of honour bound in vellum, embossed with gold. Three copies of this roll were made, one for the cathedral, one for the county and one in a copper casket, which the prince placed in a hollow in the memorial. It listed in alphabetical order 11,600 men and women 'of all ranks and all conditions' – sailors, soldiers, merchant seamen, minesweepers and hospital workers. The crowds hoping to attend the unveiling of the war memorial were let down by the railway service. When masses of wounded soldiers, Scouts, Guides, army cadets and ordinary Devonians wanted to travel to Exeter the railway service was 'partially suspended'. The *Western Times* reported that every conceivable conveyance had to be pressed into service, even a motor lorry. It sounds as if horse-drawn carts and wagons came into their own. The young Prince of Wales spent 10 days touring the Duchy lands, staying at Bicton, and regretted that his busy programme did not allow him to fit in a visit to the inside of

Exeter Cathedral. He enraptured the crowds by 'smiling in that half shy manner of his which has won hearts wherever the Union Jack is flown'. He even stood up in his car to give everybody a clear view of him. The newspaper headline read: 'Prince stands up'.

After the ceremony the prince's motorcade drove past thousands of cheering Devonians, 50,000 in High Street and Sidwell Street. The premises of Messrs Walton & Co. (they were on the corner of High Street and Queen Street, where Marks and Spencer is now) displayed a large banner reading 'You're welcome, Prince, us be praper glad to see ee' in red and blue letters on a white background with a life-sized portrait in the centre, flanked with his crest and evergreens. Messrs Ross's establishment (near Eastgate) was decorated with rosettes of purple paper and gold. The Prince's car went on to pass St Luke's College. At the top of Heavitree Road the children made good use of the raised kerbs by sitting on them. The newspaper reported that 'the garden streets, such as Blackboy, Polsloe, College and St Leonard's Roads added cheerfulness – trees in full spring blossomings: lilac, laburnum, may, chestnut, clematis'. The motorcade proceeded past the Deaf School on Topsham Road, and the prince allowed the car to slow down as it passed through Exton and Topsham. Whit Monday had been a lovely sunny day. All that was left for the happy crowds was to try to get home without the help of the railway.

The city's war memorial was also created in 1921. From Queen Street it can be seen high against the sky on the summit of the rising slope of Northernhay Gardens. The sculptor was John Angel, born in Newton Abbot. A female figure of Victory flourishes a laurel wreath overhead and pierces a dragon with a sword at her feet. She stands on a 20ft high granite plinth. Four bronze figures of representative war heroes sit against it: a soldier, a sailor astride the hull of a ship, a nurse holding a bandage and a prisoner of war in chains. This ambitious work cost over £6,000. Shortly after finishing it Angel emigrated to the United States and worked on the cathedrals in New York.

14

Between the Wars

In the 1920s an Exeter GP, Dr Lovely, was horrified by some of the slum conditions in which some of his patients lived, in cramped, sunless, rat-infested courts and alleys, mostly in the West Quarter. In 1926, with other concerned citizens, he set up the Exeter Workmen's Dwellings Company Limited, in Bedford Circus, which raised funds with £1 shares. For each family housed the local authority had to promise to demolish their former dwelling. The first project was 30 three-bedroom houses built in Looe Road. These were followed by 50 houses in Mildmay Close, Foxhayes Road and Clayton Road: built using low-interest loans from the Great Western Railway Society, these were for railway employees. By 1939 the company had built 550 houses and flats, and the 1942 Blitz destroyed most of the remaining slums. In 1954 the association became the Exeter Housing Society.

The River Exe was the scene of a bizarre activity after the First World War. A millionaire businessman, Thomas Mills, had been experimenting on the east coast of Scotland to train seagulls to detect the presence of enemy U-boats. He continued his research on the Exe, filling model submarines with fish to condition seagulls to flock around periscopes and reveal the presence of U-boats. He stayed in the Imperial Hotel in Exmouth, writing an explanation, *The Fateful Seagull*, for private circulation. The scheme was not adopted by the government.

Between the wars motor buses began to serve nearly all the villages, bringing people into Exeter for their shopping.

Memories of city life between the wars were collected by the Fountain Community Association for their series of booklets *People Talking*. Residents had fond memories of the Devonshire Regiment when they were in the Higher Barracks: 'They would play their cheerful regimental marching song "Over the fields and turnips". They used to march down to the cathedral for their Sunday morning church parade and afterwards they would give a concert on the parade ground that the public could attend. It was the

custom then to promenade around, like at Hyde Park, the women with their parasols and their Sunday dresses and the fellas just slowly walking around, while these chaps were playing their military music.'

Often bullocks were driven from Queen Street station goods yard, up York Road into Sidwell Street, through an arch to a slaughter yard on the corner of Summerland Street, about where the launderette is now. Sheep were also driven up Sidwell Street and Blackboy Road, and into the country to farms. The trams had to slow to a crawl behind the flocks.

Mr H. Aggett had some atmospheric memories of life in the city at this tiime:

> On Saturday nights, walking up Sidwell Street, there was an air of excitement. People would be queuing up in London Inn Square for the second house of the Hippodrome. The shops were open till late and brightly lit. The pavements were packed with people. The trams clattered up, bang, bang, bang, the conductor stamping his foot on the bell. The butchers were selling their meat off cheap – no refrigeration then. Greengrocers were selling off bruised fruit and bakers were getting rid of yesterday's loaves. Occasionally a pub door would open and a burst of song would be heard, the old favourites, Nelly Dean and all that.

> The electricity company had an office on Sidwell Street. Every afternoon, at teatime, just before it got dark, you'd see some fellows come out of there with a pole on their shoulders. They'd go along hooking the switch on; the lamps used to have a little catch hanging down. Next morning they used to start all over again and then they'd push them up.

Other memories of pre-war Sidwell Street, before half of it was blitzed in 1942 and much of the rest was demolished in the 1960s, include horses brasses shining on the ponies waiting outside Hammetts Dairy, their carts full of milk churns.

Between the shops and the many pubs were side alleys leading to enclosed courts with cottages packed in at right-angles to the street. These were not gloomy slums but tight-knit communities in secluded closes – 'little havens, another world, trees reaching up to the sky'. They have all been cleared away, and so have the adjacent streets of terrace houses that provided St Sidwell's Church with a large congregation.

In 1925-7 the city council constructed a bypass through the Streatham estate, from Union Road to Cowley Bridge Road, to provide work for the unemployed. This road was a condition of the sale of the Streatham estate by the Thornton-West family to the university college, which had outgrown its premises in Gandy Street. The hill-crest beside the cricket field was cut through with a pick and shovel; little trucks running on rails tipped the earth into the Hoopern valley and were pulled back by a carthorse. The new road was opened and named by the Prince of Wales, and became an evening promenade for lovers. Motorists boycotted it at first, as they wanted to drive through the city centre. Now the university finds it useful for side-of-the-road parking, and when an orchestral concert in the great hall coincides with a play at the Northcott, a tailback of cars with twinkling red lights builds up all along the valley and up the hill.

A favourite city-centre rendezvous in the 1920s and '30s was Dellers café-restaurant on the corner of Bedford Street and High Street, previously the site of the Half Moon Inn. Dellers' main entrance in Bedford Street was up steep steps through a large arched doorway, flanked by decorated columns supporting an entablature on which reclined female figures below a large scrolled pediment. The interior resembled a theatre, with three storeys of galleries overlooking all the comings and goings on the ground floor. There were bright friezes of exotic scenes and private niches for couples. An ensemble of violin, cello and piano played for quicksteps, foxtrots, tangos and waltzes on the sprung dancing floor. The waitresses wore green dresses and white aprons, with green clips in their hair. It was a treat to come for tea and cream cakes or dinner before a show at the Theatre Royal, or wedding receptions. At one 21st birthday party the surprise present, a motor car, was driven down the main staircase. Ice cream was made on the premises, while cream cakes were baked in St Thomas, in Buller Road. There was an early automatic dishwasher.

Edwin Deller, a grocer, plumber and glazier, had founded the first Dellers café in Paignton in 1844. Dellers opened in Exeter in Martins Lane, before the magnificent building in Bedford Street was opened on Tuesday 5 December 1916. The architects were Hyams and Hobgen of Paignton. In 1933 the Dellers chain was sold to Cadena Cafés but kept the name Dellers. Although the café was not directly hit in the 1942 Blitz, it caught fire from flaming debris blown along from adjacent buildings. Substantial parts still remained and the government recommended rebuilding behind the surviving façades, but the council went ahead with demolition.

There is no longer a school in St Thomas called John Stocker, although he was rightly honoured in this way for many years. When the St Thomas School Board held its first meeting in March 1871 one of its members was the young John Stocker, then aged 23. By 1921 he had served an amazing half-century on the education committee, and he was honoured by having the St Thomas Boys School named after him. This school burnt down in the 1930s and in 1936 Stocker laid the foundation stone for a new school with the same name, a little higher up Dunsford Road. John Stocker's memorial is one of a handful that survived the clearance of the parish church's graveyard by the Rev. Philip Henton. An upright stone with its inscription still clearly legible remembers the builder James Stocker, his wife Sarah and their fourth son, John Stocker, OBE, JP, born 31 January 1848, died 2 March 1940. It lists his unparalleled record of public service: chairman of St Thomas School Board 1892-1900, chairman of Exeter Education Committee 1908-40, alderman of the city and county of Exeter 1910-40, sheriff of the county of the city of Exeter 1915-16, and adds one word – 'faithful'. In 1934 he was described as one of the strongest churchmen in the city. Stocker lived at 66 Cowick Street, next to the family's building and undertaking business. He was a lifelong bachelor and liked his staff to join him in morning prayers.

Stocker Road on the Streatham campus of the University of Exeter leads uphill from the Prince of Wales Road to the Northcott Theatre. This road and Perry Road were named in 1932 after the two longest-serving members of the university council and the college committee that preceded it. Stocker Road was not surfaced until 1957 and its course was moved slightly when the new university library was built, but there has been no talk of changing its name.

Manor Road leads to Montgomery School. Alderman John Stocker laid its foundation stone on 28 October 1929, and the school was opened in 1930 by the Bishop of Plymouth. The field it stands on was previously known as the Easter Fair Field and was owned by Mr Kerswell. He kept one or two Jersey cows on it for 51 weeks of the year, then on the Monday before Easter the fair arrived, with helter-skelter, distorting mirrors, swing-boats and so on. In 1877 a novelty was the switchback railway, which did 'a roaring biz'. Once Emmanuel Church was built the congregation found the fairground organs very noisy during the Good Friday services.

St Sidwell's Church of England Combined School is the setting of two children's books, *Gowie Corby Plays Chicken* and *The Turbulent Term of Tyke Tiler*; these were written by Gene Kemp, who taught at the school in the 1970s. The latter won the Carnegie Medal. Both stories make use of the school's unusual features, its early foundation and the rich variety of backgrounds of today's pupils. Some of their surnames feature in the earliest recorded history of Exeter; some local families have come recently from Vietnam, China, Pakistan or the Caribbean; some parents are postgraduate students or lecturers at the university; some cook the best fish and chips in the city. The school is still Church of England but its pupils are of many faiths. It dates back to 1665 when it was established by the Dean and Chapter in a small schoolroom in the churchyard. There were several benefactors, including the Rev. John Bury, father of a rector of Exeter College, Oxford. The school building was relocated in 1803, and substantially extended in 1854 and 1895. By the 1900s St Sidwell's was a school ahead of its time, teaching French, shorthand and typing. The bishop opened new classrooms in 1973 for the Combined First and Middle Schools, which catered for children aged 5 to 12. The City Football Team was previously called St Sidwell's Old Boys, and Harry Snell, in *People Talking*, recalls how teacher and boys disagreed on the important subject of football:

All my family – there were seven of us – all went through the same classes at St Sidwell's school. The headmaster was Teddy Nicholls. He was a rugby player – course it was a rugby school. He tried to force rugby on you. The majority of us wasn't interested in rugby – soccer was our game. Every day at lunchtime some of us would play soccer in the playground. We'd have one fellow on the corner of the railway bridge in Pennsylvania – he could see Mr Nicholls' house. When Mr Nicholls came out, then that boy would pass it on to a boy down the corner of York Road; that one would wave his arms to the boy that was posted up outside the school gates. As soon as you had the signal, 'He's coming!' instead of playing soccer you'd be playing rugby. And if you were in Belmont Park playing soccer – if anyone reported to Mr. Nicholls that some of his boys were playing soccer, you used to get the cane the next morning. And this was for playing soccer after school.

133 Edward Ashworth's building for St Sidwell's Church of England School in York Road, sadly demolished after 150 years.

The school's log books record the naughtiness of the Govier boys, Walter, George, Charles and William. Walter was reprimanded for running to the pump instead of to prayers, and George was told off for smoking in school. Worse was to come. George was made to stand in front of the whole school while he was ceremoniously thrown out. He had kept his school fee of 6d. and falsified the entry in the register.

One of the pleasures of travelling by train is the opportunity to catch up with one's reading without any distractions. Most people carry a paperback on their journeys, but these have not always been available on the stations. It was on one of the platforms of Exeter St David's station that someone spotted this gap in the market, and Penguin Books was born. In the 1930s publisher Allen Lane was travelling back from visiting one of his authors, Agatha Christie, who had been born in Torquay in 1890 and continued to live in the Torbay area. Waiting for his connection at Exeter, Lane noticed that the bookstall had only an uninspiring selection of magazines and dated Victorian novels. Anyone who wanted a more satisfying classic or a modern work in their pocket had to smuggle in a Tauchnitz paperback from the continent, published in Leipzig since

1841. The Tauchnitz Collection of British and American Authors eventually listed 5,370 titles – but for copyright reasons they were banned from sale in this country. Lane thought people would buy good books if the price was really low. He wrote: 'We believed in the existence in this country of a vast reading public for intelligent books at a low price, and staked everything on it.' Until then he had worked for his uncle's publishing house, Bodley Head, and had risen to become managing director. In 1935 he set up his new company without any backing from his fellow directors. The offices were in a church crypt and staff had to keep quiet during services; their pay included an extra penny a day to use the public toilets at the nearest station. When the secretary suggested the name Penguin Books, a member of the office staff was sent to London Zoo to sketch a penguin. Advertisements on the back pages helped to keep the price to 6d., which was about the cost of a packet of cigarettes. Hardbacks cost about fifteen times as much. The cardboard covers showed the distinctive penguin logo and wide bands of colour: orange was fiction, green was crime and blue was biography. The first ten titles included works by Dorothy L. Sayers, Hemingway, Compton Mackenzie and Agatha Christie. When Lane overheard someone asking for a Pelican book by mistake, he picked up the idea and added a range of non-fiction with a pelican logo in 1937. Puffins for children followed, Ptarmigan puzzle books and Peregrines. The idea he had at St David's had borne rich fruit.

Between the wars, as car ownership spread, Exeter High Street became a notorious bottleneck for holiday jams, despite the 1927 northern bypass.

Slum clearance projects re-housed hundreds of families in the fields round Buddle Lane and Burnthouse Lane.

The comedian Tommy Cooper lived in Fords Road, St Thomas, as a young boy in the 1930s, sometimes helping his parents sell ice-cream out of the front window of their small house. He attended Mount Radford School, a private prep school in St Leonard's.

Dame Georgiana Buller (1884-1953), the only daughter of General Redvers Buller, devoted her life to hospital administration. She instigated the foundation of the orthopaedic hospital, built on former Veitch nursery ground, which was opened on 16 November 1927 by the Duke and Duchess of York and named Princess Elizabeth after their baby daughter. Rosemary Sutcliff, the brilliant author of historical novels for children, suffered from Still's Disease and spent long stretches in this hospital as a child, in a ward designed to be so healthily airy that it had no walls or ceiling. Dame Georgiana also founded the rehabilitation hospital of St Loyes in 1937 and its school of occupational therapy in 1944.

In 1931 there was a proposal to demolish six city churches as they were redundant, because so many residents had left the centre. St Paul's and St John's were pulled down, Allhallows was deconsecrated, and the Nazis eventually saw to St Lawrence's and Bedford Chapel; though St Mary Major survived until the 1970s.

15

The Second World War

The Odeon opened in 1937, a large luxury cinema with a restaurant on the first floor. In *Exeter Phoenix* (1946) Thomas Sharp deplored its 'great hump-backed mass on the summit of the Sidwell Street ridge – a shapeless lump of a building which rides the city like a totalitarian mammonite cathedral'.

Exeter Airport was built on requisitioned land by May 1937. The first plane to land brought films of the coronation of King George VI to be shown in cinemas, and photographs of the ceremony for the *Express and Echo*. The airport opened for business on 31 May but the official opening was not until 20 July 1938. When the RAF needed bases Exeter Airport was one of the few already in existence. From June 1940 it was an active operational fighter base for squadrons of Fighter Command, which had retreated from France. Hurricanes were scrambled here to counter attacks on Portland, Southampton and Portsmouth by Junkers and Messerschmitts. Polish and Czech squadrons also operated from Exeter and in 1944 the American Air Force came with Dakota troop carriers: 47 of them dropped troops over Normandy.

During the Second World War Exeter did not expect to be a target. Evacuees from London crowded the pavements, mostly young mothers with toddlers and perambulators, and the London School of Medicine for Women moved down here. The first year of the war, known as the 'phoney war', ended when France and the Low Countries were invaded in the Blitzkrieg of June 1940. Exhausted men rescued from Dunkirk shambled through the streets without equipment or uniforms.

The Blitzkrieg in Exeter was a reprisal for the RAF's attack on the German Baltic town of Lübeck on 28-9 March 1942. 234 of our aircraft dropped 144 tons of incendiaries and 160 tons of high explosive bombs, causing the timber town to blaze fiercely. The Nazis declared revenge, picking historic English towns from their Baedeker guide books: Exeter, Bath, Norwich and Canterbury. The foretaste came on 24 and 25/6 April, first in the Okehampton Road area, and then in the cathedral precincts, Paris Street, Prospect

134 The cathedral escaped major damage during the war, possibly because enemy pilots valued it as a landmark, just as RAF pilots would turn left for Hamburg at Cologne Cathedral. However, bombs on 24 April and 4 May 1942 destroyed the side-chapel of St James, between the choir and the chapter house.

135 St Mary Arches with its Norman pillars had apparently escaped the blitz of the night of 4 May, but when the sisters of St Wilfrid's took the girls in their care to a service there the next day, a smouldering fire-bomb burst into flames, destroying part of the roof. The nuns rescued the processional cross, although its base was burning.

Park, Regent's Park, Regent Street and Hill Barton Road. In these two raids there were 79 deaths and 121 wounded. On 4 May 30 Junkers and 88 German bombers followed the line of the River Exe under a clear moonlit sky. At a height of 500ft they unloaded flares, then 10,000 incendiary bombs and 75 tons of high explosive. For one and a half hours 30 German planes swept low over burning streets with machine-guns spitting. Flames spread along High Street, Sidwell Street, South Street, Fore Street, Paris Street, Southernhay and Belmont Road, and the districts of Newtown and St Leonards. A high explosive bomb on the cathedral wrecked St James's chapel and some vaulting in the south aisle. The flames from the blazing city could be seen as far away as Plymouth. A German broadcaster boasted: ' Exeter was a jewel; we have destroyed it.' Casualties amounted to 156 civilian deaths and 8 servicemen, and more than 550 people were injured. Of the 20,000 houses in the city 1,500 were totally destroyed (800 of these in St Sidwell's – the close-packed terraces between Sidwell Street and Paris Street, the warm communities of Russell Street, Cheeke Street and Summerland Street) and 2,700 seriously damaged. Buildings destroyed amounted to 9 churches, 6 banks, 26 pubs, 5 off-licences, 4 chemists, a cinema, over 400 shops, nearly 150 offices and over 50 warehouses. Landmarks which were destroyed included Dellers Café, Bedford Circus, Bamfylde House and the Lower Market. Important buildings that remained unscathed included the Guildhall, most of the cathedral, St Nicholas's Priory, Tuckers Hall and Rougemont Castle. The city library, St Luke's College, the post office, the city hospital and a number of churches were wrapped in flames. A string of bombs was dropped across the Hoopern valley, hitting houses in West Avenue, scarring the valley side and leaving the crater that formed the small pond outside Queen's Building. Shops burnt fiercely because their fronts were all studding – lath and plaster. Two thousand people sheltered in the city swimming baths, while others took refuge in cellars or in the crypt of St Sidwell's Church. The church was severely damaged; its tower was declared unsafe and a sapper was given orders to demolish it at noon. The rector, the Rev. M.V. Narracott, risked his life to rescue irreplaceable registers and silver from the vestry, which was under teetering masonry. The tower of St Sidwell's Church was dangerously damaged, but the body of the church was safe and used for services. Unfortunately the sappers who were sent to blow up the tower did it so clumsily that it fell on the rest of the church.

A heavy bomb came down on St Sidwell's Avenue and houses on both sides of the road went down like playing cards or dominoes. Even today York Road clearly has houses missing. Soldiers were billeted there, and when incendiaries set fire to the houses their small arms ammunition went off, sounding like machine-gun fire. An incendiary

136 Experts quickly installed steel ties across the nave to hold the main walls until the two south buttresses could be replaced, otherwise the whole cathedral could have collapsed.

bomb was about 2ft long with a flame at the end. Fire-watchers had to deal with them quickly with a shovel and a bucket of sand. While most of South Street burned, the Baptist church and the Catholic church were saved by the priest and two curates, who tirelessly doused the incendiaries with buckets of sand and buckets of water.

Along the length of the eastern High Street, from London Inn Square to past Bedford Street, only one building survived: St Stephen's Church. Its tower burned, flames leapt out of the top like a furnace, the ring holding the bells broke and the three bells came crashing to the ground. Its two safes survived, one of which held all the silverware of the five central parishes.

The strong wooden doors of the rooms holding the city's precious archives smouldered but did not give way. The city library lost 100,000 books, but an appeal went out for people to return books they had on loan in order to restock the shelves. For years afterwards the library shelves were not considered safe enough for the public to access them. They had to write down the title they wanted for the librarian to fetch.

The city hospital suffered direct hits, which killed 18 patients, destroyed many of its buildings and burnt all its records. The RD&E escaped major damage, but not the terror of bombs falling all around and fires raging. Incendiary bombs on the roof, and one which penetrated the basement stores, were quickly put out by the ARP warden, the porter and terrified young nurses, who then rushed to evacuate the upstairs wards to the basement corridor. A letter home from a 19-year-old student nurse, Betty Biggs, reassured her family that she had survived:

> The bombs came whistling down and blew the blackout down and the windows and doors off their hinges … and the children started to cry …

137   A similar fate befell the Globe Hotel, which had stood for centuries between South Street and the corner of the Cathedral Close. Weary fire-fighters and bemused office-workers saw it still standing on the morning after the blitz, but by the end of the day a raging fire had destroyed the hotel and the neighbouring shops.

A strong wind was blowing. The dive bombing and machine-gunning were dreadful … the sky was scarlet with fires … Burnt and bleeding casualties were brought in … Fires raged mountain high all round, fire brigades all chasing up and down the street and the place was swimming with water and mud.

When she finally went to her room she found it had lost half a wall and there were broken glass, bricks and dirt everywhere. For a week the nurses hardly had a chance to sleep, and no time to change out of their uniforms. Matron Stopford-Smyth was on duty all hours. Secretary John Sullivan worked for three days non-stop. Beryl Raphael began a nine-month pre-nursing course in 1943 and found it was more like domestic service: cleaning saucepans, making 40 junkets every morning for poorly people, and summoning up all her courage when a huge pike was donated for her to gut.

Bishop Curzon occupied Cumbre at the top of Pennsylvania Road from 1939 to 1944. Frank Sleeman remembered him standing in the road one day, a dignified hitch-hiker, more used to raising his hands in blessing. 'I am due to take a service at the cathedral, and my chauffeur has not turned up.'

Exeter had a well-organised Home Guard, as the Local Defence Volunteers were renamed at Winston Churchill's suggestion. They were kept busy on patrol, manning observation posts and road blocks and checking that all the petrol pumps were immobilised every night. They created a 'blue line' 14½ miles long around the city, guarded by trenches and barbed wire, and they practised increasingly ambitious training exercises simulating enemy attacks. Exeter Home Guard was the first in the country to have its own carrier pigeon service. During the Blitz of May 1942 the Home Guard helped

138   The Lower Market was destroyed. It had been designed in 1835 by the local architect Charles Fowler (as was Covent Garden). Anyone who wants to see its like must travel to Australia, where an emigrant from South Street modelled the market hall of Castlemaine, Victoria, on his childhood memories of Fowler's market.

control traffic, salvage safes from bank vaults and clear debris, especially from Castle
Street, so that new batteries could reach the telephone exchange. No. 2 Company of
Exeter's Home Guard had their headquarters in the old St James's School next to the
football ground. They saved this building and fought the blaze in the adjacent church
from 4am to 7am. Hot and thirsty, they were told that the quartermaster had tea, milk
and sugar but no gas to boil up the water for tea. An enterprising individual put the
kettle on the end of an iron pole and poked it through the church door into the flames.
The city's gas supply was shut off because of multiple fractures in the pipes and holes
in the gasometers, and therefore the danger of explosions. About 400 gas-workers were
called in from outside areas and the supply was restored in 11 days.

Willey's works in St Thomas made some of the components for the Mulberry
Harbours needed for the D-Day landings in Normandy. Before D-Day, American
troops were billeted in Exeter. The United States still practised segregation, including
in the army, and to prevent street fighting the white soldiers were accommodated on
the city side of the river. The blacks were housed in tents on the county ground in
St Thomas. They sat on the low wall of the parish churchyard in Cowick Street, tossing
pennies to the local kids, who had never seen black faces before. The swing-bridge on
the bypass at Countess Wear played an important part in the preparations for D-Day.
In May 1944 over a period of three days and nights it was used for a rehearsal of the
crucial and successful glider-borne attack on the similar bridges over the Canal de
Caen (Pegasus Bridge) and the River Orne (Horsa Bridge) on the night of 5/6 June.

Soon after the war the housing stock began to be repaired. A plaque in Isca Road
records: 'This stone was laid on 27th September 1945 by Sir Malcolm Trustram, Chairman
of the Building Apprenticeship and Training Council, to commemorate the fact that
these houses were the first war-damaged houses rebuilt in Great Britain by Apprentices
under the scheme formulated by that Council.'

A plan for post-war reconstruction was commissioned from the town-planning
expert Thomas Sharp. His report was published as a book entitled *Exeter Phoenix* in
1946. Old etchings and photographs of surviving architectural treasures illustrated

141 Allhallows' Church, Bartholomew Yard, became redundant and was used as a corset factory. One West Quarter couple were married in this church, then their daughter was employed there making parachutes, and finally their son helped to demolish it.

Exeter's individual character as a historic city set among green hills. Sharp believed that the 'intimacy of scale' of the pre-war streets could be recreated in modern architecture. The ruins of St Catherine's almshouses and the vicars choral hall should remain as a memorial of war, but he did not approve of erecting replicas of destroyed buildings, or of restoring, for example, the shell of Bedford Circus. In his view the war damage had literally cleared the way for long-needed improvements. The cathedral had been hidden from sight even from neighbouring streets, but when the ruins had been bulldozed away it stood fully revealed. Sharp suggested retaining a vista towards its north tower from a pedestrian shopping street. The result was England's first pedestrian precinct, named Princesshay by our future queen in 1949. Sharp also prized the glimpses of the Devon hills even from the centre of the city: he did not want good farming land or market gardens to be sacrificed to development. He also recommended the creation of green areas among the streets, in particular a 'green moat' of open space immediately outside the city walls, so as to expose the whole circuit to view. This has been achieved in two stretches of Southernhay at least, by opening the back gardens which abutted the wall. As for roads, Sharp saw that Exeter was at risk of 'strangulation by traffic'. He recommended an inner ring-road and a relief road for Pinhoe and Blackboy Roads (which was ready in 1949, in time for the princess to name it after her new baby, Prince Charles, born 14 November 1948). Prince Charles Road had initially been planned before the war but was built (by prisoners) after the war. Prince Charles's mother and aunt also have nearby roads named after them. On 21 October 1949, the day that Princesshay was named, Princess Elizabeth also visited the Stoke Hill estate and laid the foundation stone for a block of 14 self-contained flats for elderly people who had been bombed out. An Exeter woman told her sister in Toronto, and she initiated such a successful campaign for the Lord Mayor of London's National Air Raid Distress Fund that it was able to present half the total cost of the finished block. Birmingham, Liverpool, Southampton and Swansea also named their equivalent buildings Toronto. On 1 November 1952 the High Commissioner for Canada declared the house open. It consists of two long wings with sun-verandas that provide covered access to a central common-room. The builders were Woodman & Son, an Exeter firm acknowledged by Frank Sleeman to be even longer established than his own. Some citizens were re-housed on the airy

142 The 1930s Fearis building survived the Blitz to become the Co-op, but was demolished to be replaced by Next.

green Nine Paths Field on Stoke Hill. Exeter had built no council houses between
1933 and 1946, and this development won a gold medal in 1952 from the Ministry
of Housing and Local Government. It is considered an example of the best in local
authority building, thanks to its low density and low elevation. There are plenty of
grassy areas, and motor roads are kept separate from pedestrian ways.

144 The view of the
cathedral from the new
Bedford Street was
thought worth retaining.
The new post office had
a glazed front wall which
framed this view, and the
pedestrian precinct named
by Princess Elizabeth was
aligned to the cathedral's
north tower. Only
single-storey shops were
built on this site, as Thomas
Sharp had suggested.

143 (*Left*) In 1953 the new Bedford Street was built alongside the old one so as not to disrupt the traffic. The carriageway of Bedford Circus in the middle distance bears witness to the graceful curve of the Georgian crescents that have been cleared away.

145 The spacious post-war post office, which has been replaced by a small upstairs one.

146 Princesshay, by the 'feature' where Princess Elizabeth stood to inaugurate Britain's first pedestrian precinct.

147 In February 1958 the opportunity was taken to widen South Street (again), while carefully retaining George's Meeting and Holy Trinity on the left and the White Hart and its neighbours on the right.

148 Paul Street became a traffic-filled bypass between car parks.

16

Mid-Twentieth Century

Bishop Mortimer, licensing the curate in charge of St Stephen's in 1957, told him that his mission was to bear evangelical testimony in the city centre, to justify occupying such a valuable central site. Prebendary Willis explained in 1976 why the church would be used for festival events: God is as interested in our everyday activities as in sacred services on Sundays. The church is in constant use for coffee mornings, exhibitions, jumble sales and concerts as well as christenings, weddings and funerals. There is a welcoming inscription over the door: 'Come ye yourselves apart and rest awhile.'

Airy estates on green hillsides at Whipton, Exwick and Cowick continued to be built, primarily for those made homeless by the bombs. Western Way was built in the 1960s across the devastated hillside between Sidwell Street and Newtown, along a rubble viaduct dumped onto housetops in the Barnfield and elbowing aside the 15th-century Frog Street house as it swept down to Exbridge. There was also a new outer bypass, which became notorious for summer holiday tailbacks. Indeed, the more new roads were built the more traffic came to fill them. John Betjeman spoke out against the motor-car in Exeter in the 1960s, and the distinguished scholar W.G. Hoskins did the same. Honiton Road was to be widened, at the cost of losing two handsome historic houses at the entrance to Exeter, 74 and 76 East Wonford Hill. In his maiden speech to the city council, Hoskins said: 'I think people are more important than roads, and houses more important than cars.' Nevertheless the houses were lost. One of them had a 'highwayman's step' – one stair a different size so that a marauder would trip. Hoskins also felt that Bedford Circus could have been saved to the benefit of the city's landscape and he was concerned about what else might be lost. A cartoon in 1959 was captioned 'Come to Exeter and watch the natives pull it down.' Indeed, part of the Roman wall was cut away for Western Way to be built. Hoskins said of the Luftwaffe: 'They did terrible damage, but since then the city council to my mind has nearly finished the job off.' Planning applications were

not advertised in those days and decisions were taken behind closed doors. Hoskins suspected bribery, and was sued.

There were several areas that caused deep concern. Holiday traffic still went through the High Street. The eastern stretch of it had been widened from 52½ft to 70½ft and there was a proposal to continue the widening through the Tudor part of the High Street, which had survived the Blitz. Unbelievably this might have involved moving the

149 Commentary in November 1959 by Frederick Beamiss, published in the *Express and Echo*.

iconic and historic Guildhall. Hoskins demonstrated that nos 225-6 were Tudor, not later imitations, and felt strongly that the road should not be widened; neither should there be a 'spaghetti junction' over Bull Meadow to cut through the judge's lodgings and reach a new bridge over the Exe. Nor should the scheme to develop the 'golden heart' of Exeter allow the demolition of the Higher Market.

A packed meeting was held in the Civic Hall to set up a civic society (the first outside London) to protect Exeter's distinctive nature. Founder members were Hoskins himself as chairman, Aileen Fox, the archaeologist who had been excavating Roman remains in the post-war rubble aided by a team of Italian prisoners of war, architect John Radford, James Smeall, principal of St Luke's College, Bishop Wilfrid Westall, Dr Fortescue-Ffoulkes and historian Robert Newton. Their original aims were to secure a new library, to create a riverside walk and a walk round the city walls, to win green belt designation and protect open green spaces in the city, to open a museum of local history and archaeology and screen the new reservoir behind the university. Although the Junior Chamber of Commerce wanted the lawns of Southernhay to become car parks, this idea was fought off, and the Hoopern valley was saved from becoming a car park for the university. In 1977 a booklet was produced: *Exeter, A City Saved?* Plaques were put up, including on the city wall, on the site of St Lawrence's Church and on Bodley's birthplace.

Dame Barbara Hepworth, the sculptress, has a worldwide reputation, with deep roots in Yorkshire and in St Ives in Cornwall, but Exeter can claim several important connections. Barbara and her sister each gave birth to triplets. One of Barbara's triplet children, Sarah, was stricken with osteomyelitis in 1943. This was before antibiotics were available and she was treated during a lengthy stay in the Princess Elizabeth Orthopaedic Hospital in Exeter; the distinguished surgeon Norman Capener ensured that she made a complete recovery. This episode led to a lasting friendship between the surgeon and Sarah's mother, which brought her back to figure drawing after years of concentrating on abstract shapes. Capener allowed her to do drawings in the operating theatre of the PEOH, where she stood masked and gowned on a box and used a pen and a sterilised notepad to sketch the skilled hands and tense dedication of the surgeons and nurses. Barbara also attended operations in London hospitals and completed more than 50 drawings in Exeter and London of medical teams at work. Capener was inspired to take up sculpture himself. He stayed in the Hepworth household on the cliffs above St Ives and worked alongside Barbara in her studio.

The Rev. Moelwyn Merchant, professor in the English department of the University of Exeter, also became a friend of Barbara and took up sculpture with such enthusiasm that he eventually left his university chair to spend more time on it. It was he who organised the arrival of the first Hepworth sculpture on the university campus in 1965. The rounded abstract bronze of Mother and Child stands among the trees opposite Queen's Building. In 1966 the University of Exeter made Dame Barbara an honorary doctor of letters. The following year she had a spell in the orthopaedic hospital herself, when in the wet spring she fell and fractured a hip. Norman Capener set it. Barbara looked at the X-rays and decided that the head of her femur looked like the vaulting in Exeter Cathedral.

It was also in 1967 that the Northcott Theatre was built on the university campus; a bronze figure by Barbara Hepworth formed an integral part of the design. It was to stand at the junction of the stairs leading up to the auditorium. Barbara attended the unveiling of the sculpture by the university's chancellor, the Duchess of Devonshire, on 2 November. Moelwyn Merchant officiated at her funeral in 1975.

Exonia Park nestles in the sun-trap of the disused quarries. Blasting stopped in the 1930s, and the land was used for a market garden for a time. The cliff-face shows the characteristic white-veined reddish-mauve of the Pocombe stone, which is a volcanic basalt like Rougemont. Semi-permanent mobile homes with pretty gardens now stand on winding lanes called after birds: Sandpiper Green, Swallow Drive and so on. Eagles' Nest is a grass-verged promenade along the western fringe with beautiful views over the green hills. On 1 April 1988 the boundary of Teignmouth moved south-west to the motorway, and this area was welcomed into Exeter.

St Sidwell's Church was rebuilt in 1957-8. Between 1948 and 1958 services were held in a Nissen hut in the churchyard. (Tesco's, built in 1969, was designed by the same Exeter firm as the church, Lucas, Roberts & Brown.) The church is yellow brick with concrete arches. The war-damage compensation was not enough for a tower: there is a structure supporting one bell behind the east end of the church. The stained-glass west window was designed by James Paterson of Bideford Art School. It shows St Sidwell, and Nazi bombers flying over the blazing church. The great mural on the east wall is by Hans Feibusch, a converted Jewish refugee. He always created his works *in situ*, and used such modern materials as Walpamur distemper: 'Modern people come into church with the impressions of the outside world and all its images, posters, slogans still quivering in their mind … If there are paintings and sculpture around them, their minds can fix on these, quieten gradually and make their ascent into the world of which the pictures are only the shadow … The feeling of our time is of an infinity, but in which we are here and far away at the same time.' His mural shows Christ in glory,

150 The new St James's Church at Stoke Hill roundabout was consecrated in October 1956.

with people of all times and all places joining the angels in praise of the risen Lord. After the restructuring of the church the mural survives behind a wall.

The Stoke Hill estate provides the congregation for the new St James's Church, which was built at Stoke Hill roundabout on Prince Charles Road. The older church of 1836, rebuilt in 1878, destroyed in 1942, still gives its name to the city football field, but its old foundation stone has been brought to the new site. The foundation stone of the new church was laid on the evening of 31 May 1955 by Bishop Mortimer, watched by a crowd overflowing onto the sloping grass verges on the opposite side of the road. There was an unaccustomed stillness, because of a train strike. The new church was designed by Gordon Jackson and built by Soper and Ayers. Scallop-shell decoration, the balconied open arches in the tower and the little pagoda-roof on stilts give a flavour of Compostela. The War Damage Commission paid £42,000 of the cost and the parish raised the remaining £12,000. At the consecration on Saturday 27 October 1956 Bishop Mortimer anointed the font, altars and three consecration-crosses in the walls made from stone salvaged from the blitzed church. The adjoining church hall was opened on 20 June 1968. The architects were Salisbury and Chandler, but wishing to involve young people they invited senior pupils of Exeter School to design an exterior sculptured wall. The one they used is by David Scott, and is said to be based on the letters that spell St James.

There has been repeated flooding over the centuries in the low-lying parts of the city. Exceptional floods came in October 1960. There had been heavy rain in the weeks before, half the year's average falling in that month. The ground was saturated and the river level was high. On 'Black Thursday', 27 October 1960, more heavy rain had nowhere to go but the streets of St Thomas. 42,000 tons of water per minute swept through the lower parts of the district, inundating 2,500 houses, factories, churches and pubs. The children in Montgomery School had to be led out through a house in Maple Road. Amphibious DUKWs rescued householders and transported stranded workers trying to get home. In Emmanuel Church pews were overturned by the force of the water and wooden floor blocks were torn up. Two choirboys took refuge in the pulpit until firemen came and rescued them. A beer barrel reputed to be from the Royal Oak pub in Okehampton Street was found bobbing about in the water off Portland Bill. Eventually the waters subsided, leaving a stench of rot and sewage. A greater flood just five and a half weeks later strengthened the general feeling that drastic countermeasures were called for. Experts recommended digging two tunnels 3½ miles long and as high as a house through the rock that Exeter stands on; or else redesigning the river. The latter plan seemed more sensible, though the vast expense, £4m, made some wonder whether it might be cheaper to rehouse the entire population on higher ground.

In 1973 Devon River Authority started digging a mile-long relief channel, straightening the river and filling in Exwick Leat between Higher Mill and the river. This work may have helped cause the devastating damage in September 1974. Harold Ackland remembers gazing fascinated as the flood waters demolished Station Road. 'The water was that rapid and that forceful you could see it washing a whole circle out of the field. The force of the water literally ate that field out. You could see lumps just dropping into the water – hunks as high as this table – and then it washed out the next part. No machine could clear earth like that. I told the inspector he would be back by 12 o'clock ordering a new bridge over the river. The bridge collapsed at 11.30pm.' Last across were GPO engineers, to cut the telephone lines.

In the end the Exeter Flood Relief Scheme cost £8m. The chief engineer was Clive Gosling. Twin sluice gates at Exwick were designed to close automatically when the river level is high, limiting the flow downstream to a safe volume. The excess is diverted over a side weir into a wide flood relief channel. This channel is used by anglers and model boat-owners. The banks are made of stone-filled gabions covered with turf, which can be replaced if a flood scours it away. The scheme was opened on 23 September 1977 by John Silkin; and 50 years later engineers are investigating whether the existing flood measures are adequate.

Battersea Park in London has been restoring the delightful Festival Gardens from the 1951 Festival of Britain. These gardens were designed by the artist John Piper. We can still admire the grand vista, the fountain lake and the colour scheme of pink, cream, white and blue flowers. The concrete paths and terrace edges are coloured to match the planting. Meanwhile, Exeter faced the demolition of its post-war buildings inspired by the Festival of Britain. We still have the wavy porch of Southernhay Church and the wavy roofline of Boots and the rotunda of the former Fine Fare on the corner of Paris Street and Sidwell Street. But we lost the exuberant facade of Eastgate House at the top of Princesshay. Its loss will be lamented by the Twentieth-Century Society and many Exonians.

2003 was the centenary year of the artist John Piper, born in 1903. It was marked by exhibitions of his work in London galleries, Eltham Palace and elsewhere. He was extraordinarily wide-ranging in his interests, designing stage-sets, textiles, stained-glass windows, pottery and book illustrations. He is also said to have made the most extensive record of the buildings of Britain by any artist of the 20th century. At the same time Piper was attracted to the abstract movement of the 1930s led by Ben Nicholson and

151   The Yaroslavl Bridge over Western Way leads from one surviving stretch of Roman wall to another. The council wanted to demolish the part at the top of South Street to fit in one more shop unit but Lady Aileen Fox said that more people would come to see the wall than would use one more shop.

Barbara Hepworth. John Betjeman recorded that when Piper was about to marry Myfanwy Evans (the Myfanwy immortalised in Betjeman's poem), he told her, 'I am afraid I never take a holiday. Do you mind?' Exeter owns a large mural by John Piper but it is rarely on public view. It was commissioned for the end wall of St George's Hall when it was built in 1962, but was later replaced by panelling and moved to the back of the stage, where it hangs behind curtains. The mural is an abstract relief. Three pieces of board are joined like a triptych; the surface is three-dimensional. Rhomboid shapes have been jig-sawed from the backing and are reattached horizontally or vertically. Some are hollowed out like frames. The shapes are painted in flat shades of red, yellow, tan and brown. The background is a stippled blue, black and white roughened surface, giving the effect of water. The whole work was designed to echo the lines of St. George's Hall. Perhaps it should have an airing sometimes.

The Theatre Royal was demolished in July 1963 after audiences had dwindled to single figures, even for visiting ballet companies. Its loss is still regretted by those who find the Northcott comparatively inaccessible and lacking the atmosphere of a large Victorian theatre with gallery and circles. It also has less spacious backstage accommodation.

Exeter is twinned with four cities in Europe: Rennes, Bad Homburg, Terracina and Yaroslavl. Their coats of arms are displayed around a mosaic map of Exeter at the entrance to the Mary Arches car park from the footbridge across North Street. The names of our twin cities also feature here and there in Exeter's landscape. The tower block of residential flats in Whipton was built in 1966-7 and named Rennes House. Also in 1967 a new

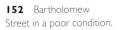

152 Bartholomew Street in a poor condition.

road on the Streatham estate of the university was named Rennes Drive, and declared open by the mayor of Rennes. The mayor of Bad Homburg planted a tree outside Boots, now felled in the make-over of the High Street, because it did not match the other trees. Bad Homburg Road is a new road on the Matford industrial estate, lined with one of Germany's favourite trees, the lime, so Devon now has an Unter den Linden. The friendship with Terracina is commemorated by an Italian-style piazza alongside the canal basin, laid out in 1995. Yaroslavl in south-west Russia became one of Exeter's twin towns

153 Bartholomew Street restored.

154 Cars could park under the elms of the Close until 1970. A scheme to accommodate them underground led to the demolition of the Victorian church of St Mary Major, revealing remains of the 15th-century church known from drawings, but below that – amazingly – the 11th-century apsed cathedral of Leofric, and earlier graves confirming 1600 years of continuous Christian practice on this site.

in 1989, and the Yaroslavl footbridge crosses Western Way, from the top of South Street near the site of the Southgate to the top of the section of Roman wall that borders the quay and cathedral car-park. This footbridge was constructed in several sections. Before being assembled on site they were loaded onto lorries and sent across the Severn Bridge to Newport in South Wales to be given an anti-corrosive finish, which would stop the material rusting. While this was taking place the Severn Bridge changed hands. The new owners would not allow the lorry carrying the 60ft-long main section to drive back across the bridge because there were roadworks, and it was considered to be dangerously wide. It had to be driven north as far as Gloucester before it could cross the river, and come all the way south again. The Yaroslavl bridge was put in place in May 1992 and opened for use in November. It has a wooden handrail and non-slip surface and is adorned with plaques and coats of arms.

Some episodes of the television comedy series *Monty Python's Flying Circus* (from 1969) were filmed in Exeter High Street and other areas. Michael Palin, John Cleese, Terry Jones, Terry Gilliam and Eric Idle were seen acting out such scenes as the inauguration in French and English of an Euro pillar-box on the corner of Maryfield Avenue and Higher Kings Avenue. In another sketch, housewives came out with their hair in curlers to sell mangles to a rag-and-bone man.

The Rosebarn Dairy, a small rough-cast farmhouse and its thatched outhouses were demolished in the 1960s to make way for executive residences. During the following 20 years the whole green valley has been filled with roads and houses, despite the uneven terrain. The road-namers seized on the trans-Atlantic connotation of Pennsylvania, and branched off into Florida, Michigan and even Mayflower. Future historians will be able to date the development from the roads called after American astronauts. Doubtless rightly thinking that nobody in Exeter would buy a house in a Yuri Gagarin Avenue (first man in space, April 1961), the developers commemorated the first American spaceman, Alan Shepard (5 May 1961) by spelling his name wrong. Senator John Glen made a three-orbit flight in 1962, and has a (mis-spelt) pedestrian way called after him. Surely it would have been more appropriate to have had an Armstrong Walk ('One small step for a man, but an awfully long steep way to the nearest post office for a mother with a pushchair.') Edwin Aldrin joined Neil Armstrong on the moon's surface in July 1969, while Michael Collins stayed in Apollo 11. Taxi-drivers have to have their space-history at their finger-tips to know when to head for Higher Pennsylvania.

The 1905 Exe Bridge had obstructed the flood-waters, and the study of a model established where to site new twin bridges. This new layout was also supposed to relieve the traffic-jams at the crossing. A start was made by demolishing the long-established shops and businesses that stood between the river and the railway, and a cat's cradle of underpasses and loops was devised. Mayor Hallett opened Exe Bridge North on 30 July 1969 with a plaque-unveiling and a tea party, and Mayor Sargent its southern counterpart on 15 May 1972, with less junketing. The 1905 bridge was then demolished.

Gateway developed a shopping precinct west of the railway bridge, planned around the car, with most of the area devoted to 100 parking-places. The Albany site stood derelict during many years of discussion, until finally a large supermarket and indoor-sports complex were built just where their car-borne customers would block the traffic as they left. As with all new road-schemes, such unforeseen increase in use soon brought it to a standstill. Exeter really does need to return to its excellent rail network. Let this be the lesson learned from St Thomas, the railway town.

155 The blitzed eastern end of the High Street was redeveloped with wider pavements and wider carriageways. After compulsory purchase of bomb-sites, purpose-built accommodation for chain-stores could be designed a block at a time, contrasting with the older western end of the street where the shops continued to adapt centuries-old merchants' dwellings on medieval burgage plots.

Bartholomew Street zigzags round the lovely Bartholomew Burial Yard with its tall trees and precious green lawn. A road scheme in the 1970s proposed cutting across the burial yard, simplifying the route for drivers. Exeter Civic Society published a study of the area and campaigned to preserve the Georgian houses along this part of the street and make it a conservation area. The road widening was implemented as far as the first bend, including changes to the pavement, which was part of the scheme to go straight ahead through the cemetery; it ends dramatically at its wall. Bartholomew Yard still holds several memorials, but estate agents have started describing the nearby houses as overlooking a park.

156 The ABC cinema replaced the New London Inn. The open space in front of it was a reminder of the Old London Inn Square outside the Eastgate.

17

The Royal Devon and Exeter Hospital

From the 1940s Exeter had been hoping for a new hospital on a larger site. In 1944 the honorary staff of the RD&E produced a report that foresaw the need for expansion, more than there was space for at Southernhay; they were the first to propose 'a large new hospital of 700 beds, south of the city near Countess Wear'. In 1949 the Exeter & Mid-Devon Hospital Management Committee proposed that a new general hospital be built on the Wonford Hospital estate, and this was approved in February 1950 by the Regional Hospital Board in Bristol. In December 1950 Dr Harry Hall-Tompkin (an Exeter GP) was still reporting a shortage of rooms and staff – but hopes subsided until 1960, when the Minister of Health Derek Walker-Smith was in Exeter and inspected the Wonford site. It lay on a prehistoric ridgeway, near the ancient village of Wonford, which had been head of the Saxon hundred which stretched as far as Okehampton; 1,000 years later the Health Area had the same territory. Across a Saxon lane lay the Princess Elizabeth Orthopaedic Hospital (PEOH), and on the site itself was Wonford House, which had been built in 1866-9 to house 120 mentally ill ladies and gentlemen and their staff. Its grounds were now used as playing fields by Endsleigh School, St Margaret's School and University of Exeter women's teams, the Christchurch cricket field and public allotments. The patients could go for a good long walk without leaving the grounds.

Enoch Powell became Minister of Health in 1961. He soon announced a vast programme of new district general hospitals and a definite start on Wonford in 1964 – but this was put off in 1967 for yet another year. For the first 25 years of the NHS Exeter's hospitals functioned on cramped sites, separated from each other by distances that ranged from just across the road to many miles

BBC TV recorded *Songs of Praise* in the RD&E chapel in December 1963. Nurses, doctors and some of the patients formed the congregation; others followed the service from loudspeakers and screens in the wards.

Many pioneering schemes sprouted in the cramped seed-bed of Southernhay, one significant venture being the Postgraduate Medical Centre – from 1963. Its purpose was to provide in-service training and refresher courses for doctors, many of whom came from abroad. Exeter University provided lectures on non-medical subjects – the first time that such a centre was opened in association with a university without a medical school.

In the 1950s and the 1960s Exeter took part in an integrated scheme of training with the Hospital for Sick Children in London, whereby the Great Ormond Street nurses in their pretty little white caps came for general experience.

Exeter had built its isolation hospital in 1878 at Whipton, a long way out of town among green fields. It was used for patients suffering from such infectious diseases as diphtheria, scarlet fever and chickenpox. In 1914 extensions to the hospital were built, including admin rooms. By the 1960s many previously life-threatening diseases could be cured with antibiotics and the isolation hospital was not needed for them, but when a penicillin-resistant staphylococci infection entered hospitals from Australia, 'hospital staph', Whipton was used to house affected patients from the RD&E while its wards were vigorously cleaned and disinfected. The Whipton Hospital Campus has been adapted since to house physiotherapy and other services for the disabled and elderly, including help with rehabilitation. Hip-joint replacements began at the PEOH in 1965, with six pioneering operations; and 200 were done before 1970, when numbers accelerated, the PEOH being one of four British centres licensed to do these operations. The Ling-Lee joint was developed here by Robin Ling, consultant orthopaedic surgeon at Exeter University, and engineering scientist Dr Clive Lee. When they heard it reported as a Chinese invention they changed the name to the Exeter Hip. It became the standard across the world, and after continual improvements the Exeter Universal Hip was launched in 1988: 9,000 are produced every year.

On the freezing winter night of 22 February 1968, just after 7pm, the fire alarms went off in Southernhay. A fire in the roof above the kitchen spread into a lift shaft, and flames roared 60ft from the roof, destroying the original cupola. Fortunately there were no longer wards in the central block and no lives were lost. Sixty firemen fought the blaze, while 130 patients were carried to safety in their beds or dragged on mattresses in an evacuation that took only 14 minutes. The Civil Defence was holding a first aid class in Barnfield Hall and they were quickly summoned, as were the boys of the Spartan Boxing Club in the Trinity Youth Centre to help the Red Cross and St John's Ambulance. People came from miles, not all to help: some, knowing the need for a new building, offered to fan the flames! The paintings and furniture from the board room were carried to the car park, and later to the Royal Albert Museum for temporary storage. Some patients were transferred to the Nurses' Home, and others were taken by bus or ambulance to other hospitals.

By Saturday 24 February six wards were reoccupied, and the board room was fitted out as a temporary kitchen. The weather-vane from 1742 survived the fire, but the cupola was replaced by a low-maintenance fibre-glass replica.

In March 1970 visiting members of the College of Physicians gathered in the board room for a lecture. They were greatly surprised when Sir George Baker (who had died in 1809) appeared to enter, and delivered his 1767 lecture about the Devonshire Colic, which arises from the presence of lead in the cider presses. Professor. David Mattingly had conspired with Tony Church, director of the Northcott Theatre, to dress in costume and bring off this illusion.

In the 1970s, when the public were taking package holidays and acquiring a taste for foreign food, Miss Theo Churchyard, catering officer at the City Hospital, told the *Express & Echo* that, while varying the menus, she always included potatoes, gravy and custard – or the patients complained. She was gradually offering foreign alternatives, such as ravioli, and even dared to offer curry to the nurses.

In late August 1968 the cricket ground at Barrack Road had been bulldozed and Dr James Westwater once again cut the first turf – for the new general hospital. Groundwork now began: 77,000cu. ft of earth were removed and 17,250cu. yds of concrete were laid. Nobody gave a second thought to the fact that it was being poured straight onto soil that tests had shown to be unusually rich in alkali.

What would the new hospital be called? The Exonia Hospital? Should the constituent parts be called after the roads they stood on: Magdalen, Barrack, Heavitree Road? Wonford was already the name of the mental hospital on the new site. Really, the hospital's name should continue to reflect the fact that it served Exeter and the greater part of Devon, so 'Devon and Exeter' would be ideal. But would the Queen allow the 'Royal' to be transferred? In March 1970 it was announced that the names would be RD&E (Southernhay), RD&E (Heavitree) for City Hospital, and RD&E (Wonford) for the new district general hospital. On 1 July 300 people gathered, including the mayor and mayoress, the sheriff and his wife, to watch the foundation stone being laid.

The planning group was made up of representatives of the consultants and management, and Matron Furze to speak on behalf of the nurses. An architect sat in on the group meetings and made instant sketches of possible designs. They eventually decided on a seven-storey block of wards standing on a two-storey podium. Inside the tower the layout was what is called 'race-track' – services and the nurses' stations in the middle, rooms on the outside with picture windows. There were six-bed bays plus some single rooms; a ward could be mixed, which created a flexible arrangement. Because of the vertical design (wards piled on top of each other with a liftshaft in the middle and stairs each end), the area allotted to circulation was only a tenth of the total. On the other hand, the corridors on each floor were wide, in case they had to hold extra beds after a nuclear attack. Advances in medicine necessitated a coronary care unit, an enlarged cardiology department, a department of anaesthetics, improved accommodation for the blood transfusion service and a state-of-the art radiotherapy department. Management and the Ministry of Health insisted that the restaurant should be open to the public and all the staff, with not even one private table reserved for the consultants.

A Scandinavian-style residential village for 260 people in T-shaped three-storey red-brick blocks of flats was built in 1973-4 on a knoll above Bovemoors Lane, looking across to a ridge of green fields, to attract young doctors to come to Exeter. This land had previously been the farm for Wonford House, providing fruit and vegetables.

In the run-up to the great move in 1974 Southernhay was allowed to run down: hardly any new patients were admitted so that they would not have to be moved, and those that were left were put into a mixed ward as there were so few of them.

The move to Wonford was delayed to November 1973 and then to March 1974. For a fortnight in March the hospital opened to hundreds of sightseers. On 1 April

1974 the new hospital opened for outpatients only. It took three months to move all departments, although the major move was accomplished in one weekend, and WRVS volunteers were at hand to guide people along the shiny new corridors.

The new Duchess of Gloucester was to have opened the new hospital on 15 May 1975 but as she had hurt her ankle her husband stood in for her. One of the consultants pointed out to the duke that 'This is the largest and most expensive building put up in this city since the cathedral and it is like a concrete German bunker.' Lunch for 500 was laid on, although the duke had already moved on to the Devon County Show.

157 The new, third, Royal Devon and Exeter Hospital had to be built while the second, the tower block, was still standing.

The Regional Hospital Board had hoped to sell the Southernhay site, but the premises first had to be offered to other government departments and then to the local authority. By 1977 the Area Health Authority had taken it for its pay office, accounts and audit sections, health clinics and so on; the building's name was changed to Dean Clarke House.

The exterior of Wonford was thought ugly: the cheap yellow bricks of the lower storeys were slow to weather, and after rain there were smudges on the concrete tower. How much worse than merely unsightly this was to prove! The main entrance was not easy to find, but all agreed (at first) that the inside was superb. However, once the honeymoon was over the complaints began. The reception area was draughty if there was a gale; radiators leaked; the windows were not cleaned for two years because the gantries could not be used. Soon people began to comment on the web of surface cracks – first like a cobweb, then larger – which started to exude a white starchy gel. Geoff Hingston, technical officer for Wonford, could see that these were not just compression or intension cracks, and soon realised it was Alkali Aggregate Reaction – 'concrete cancer'. There was no cure. There had been a seam of silica in the sand quarry, which was reacting with the alkaline cement to form a gel. The chemical reaction causes the concrete to expand, pushing off the surface layers until they crumble and fall off. Condensation in the hospital kitchens could have started it; alternatively improperly mixed concrete could have led to cracking. There was also a carbonisation problem: steel reinforcement bars were not inserted according to specification, as they were too close to the surface.

Soon little bits of concrete the size of half a crown began falling from the lintels, and a scaffolding tunnel was put up over the entrance to keep this off the public. The roofs and seventeen courtyards were put out of bounds to staff, unless wearing hard hats. The cracking increased to nightmare proportions, with deep cracks each side of the vertical pillars on which the hospital stood; then it spread to the central core with the lift shafts. This was where it could do most damage: the central section only had to shift 10mm out of true to fracture all the piping and wiring.

The hospital had been built for £7m. Could the building be saved and patched up? It was too far gone. It had to be rebuilt, and the money would have to come from central government. It was also suggested that the builders, Higgs & Hill, were liable: the twelve-year guarantee had only a fortnight to run. The Treasury released £40m in 1986, towards a £50m rebuild, with the first £5m allocated for 1988-9. The region had to find the shortfall by selling its newly vacated mental hospitals.

The builders successfully pleaded that 'concrete cancer' was an unknown phenomenon, and they offered to put things right for £3m rather than pay out £6m compensation. However, they offered a settlement relating to the charge that the building had not complied with specifications, rather than risk losing.

Soon demolition began, although two unaffected ground-floor wards (not built until 1984) were retained. The low-rise new building is on a human scale, being what estate agents call 'deceptively spacious' – although it is smaller than its predecessor it feels larger. On 17 March 1994 the Duchess of Kent officially opened the new hospital. An enthusiastic throng welcomed her into the new concourse, and she toured the hospital before performing the opening ceremony. This was just one part of a day of celebration of 250 years of healthcare in Exeter, which included an exhibition at the cathedral chapter house, a civic luncheon and a service of thanksgiving.

An illustrated sheet that was sold to raise funds for the hospital at a 'fancy bazaar' on Northernhay, in 1849 expresses sentiments that still ring true today:

Where pain finds refuge, – Mis'ry dries her tears …
There pining sickness may in peace recline
Whilst godlike Science lends its aid divine …
Devonians glory in these works of love
Which find their recompense in realms above.

18

Later Twentieth Century

Along Pennsylvania Road we come to a bend, and lodge gate-posts. Here in the early 20th century Sunday strollers could have a glass of lemonade and admission to the breath-taking vistas from Belvidere and Argyll Roads, for 1d. A property developer wished to build on the steep fields in the 1980s, but was prevented by a campaign to save the Duryard valley for a park and nature reserve, to form part of a green belt around the city. The fields and hedges still harbour the rich variety of plant and animal life (including 17 species of butterfly) that has been wiped out elsewhere by intensive chemical farming. The hedge along Belvidere Road is estimated to be 600 to 700 years old, while interesting trees include Turkey oaks, red and pink hawthorns and barberry bushes.

Pennsylvania Road climbs yet higher to the famous view at Prospect Gate. Picnic tables and parking space for about 13 cars were put here by the council in 1983, but it was already prized 100 years before. In Gissing's *Born in Exile*, Sidwell Warricombe decides that they shall drive along 'the Stoke Canon Road, so as to let Mr Peake have the famous view from the gate … A gate, interrupting a high bank with which the road was bordered, gave admission to the head of a great cultivated slope, which fell to the river Exe … three well-marked valleys – those of the Creedy, the Exe and the Culm … Westward, a bolder swell pointed to the skirts of Dartmoor … Exeter was wholly hidden behind the hill on which the observers stood, and the line of the railway leading thither could only be described by special search.'

Half a century before that, Besley's directory for 1831 describes the view from the field on the other side of the road: 'A panoramic view, extending for many miles over some of the richest country in the kingdom: to the north-east as far as Lord Wellington's monument on Brendon Hill in Somersetshire; to the east, beyond Honiton, to the south and west, the sea from Portland almost to the entrance to Torbay, with the intervening country, esteemed the garden of Devonshire, and to the north-west and north, the

rocks and hills of Haytor and Dartmoor, the vale of Crediton, and the mountainous tract which divides the county of Devon into two parts.'

From 1895 to 1929 the Exeter Golf Club had its course here. It was well-drained, unlike the present course by the river, and members enjoyed playing the nine holes, stopping for tea in the Panorama Café, then playing nine again. The entrance was at the corner of the first field, now used by Hilltop Riding School. The café continued serving walkers after the golfers had moved away.

Exeter boasts the earliest mosaic found in the United Kingdom – fragments from the floor of the legionary bath-house built by the Romans in about A.D. 55. It is a happy coincidence that mosaic work is once again decorating our public buildings. The city now has 14 community mosaics, all created by the internationally renowned mosaic artist Elaine M. Goodwin and her team of helpers. While teaching at the college of art, Elaine wrote to Bob Clement, schools art adviser for Devon, saying that she would love to work outdoors with her students to create something large-scale for the community, using recycled materials. He suggested a playground mural for Cowick Street First School. The Wall of Play became the first of many projects, undertaken on this occasion with nine students. It took a year, working one day a week. Elaine showed the children methods she had learned in India, and they brought treasures to embed in the mosaic – including magnetic letters from a fridge and a loose tooth that came out one lunchtime! The Wall of Play reflects life in the playground: conkers, kite-flying, sliding on the ice, playing 'wheelbarrows', skipping, fighting and clapping games. There are 28 life-sized children portrayed, together with 33 animals ranging from a woodlouse to the school cat. An aeroplane breaking into the nucleus of an atom was inserted as the news came through of the accident at Chernobyl. There was a grand opening in June 1986.

In 1986 Elaine founded Group Five to work on further public commissions. She named the group after the number of members (Glen Morgan, Eve Jennings, Sue Sims, Rhonwen Vickers and Liz Badger). They work as a team and there is no egotism; no one says: 'I did that bit'.

158 Wall of Play – the winter section of the playground games portrayed in Elaine M. Goodwin's mosaic made for Cowick First School in 1985-6.

159 King William car park mosaic made in 1992 by Elaine M. Goodwin. The Bayeux Tapestry theme continued in the passageway to Sidwell Street by Elaine M. Goodwin in 1994.

John Clark of the city council's planning department explained how the group's car park mosaics came about:

> In the late 1980s, Exeter City Council started to tackle the legacy of the 1960s multi-storey car-parks, mostly forbidding concrete structures covered in graffiti … It was decided to make them more welcoming and humanise them by improving the lighting and painting the bare concrete walls and ceilings white. After seeing the wonderful cheerful mosaic mural … in the Cowick Street First School playground, I persuaded the City Council to commission a mosaic mural for the Guildhall Car-park. The experiment was a great success. Many local people brought old pots and crockery as well as badges from every make of motor car as features in the mural. By the time it was completed it had become a talking point – the car-park attendants said that it had changed the whole feeling and ethos of the car-park. … Miraculously the graffiti vandalism ceased overnight! I had no difficulty persuading the Council to commission murals … for the Mary Arches, King William and Broadwalk Car-parks. These bright and colourful mosaic walls of art are now a unique feature of Exeter's car-parks, and have helped transform ugly places into pleasant ones. One American lady touring England to find a new home decided to settle in Exeter because she felt that any city that commissioned quality works of art in its car-parks must have the right values and be a good place in which to live.

The King William Street car-park mosaic decorates what was an underused and dirty facility. Elaine and her team were invited to make it brighter and more distinctive. The car-park attendant made them very welcome, and collected discarded hub-caps for them: the design was to combine the theme of Conqueror and car-park by marrying the Bayeux Tapestry and old car parts. The result is stunningly successful. The side wall is a faithful replica of mounted Norman soldiers from the tapestry, but their round shields are petrol caps and the militant slogans are car-names: Avenger, Allegro, Cavalier.

Exeter City Council and British Rail jointly funded a Cowick Street improvement scheme, including paving, tree planting, screen walling and cleaning the railway bridge. Group Five were sponsored by the council and by British Rail to decorate the inside of the railway arch to discourage pigeons, which roosted there and messed the pavement. The group worked for two days a week for a year and became rather fond of the pigeons: each time they came back they found another nest on the scaffolding, another two eggs laid. They incorporated pictures of pigeons among the railway motifs until in the end it became known as the Pigeon Mural. It was a cold and draughty site. The bridge juddered every time a train crossed it, and the mosaicists had to keep going into the adjacent ladies' loo to warm their hands. They used Italian granite and donated crockery, brought along by local people. The design includes an old train from Brunel's time and an InterCity 125, Brunel himself and Ann, the 'pigeon lady' who cycles all over the city to feed the flocks. Group Five are there too, looking over the parapet of the bridge. The mural was declared finished by Mayor George Clark in April 1991, on Brunel's birthday. The public was invited to guess the number of pigeons portrayed, and the prize of a small square pigeon mosaic was won by Karen Read, aged seven, and her younger brother Simon, who correctly counted 91 pigeons.

Once again the team was called in to transform a squalid corner. The passageway from Sidwell Street to the King William car-park was a dark and unsavoury shelter for dossers and beggars; it was to be improved with lighting, fresh paint and an extension of the Bayeux Tapestry mosaics. Once again the feel of the tapestry has been captured in this very different medium.

When a developer applies for planning permission the decision is often based on the suitability of the design to the proposed site. Will it look good in context? Will it contrast with the neighbouring buildings in a stimulating way or will it wreck

160 The Pigeon Mural under the railway arch in Cowick Street, made in 1991 by Elaine M. Goodwin and her Group Five.

161 Next store and multistorey car park on corner of High Street and Paris Street.

the 'feel' of the neighbourhood? A prime example of this clash was the discussion about whether to site a modernistic sports centre on Clifton Hill; on either side were the sturdy, fairly ornate Victorian residences of Belmont Road and Clifton Hill. When the sports centre was built in 1983-4 it was accused of looking like a grounded pleasure boat, with its red and blue stripes, the rail along the walkway leading to the entrance and the round portholes in the walls. To the untutored eye it looked as if it was built of corrugated iron; in fact it is corrugated aluminium. In *Buildings of Devon* by Cherry and Pevsner, the sports centre is described as 'a large strident box of one and two storeys, clad with horizontally reeded sheet'. It was designed by Nicholas Grimshaw, who has since become a household name as the architect of the amazing biodomes of the Eden Project in Cornwall. It is one of 21 similar modular low-cost buildings commissioned by the Sports Council in the 1990s, and is arguably one of the best, with the clever use of its sloping site. Opposition to this ultramodern edifice was based on its looks, but also on the fact that it would replace several well-used allotments. There was a feeling that gardening provided plenty of healthy physical exercise without the need to provide those things that are apparently essential for a work-out today: a large car-park and a well-stocked licensed bar. But the centre was built, it proved a success, and in 1999 it was enlarged during a £200,000 refit. Perhaps we should start regarding it as one of Exeter's architectural treasures.

162 Corner of Queen Street and High Street, attempt not to clash architecturally.

The author of the Harry Potter books, J.K. Rowling, studied at the University of Exeter from 1983 to 1986. Her series is a publishing phenomenon, and her intricate plotting fascinates adults as well as children. Harry's adventures are in turn terrifying and funny, always based on a firm moral foundation and promoting decency, courtesy and courage. J.K. Rowling came to Exeter to study French with German but soon switched her second subject to Greek and Roman Studies. Her course included classes on mythology and narrative, which clearly fell on fertile ground. Nobody could have foreseen the use she would make of centaurs, hippogriffs and the classical three-headed dog. One staff member of the time is acknowledged to have been the model for the diminutive Professor Binns. Numerous prizes have been showered on the books, and J.K. Rowling received an OBE for service to children's literature, as well as numerous honorary degrees. It is tempting to comb the books for echoes of Joanne's student years. 'Parents are reminded that first years are not allowed their own broomsticks' is a clear parallel with Exeter University's parking policies. There is a nod towards Devon's ageing population: the 665-year-old alchemist Nicholas Flamel, discoverer of the Elixir of Life, 'enjoys a quiet life in Devon with his wife Perenelle (658)'. Readers familiar with Devon will spot Madam Z. Nettles of Topsham, and the Beesley family's home village, Catchpole St Ottery (combining Ottery St Mary with a university professor of theology). Did the clock in Exeter Cathedral with its circling sun and moon inspire Dumbledore's gold watch, which has little planets moving round the edge? And Hogwart's tunnels, so important to the plot – did Exeter's Underground Passages perhaps provide the germ of an idea? Gandy Street may have been the model for Diagon Alley. Sir Cadogan the bold knight, madam Pince the librarian – we clutch at crumbs of reflected glory from an Exeter graduate's amazing creation.

The elegant Cricklepit footbridge was designed by David Hubbard and opened on 29 June 1988 by Mayor O. Callaghan; Montgomery School pupils processed in costumes from the times of previous bridges. When the hole was dug for the bridge-support surprising new evidence for the age of Whipton stone was discovered – fossil spore that was 250 million years old.

The Met Office came to Exeter in 1993, choosing from several possible destinations. It had been based in Bracknell since 1960, using several scattered buildings. Exeter offered a green-field site east of the city, near the Honiton Road, for a landmark building. Established in 1854 to provide forecasts for mariners, the Met Office was part of the Ministry of Defence, since it supplies essential information for the battlefield. For example, it had to advise on a calm moonlit night for the D-Day landings in June 1944. Together with a centre in Kansas it supplies information for all world aviation. It is a 24-hour, seven-days-a-week operation. The Met Office has provided BBC radio forecasts since 1922 and TV forecasts since 1954, and now it advises the National Health Service if weather may affect admissions for heatstroke or broken bones from slipping on ice; tells supermarkets when to lay in stocks of salads and ice-cream; advises councils when roads might need gritting.

Over 1,000 staff moved from Bracknell to Exeter. The service had to continue without a break, even when it involved moving the two super-computers, known as the Cray Twins, which had been used since 1981, in one of the biggest IT moves ever undertaken in Europe. These were capable of carrying out 1,500 billion calculations a second – among the most powerful computers in the world used to forecast the weather.

163 The twin Exe Bridges under construction.

They were soon upgraded to NEC computers, with a sixfold increase in power. The new building was designed round a central 'street' with a stream running down the centre, fed by a 60ft waterfall, as well as a shop, a café and a keep-fit centre. There is a sun terrace for staff to use in their breaks. In September 2003 the first forecast emanated from here. In 2004 the Met Office celebrated its 150th anniversary.

From 1969 the quay warehouses contained the Exeter Maritime Museum, Major David Goddard's unique collection of boats from every continent. Some had a story – a rowing boat used to escape from Nazi-occupied Holland, others that had been recovered from attempts to row across the Atlantic single-handed, although the rower had been lost at sea. Some were working boats, rescued at the moment when mass-produced outboard motors and fibre-glass hulls were replacing boats crafted locally from local materials. The boats filled the warehouses on the quay; a ride on the ferry across the river was part of the fun; and the canal basin held large boats to explore, including a Danish steam tug and a Chinese junk. Under cover there was a Venetian wedding gondola, together with a reed boat from Lake Titicaca, dug-out canoes, catamarans and coracles. The city council evicted the Maritime Museum at short notice in 1996, just as it was on the point of applying for lottery funding. Many of the exhibits can now be seen at World of Boats, Eyemouth, East Berwickshire. The area is now promoted as 'Historic Quayside'. On sunny days it is busy with visitors enjoying the cafés and antiques showrooms or canoeing on the water, but many people still come looking for the maritime museum. It was Exeter's major tourist attraction, second only to the cathedral.

Another sad loss was the Princesshay precinct. This unique asset was enjoyed for its fresh air, view of the cathedral, lovely flower beds and trees, shops supplying real needs – hardware, groceries, dentists, bread, cameras, the Chapter and Verse bookshop, the Blue Boy gift shop and Carwardine's roasting coffee beans. A tablet commemorated the day

164 The warehouses on the Quay are used for offices. They are now linked with a glass atrium holding a lift, so can no longer figure in historic films, as they did for *The Onedin Line* on TV. Older residents remember French 'onion boys' sitting with their feet out of the windows while they prepared the strings of onions to hawk around on bikes or poles.

165 Eastgate House, a loss lamented by the Twentieth-Century Society.

– 21 October 1949 – when Princess Elizabeth inaugurated the development. Temporary post-war shops were replaced with first class architecture inspired by the light-hearted ideas of the 1951 Festival of Britain: the red, white and blue scheme of pillars, lamp-posts and paving, the undulating roof line and orb motif on Eastgate House. In September 1999 English Heritage sponsored Jeremy Gould of the Twentieth-Century Society to report on the architecture of High Street and Princesshay, and it was published under the title of *Phoenix Flying*, referring to Thomas Sharp's *Exeter Phoenix*. He pointed out that Princesshay was slightly wider than the height of the buildings, 'seeming to give exactly the right sense of enclosure'. Hughes Garage, built by Redfern and Gilpin in 1955-7 with a pioneer steel window curtain wall was just one example of cutting-edge architecture. Gould wrote: 'This mid-20th-century architecture is unique to Exeter; it is as important to the history of Exeter as its medieval remains and its Georgian terraces.' Despite campaigns to keep Princesshay the area was handed over to developers, who put up boutiques filled with expensive luxury goods, replaced the spacious post office with cramped upstairs counters reached by an escalator and a lift, blocked the view of the cathedral with a cube-shaped café and built out over Post Office Street nearly as far as the Roman Wall. At least the archaeologists were pleased. They were able to examine the site thoroughly, finding remains of Roman houses and streets and workshops, the tiled floor of the Dominican church, coffins and the foot of a pillar decorated with three little rabbits looking out of their holes, and remaining wells and cellars from Bedford Circus.

The Blue Boy statue was the only listed artefact in the area and had to be retained. Several Exeter schools trace their origin back to the site marked by this statue. The medieval St John's Hospital, just inside the Eastgate, was shut down by Henry VIII, but in the 1630s a workhouse was opened in part of the premises. Eighteen orphans of Exeter citizens were given blue caps and gowns and taught to make pins. By 1637, and thanks to gifts including money from Eliza Hele, the orphans became scholars in a 'free English School'. A high spot for the boys was Ascensiontide, when they beat the city's bounds, setting out at 5am from Larkbeare, proceeding to the quay, Cowley Bridge, Marypole Head, Denmark Road and finally back to Larkbeare. On leaving at the age of 14, each Blue Boy was given a Bible and a seven-year apprenticeship. There was originally one stone statue: a likeness of a scholar called George Wall, apprenticed to a sculptor in 1733-40. It was placed in a niche overlooking the playground, and after losing its head and hands at some point was restored – the new head had delicate features and flowing curly locks. Four cast-iron figures were made when the school was rebuilt in 1859-60. They have fewer curls than the original, but George Wall's initials still appear on the inside of the cap. Two of the figures have hollow backs and were designed to stand against walls, each side of the hall fireplace at first, then when the Bluecoat

166 Belle Isle, new city park by the river, opened in August 1997.

Orphanage closed in 1908 at each side of the main gate. These figures were not painted blue; a boy had to clean them with black lead once a week. The one in the Royal Albert Museum is authentically black. The Maynard School has a hollow-backed Blue Boy, which was presented in 1996. Exeter School's cast-iron boy is beautifully painted with white collar and buttons, brown hair and pink face and hands. On 12 October 1957 the Mayor unveiled the Princesshay Blue Boy in the recently built precinct. Exeter City Council undertook to maintain it on the spot where it originally stood in the school playground.

A tourist attraction of great interest is housed in the old library of the university: the Bill Douglas Centre for the History of Cinema and Popular Culture. The display cabinets illustrate the history of the moving image from 17th-century shadow puppets to recent blockbusters. There are stereoscopes, magic lanterns, Disney souvenirs and mementoes of the Shirley Temple Club – something to awaken a response in nearly anybody. This unique collection also forms the basis for research into the history of popular entertainment. Film-maker Bill Douglas died in 1991 and the centre opened in autumn 1997.

Towards the end of the 20th century historic buildings in the city found new uses. The army pay offices moved out of Higher Barracks and the buildings were converted to a secluded enclave of houses and apartments, retaining the stately trees and using the riding school for garaging. The development was given the pretentious name of Horseguards (though admittedly it was a cavalry barracks) and the roads have an assortments of names: Martingale is a piece of harness, Lancers is the name of a regiment with no connection with Exeter, Johnson was an American general after the Second World War and Imphal was the name of a campaign in India.

The ornate 19th-century post office in Queen Street gave its ground floor to shops and the former upstairs sorting office became a high-ceilinged café. St Sidwell's Church, no longer standing amid a congregation, was converted to a community centre, retaining a small upstairs chapel and Mother's Union centre, but using the remaining space for a community café and several residential units. Vegetables are grown in a garden. Digby Asylum and Exminster Mental Hospital were also converted into residential units, after the developers had gouged the words 'lunatic asylum' from the foundation stones. The 1905 Eye Hospital became the Barcelona Hotel, while Wynards Almshouses became owner-occupied cottages; its picturesque cobbled courtyard and chapel are no longer accessible to sightseers. The Georgian family houses in Southernhay, Barnfield Crescent and most of Colleton Crescent had long been taken over for offices and estate agencies. The warehouses on the quay are used by offices and nightclubs.

In the 1980s and '90s the land between Southernhay and Western Way was developed as Southernhay Gardens, with purpose-built office accommodation in 'campus style' pedestrian-only landscaped courtyards, enhanced with inlaid quotations and mottoes. Parking was provided underground. In 1990 the large Forte Hotel was built at the west end of Southernhay, with a large car-park on the old Trinity Burial Ground. It was Exeter's first purpose-built hotel since the Railway Hotel.

When the Postgraduate Medical Institute was established in 1963, there was considerable disappointment that it did not immediately lead to an undergraduate medical school in Exeter. However, this came to pass 40 years later, when collaboration between the universities of Exeter and Plymouth and the NHS led to the opening of the Peninsula Medical School in 2002. The 200 students had three bases, Exeter,

Plymouth and Truro. In Exeter they are accommodated on St Luke's Campus and in a splendid new building on Barrack Road. The students do part of their training in the Royal Devon and Exeter Hospital, Plymouth's Derriford Hospital and Truro's Royal Cornish Hospital. Unusually for medical students, they also train in local health centres and GP surgeries and care homes for the elderly, with an emphasis on communication skills. Professor John Tooke was appointed as the first dean. The Peninsula Dental School was added in April 2008, with practice rooms in Heavitree Hospital, across the road from St Luke's.

Sixty years after the Blitz, the builders repairing the tower of St Stephen's Church made a remarkable discovery. The walls of the tower were too thin to bear the weight of their platforms, and they had to erect scaffolding inside the tower. When they reached the roof they could hardly believe what they saw. The beams had continued to smoulder away after 1942, and no longer reached to support the roof. Vigorous fundraising continues to preserve this historic and useful city-centre church.

The Exeter Book is one of only four surviving collections of Anglo-Saxon poetry and is therefore a source of great local pride. It can be admired in the cathedral library, along with a unique full Domesday listing – dating from before it was summarised for the national record.

The enhancement of the wide eastern section of the High Street from London Inn Square to Bedford Street was completed in 2005, with Chinese granite paving (now cheaper than Dartmoor granite), wiggly stainless-steel seats and flower standards, and trees matching each other. Devon County Council and Exeter City Council commissioned a work of public art of local significance, based on some of the riddles in our unique treasure. The Riddle Obelisk, 18ft high, is made from a sheet of stainless steel, folded to create an eight-pointed star that tapers from its stone base to its cone at the top. The fins are inscribed with translations of some of the riddles, teasingly written back to front in mirror writing, which has to be read in the reflections in the adjacent fins. The suggested solutions are inscribed on the shiny spheres at the foot of the fins. The sculpture was designed by Michael Fairfax. He used modern translations of the Anglo-Saxon made by his father-in-law, Kevin Crossley-Holland.

Michael Fairfax designed another piece of public art for Heavitree, Fore Street, in collaboration with poet Ralph Hoyte and blacksmith Peter Osborne. The Gateway to Heavitree straddles the busy main road. On one side is an illuminated arch more than 15ft high, made of stainless steel and glass. The arch is the same shape and dimensions as the door to the parish church near the Heavitree yew, and is inscribed with quotations from Richard Hooker, the theologian and Anglican priest who was born in Heavitree in 1554 and whose statue sits on the cathedral green. The arch frames a tablet inscribed with words about the Heavitree yew.

On the other side of Fore Street a mature oak tree has been planted outside the Royal Oak pub, along with three ornamental apple trees. The trunk of the oak is held by a metal grille consisting of words relating to nature. A poem based on the memories of local people refers to the brewing industry and the famous footballer Cliff Bastin.

York Road has seen many changes. The tall houses used by St Hilda's School still display the break where houses were shaved off after bomb damage. The adjacent field housed a Nissen hut used by the Spiritualist church until 1963 when they built a brick church nearer to the top of the road. Eminent members of the congregation were the Shakespearean scholar Wilson Knight and his Classicist brother Jackson Knight.

169 The Riddle Obelisk
on the High Street, with
Anglo-Saxon riddles from
the Exeter Book in mirror
writing and the answers on
the globes.

The Islamic Centre for the South West has been using one of St Hilda's former buildings as well as the disused swimming bath in its grounds, but in 2010 a proper mosque was built with dome and minaret. Local Buddhists have acquired a house in Union Road for the Pure Land Kadampa Buddhist Centre. The Hindu community is planning a fundraising drive to acquire a site and build a temple and community centre within the next five years, the first west of Bristol, 'to enrich the county of Devon with traditional Indian culture'.

St Sidwell's Church of England School teaches children of many different faiths.

Despite efforts to save its historic premises its handsome building of 1854 was demolished because the government offered funding for a rebuild but not a refurbishment, to be accepted during a limited 'window'. The Victorian architect was Edward Ashworth (1815-96), who trained under Charles Fowler (designer of London's Covent Garden). Ashworth settled in Exeter in 1866. He was a member of the Diocesan Architectural Society, which promoted Victorian Gothic. He restored or rebuilt many churches in Devon. For St Sidwell's School he provided neo-Gothic pitched roofs, a school bell in a turret and panelled classrooms. Boys and girls had separate playgrounds and separate classrooms. The girls' room had roof beams supported by unusual scissor trusses, with curved feet resting on ornamental corbels. The boys' schoolroom had a more conventional arch-braced roof, resting on wall-plates without corbels.

The replacement building was put up alongside: the older beautiful building could have been kept, perhaps for practice rooms or library space, but it was taken down, losing the roof and bell and outbuildings immortalised in Gene Kemp's stories of Cricklepit School. The new school has the famous bell in a blue tower and cedar cladding on an outside wall, which is intended to memorialise the giant cedar taken down after the gales in 1994.

Applications to protect Ashworth's building by listing it were refused because Exeter had one listed 19th-century school building already: Butterfields's Exeter School. When the Exeter School system was re-organised in 1870, William Butterfield (1814-1900) designed the new premises near Barrack Road. He was inspired by the churches of Northern Italy, which had bands of bricks of different colours making striking patterns; his most famous work is Keble College in Oxford. Butterfield's style was ridiculed for many years: the walls of Balliol College chapel were said to look like rashers of streaky

170 The new mosque for the south and west, built in York Road in 2010.

171 (Left) The university college became a full and independent university in 1955. After outgrowing the museum rooms and adjacent buildings in Gandy Street it scattered pink brick buildings on the hills of the former Streatham estate. Extensive tree-planting complements the century-old arboretum that surrounds the Thornton-Wests' Italianate mansion of 1867.

bacon, and Keble's architecture was described in the *Building News* as 'holy zebra' style. Exeter School's outer walls are of Culm Davy brick with diaper patterning in thin lines of dark blue. The end wall of the library could be said to resemble streaky bacon to some extent, its red brick being divided by white stone courses.

The university gained a royal charter in 1955. This gave it full independence (it had previously been an outpost of London University), including the right to award its own degrees. It expanded rapidly, attracting scholars from many parts of the world, and a yearly invasion of young people comparable in numbers to the thousands in Vespasian's Second Augustan Legion of A.D. 50.

In 1966 the city annexed Topsham. In the reorganisation of local government, Exeter was told that it would cease to be a county after 30 March 1974: it would become

172 (Left) An anonymous romantic sign on a wall by the railway in Blackall Road: 'I don't like text in art, but walking along this road holding the hand of the girl I loved was the happiest I've ever been.'

173 Ornate lamp post in Martin's Lane.

subject to Devon County Council and no longer have its own sheriff, but the queen granted the city the right for the elected chairman of its council to retain the title of mayor. In 1977, the jubilee year, she upgraded the title to lord mayor. The Exeter police force also lost its autonomy. Devon police had previously exercised authority only in certain enclaves of Exeter: the castle, the judge's lodgings and County Hall. The amalgamation wiped out the boundaries that had served as reminders of the city's long history. But Exeter continued to play its varied roles of capital of Devon, cathedral city, gateway to the west, always loyal. As Hooker wrote in 1587, 'the situation of this City is very pleasant and delicate, being set upon a little Hill among many Hills'. Sunlight and shadow still chase across the dumpy wooded hills, the city clusters around the cathedral towers, and the shining estuary flows out to the sea.

Index

Numbers refer to pages in the case of both illustrations and text.

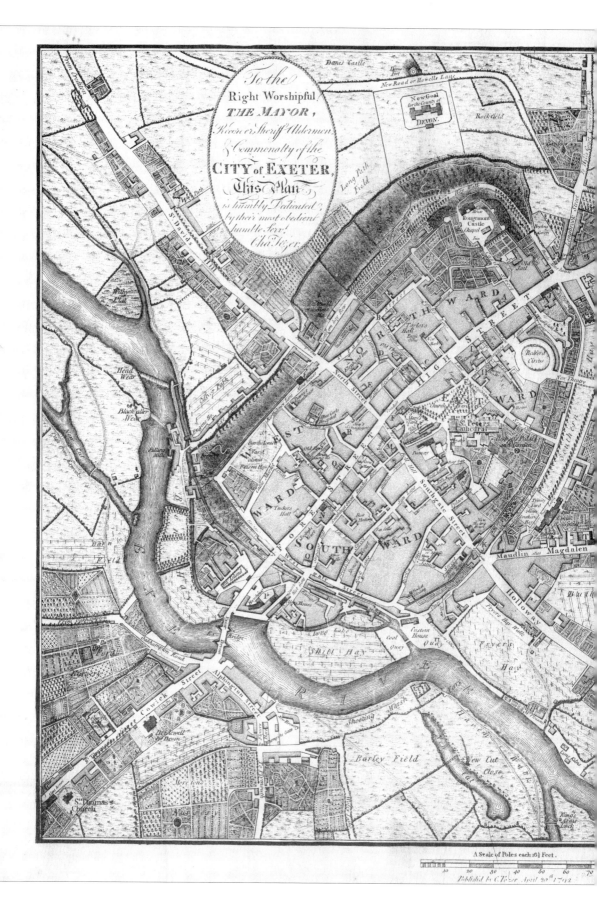